Ladies First

Ladies First
*A History of the
Queen Margaret Union
of the
University of Glasgow*

Edited by Gary R. Brown

The Grimsay Press

The Grimsay Press
an imprint of
Zeticula
57 St Vincent Crescent
Glasgow
G3 8NQ
Scotland.
http://www.thegrimsaypress.co.uk
admin@thegrimsaypress.co.uk
First published 2010

Copyright © Gary Robert Brown and contributors 2010
A full list of copyright holders can be found in the Acknowledgements.

Every effort has been made to trace possible copyright holders and to obtain their permission for the use of any copyright material. The publishers will gladly receive information enabling them to rectify any error or omission for subsequent editions.

ISBN-10   1 84530 061 0 Paperback
ISBN-13 978 1 84530 061 6 Paperback

All rights reserved. No part of this publication may be reproduced, stored in a retrieval system, or transmitted in any form or by any means, electronic, mechanical, photocopying, recording or otherwise, without the prior permission of the publishers.

To all the Q-Emmas and Q-Em-men
who made this possible

Acknowledgements

This book would not have been possible without the help, enthusiasm and support of a huge number of people.
First, I should like to thank Celeste Francis, Zoe Grams, Erin Haig, Ally Hunter, Laura Kane, Anthony McConachie, Jamie McHale, Terry Murphy, Tom Quinn, Francesca Sapsford and Gill Turnbull for their support throughout.

In addition, I should like to thank the following people

for contributing articles:
Dominic d'Angelo, Mae Baird, Irena Brichta, Stuart Buchanan, Moira Corrigan, Margaret Fairlie, Hannah Frank, Marion Fraser, Richard Gass, Gillian Govan, Mark Graham, Alasdair Gray, Elizabeth Greene, Erin Haig, Christine Hamilton, Nora Hamilton, Lady Hetherington, Jane Hook, Ally Hunter, Molly Illife, Ann Ingleston, Laura Kane, Jean Kelvin, Maire Kimmins, Omar Kooheji, Tim Laver, Sarah-Louise MacAdie, Donald MacAlister, Katie McDonald, Michael McGovern, Jamie McHale, Jimmy McLaughlin, Jane McMinn, Moira McQueen, Liz McSkeane, Rona Mackie, Frances Melville, Aaron Murray, Alec Nicolson, C.A. Oakley, Marion Neill, Jennifer Paterson, Jessie Pattie, Sam Phillips, Marcia Pirie, Margo Pitt, Jean Reid, Grahame Riddell, Stephen Rixon, Catherine Savage, Jake Scott, Margaret Sinclair, David Tait, Lizzy Toon, Gill Turnbull, Andrew Whincup, Elma Willocks.

for their time in researching for this book:
Lesley Aylward, Gordon Brady, Maren Caldwell, Sandy Cormie, Alistair Deutsch, Craig Egdell, Sheila Findlay, Brenda Graham, Rosemary Jackson, Caroline Johnston, Laura Kane, Dianne Kerr, Anthony McConachie, Joy McCracken, Alec Nicholson, Sam Phillips, Jennifer Roe, Jill Simmons, Emma Tate, Jamie Wakefield.

and for helping to track down former Queen Margaret Union Board Members and Presidents:
Marion Fraser, Brenda Graham, Mark Graham, Christine Hamilton, Nora Hamilton, Jane Hook, Ann Ingleston, Omar

Kooheji, Anthony McConachie, Michael McGovern, Terry
Murphy, Joanne Neill, Margo Pitt, Grahame Riddell, Stephen
Rixon, Alec Scrimgeour, Margaret Sinclair, Lizzy Toon.
Special thanks go to Liz Napier and Lady Russell for their
support.

*for contributing photos, scans and printed materials (including
handbooks and magazines) from their personal collections:*
Dominic d'Angelo (courtesy of Glasgow University Archive
Services), Sheila Bircumshaw, Stuart Buchanan, Morag
Doig, Marion Fraser, Richard Gass, Mark Graham, Alasdair
Gray, Nora Hamilton, Jane Hook, Ally Hunter, Molly Illife,
Ann Ingleston, Laura Kane, Marie Kimmins, Omar Kooheji,
Anthony McConachie, Michael McGovern, Jamie McHale,
Caroline McKillop, Fiona McKinlay, Jane McMinn, Margo
Pitt, Jean Reid, Grahame Riddell, Margaret Sinclair, Lizzy
Toon, Gill Turnbull, Elma Willocks.

Special thanks go to Andrew Ramsay and his studio
Developing Perception for the work done on the Presidents'
Photos and for contributing several others to Queen Margaret
Union and the History Project.

Thanks go to Lesley Richmond, Claire Daniel, Clare Paterson
and Emma Yan from Glasgow University Archive Services
for their help in locating the many pictures from their records,
and for their help in accessing the many collections held by
the University of Glasgow in initial research for this book.
Thanks go to Helen Durndell, Erika Jagielko and all the
other staff at the University of Glasgow Library for their
help in tracking down photos of all the Presidents of Queen
Margaret Union, and for their help with initial research.

*The following scans and articles (used for research and publication)
were kindly donated by or purchased from Glasgow University
Archive Services:*
DC240-4-2 Bazaar Guide; DC240-7-45 Committee Meeting;
DC240-7-59 Board Meeting; DC240-7-95 Debate in
Progress; DC240-7-97 Chair; DC240-7-107 Reception Area;
DC240-7-109 Panel; DC240-7-114 Point of Order; DC240-
7-116 Dormitory Room; DC240-7-117 Library; DC240-7-
118 Lounge; DC240-7-119 Reading Room; DC240-7-127
Catering Area; DC240-7-130 22 University Gardens; Air

Raid Precautions 1939 (ref: PHU72/3); Janet Galloway (ref: UP1/528/1); DC233/2/23/6 Playbill for 'Goblin Market' Play; DC233/2/11/3 War Fallen Memorial; DC233/2/22/3/2 Queen Margaret College Booklet; DC233/2/17/1/1 Invite from Janet Galloway; DC233/2/17/4/8 Letter from Mabel Vaughn; DC233/2/11/4/3 Letter from Frances Melville; DC233/2/19/7 Janet A. Galloway Memoir Book; DC233/2/19/6/1 GUM Special Supplement; DC233/2/22/2/69 Queen Margaret College Students and Staff; DC233/2/22/1/5/3 Frances Melville sitting; DC240/2/1 Minute Book 1890-1924; DC240/4/20 Circular Letter to Queen Margaret Union members; DC240/4/10 Invitation to Janet A. Galloway 'At' Homes'; DC168 ½ Queen Margaret Union Broadsheets Collection; DC240/7/132 Queen Margaret Union Christmas Card; DC94/8/44 Photo of Men's Union Exterior; DC240/4/1 Queen Margaret College Students' Union Bazaar Prospectus; DC240/5/1/58 Queen Margaret Union Diary 1979-1980; DC240/5/1/1 Queen Margaret College Union Diary 1923-1924; DC240/5/8/2 Lest We Forget – Memoir Book; Book Scan – University: City and State – The Hetheringtons Returning to Glasgow

Thanks also go to the staff from the University of Glasgow for their support throughout this project:
Fiona Black, Sheila Craig, Janice Douglas, Jan Hulme, Lee McClure, David Newall, Sir Muir Russell, Alec Scrimgeour, Scott Sherry, Judith Stevenson, Susan Stewart, Susan Stuart, Emily Wallace.

Proofs were read by
Zoe Grams, Jan Howden, Ally Hunter, Laura Kane, Jamie McHale, Tom Quinn, Francesca Sapsford, Gill Turnbull, Alison Wilson.

Translations were provided by:
Simon Fatoux and Aurélien Couzigné

All other photos are from the private collection of Gary R. Brown or from the Queen Margaret Union private collection

Thanks, also, to the following for permission to use copyright material, as listed:

The University of Glasgow Archive Service and Queen Margaret Union
Queen Margaret College; The Charmed Circle
The University of Glasgow Archive Service
First Meeting of Queen Margaret Union
The University of Glasgow Library
The Great War
The University of Glasgow Students Representative Council
Queen Margaret Types
The Glasgow Herald
Farewell to Queen Margaret College
Hannah Frank and Fiona Frank
Excerpt from Hannah Frank Diary and Drawings
Lady Marion Fraser
Janet Galloway; Frances Melville; Life Before the War
Lucy Hetherington
Memories of Gilmorehill
Caroline McKillop (nee Oakley)
Co-Eds of the Twenties

All other articles are included with the permission of the respective author, whose copyright they remain.

To anyone I've missed, my apologies and thanks.

Finally, a request: to anyone who can add names to the photographs, or is willing to share any archive or memorabilia: please contact me at grbrown85@gmail.com or via the publisher.

Gary R. Brown
September 2009

Contents

Acknowledgements	*vii*
Foreword	*xv*
Introduction	*xvii*
1890	**1**
Queen Margaret Herself	3
Queen Margaret College	7
First Meeting of Queen Margaret Union	11
1900	**15**
Bizarre Bazaar	17
Janet Galloway	25
1910	**31**
Queen Margaret Types	33
Life Before the War	35
The Great War	39
1920	**43**
Diary Excerpts	45
The Charmed Circle	51
Co-eds of the 'Twenties'	53
Frances Melville	57
1930	**61**
Playing with the Big Boys	63
Farewell to Queen Margaret College	67
Memories of Gilmorehill	71
1940	**75**
A World at War	77
Memories of a Diary	81
The Post-War Years	85
1950	**89**
Presidential Memoirs	91
The Professors' Wives	103
The Late Fifties	107
Annual Ball	113
Memories of Student Days	115
1960	**119**
A Past President Reflects	123
The Staff: Backbone of Queen Margaret Union	135
QM Memories	139
The New Union	149
The Late Sixties	157

1970	*161*
Extract from *Toast to Queen Margaret Union*, June 2005	165
Debating in the Early Seventies	171
The Mid-Seventies	175
The Fire That Never Went Out	181
Tales from the Seventies	183
Sisters are doing it for themselves	185
A More Perfect Union	187
A View from the Staff	191
1980	*197*
First Male President	201
Queen Margaret Union – LIVE!	207
Charities Week	217
Inspiration, Innovation	225
A Change in the Air	235
Memories of a Staff Member	241
1990	*245*
Bring on the Nineties	249
The Times They Are A-Changing	257
Goodbye Mr MacKenzie, Hello Mr McConachie	267
Heart of the Nineties	281
Words of Wisdom	289
Toast to the Union	293
The Presidents' Dinner	297
We Belong	303
Andy's Year at the Top	309
2000	*317*
Cheesy Pop	319
Clubs and Societies	327
The People Make The Union	333
Freshers' Week	339
Save the Green Planet	349
Roxanne	355
The Legend of Matron	359
Age of Innocence	365
The Space Between	377
The Love-Hate Relationship	379
Thank You and Good Night	385
The Presidents	387
Index	*415*

Illustrations

Students leaders together in the 1940s, Nora in centre	xviii
Gary outside the recently refurbished entrance in 2006	xx
View of the West Side of Queen Margaret College	6
View of Queen Margaret College from Queen Margaret Drive	6
Entrance hall to Queen Margaret College	10
Pin Badge	10
Minute Book	14
Bazaar Guide, 1906	16
Bazaar Prospectus, 1906	20
The Stray Pearls of Queen Margaret	22
A collection of favourite quotes and proverbs	22
Janet Galloway	24
Interior of the office of the Mistress of Queen Margaret College	27
Invitation from 1906-07 to join Janet Galloway	28
A commemorative book of memories of Janet Galloway	29
Christmas Card given to members of Queen Margaret Union	30
A Q-Emma	32
"Lest We Forget"	37
Earliest known photo of the Queen Margaret Union Board	38
Order of Service, 1915	41
Interior of classroom from Queen Margaret College	42
West Kilbride - self-portrait by Hannah Frank	44
QMU Diary 1923-24	50
Frances Melville	56
Playbill cover from the 1920's for a play in aid of student welfare	59
Exterior view of Glasgow University Union	60
Sketch of Queen Margaret Union after it moved	62
The Principal and Lady Hetherington	70
Students sandbagging the main Gilbert Scott Building	76
G.U.M. - Glasgow University Magazine	79
Members of Queen Margaret Union taking part in Charities Day	80
A Q-Emma enjoys a relaxing read next to the fireplace	83
A badge given to former Presidents of Queen Margaret Union	83
Q-Emmas studying	84
Board of Management of Queen Margaret Union	88
Maiden Speaker's debating prize given to Elma	90
Second Parliamentary Debate, 1949	93
Third Parliamentary Debate, 1949	94
Queen Margaret Union students on campus at the University	99
Board of Management of Queen Margaret Union from 1950s	106

Board of Management of Queen Margaret Union from 1950s	106
Students gathered in the reception area	111
Members of Queen Margaret Union Board of Management	111
Queen Margaret Union Ball decorations	112
Queen Margaret Union Board Members gather together	114
Students taking part in a debate	118
Students at the Freshers' Camp, in the early 1960s	120
Queen Margaret Union members relaxing in the 1960s	122
Group of Queen Margaret Union Board of Management	122
Decorations from Queen Margaret Union in the 1960s	133
Staff members from Queen Margaret Union in the 1960s	134
Board meeting, 1965-66	134
Freshers Camp Staff, October 1965.	137
From *Glasgow University Guardian*, 14 March 1967	138
From *Glasgow University Guardian*, 29 November 1966	141
From *Glasgow University Guardian*, 28 February 1967	142
From *Glasgow University Guardian*, 30 November 1967	143
Queen Margaret Union Ball	145
From *Glasgow University Guardian*, 24 January 1967	146
From *Glasgow University Guardian*, October 1967	147
From *Glasgow University Guardian*, 30 November 1967	148
Freshers Camp at Auchendennan in the late 1960s.	152
Glasgow University Guardian lead story, 11 February, 1968	154
View of the new Union at 22 University Gardens	155
Lounge area of the new Union at 22 University Gardens	156
Catering area of new Union shortly after opening	158
From *Glasgow University Guardian*, 24 January 1967	162
View of the new Union at 22 University Gardens	164
Queen Margaret Union Board of Management	166
Speaker at the main debating chair at debate	174
Queen Margaret Union Board of Management, 1974-1975	176
Queen Margaret Union Board of Management 1975-1976	176
QMU diary, 1979-1980	178
One of the several overnight rooms in Queen Margaret Union	179
Jane McMinn at protest on University campus	180
Students during a debate in Queen Margaret Union	188
Students during a debate in Queen Margaret Union	188
From *Glasgow University Guardian*, 1982	193
Group of Students in the 1970s	194
Cartoon published after the 1982 fire	198
National newspaper report from mid-1980s	199
From *Glasgow University Guardian*	200
Bands that played Queen Margaret Union	206

Bands that played Queen Margaret Union	209
QMU Broadsheet, October 1982	210
Article stapled to the cover of Glasgow University Guardian	213
Selection of Queen Margaret Union broadsheet magazines	214
Student leaders meet the Principal in the Quad	216
From a 1980s QM Handbook	219
Glasgow University Guardian article	222
Main Venue of Queen Margaret Union	223
Ballot paper, November 1982	224
Queen Margaret Union Board of Management 1986-1987	229
Ceasyer Cash and Michael Kelly	230
Glasgow University Guardian article	234
Tally sheet of results for recent President election in 1980s	237
Office Bearers	238
Dafter Friday Poster, 1989	246
Queen Margaret Union foyer from 1980s	247
From *Glasgow University Guardian* 1988/1989	251
From *Glasgow University Guardian*, 19th May, 1983	252
The Centenary Celebration Fashion Show	255, 256
1990 Queen Margaret Union Handbook Cover	259
Quodos at Cheesy Pop	260
Logo for the 1990 Queen Margaret Union Handbook	264
Queen Margaret Union Board of Management 1990-1991	265
From *Glasgow University Guardian* 1991	265
From *Glasgow University Guardian* 1990-1991	266
From *Glasgow University Guardian* in early 1990s	269
Queen Margaret Union Board of Management 1989-1990	270
Queen Margaret Union Board of Management 1993-1994	270
Cover of 1992 Queen Margaret Union Handbook	273
From *Glasgow University Guardian.*	274
The infamous ticket from the Nirvana gig	274
From the QMU Handbook in the 1990s	280
Display from the 1994 Bazaar	283
The 1994 Bazaar	284
From *Glasgow University Guardian* updating on the Unions	284
Local press coverage of UK group Space pulling out of a gig	287
Outside the old bar in Queen Margaret Union	288
Former President Craig Egdell on the top of the Union	288
Queen Margaret Union Executive 1996-1997	292
Queen Margaret Union Board of Management 1997-1998	295
Cover of 1997 Queen Margaret Union Handbook	296
Queen Margaret Union Executive 1998-1999	299
Queen Margaret Union Board of Management 1998-1999	300

From *Glasgow University Guardian*	306
From a 1990s QMU Handbook	307
Student Theatre at Glasgow and Amnesty International	308
Inside the old Games Room at Queen Margaret Union	308
A forgotten and mysterious space – known as the Rat Hole	311
President Andrew Whincup at his desk	312
Queen Margaret Union Board of Management 1999-2000	316
Queen Margaret Union Board of Management 2000-2001	316
President Caroline Johnston outside Queen Margaret Union	318
From a 1990s QMU Handbook	321
Cover of Queen Margaret Union Diary, 2002-03	325
Board Member Ruairidh Anderson voices his opinion	329
Stop the War Coalition society at an event	329
Roslyn Scoular shows off the latest addition in the Games Room	330
Pause Gaming Society taking over the second floor	330
The refurbished Games Room	332
President Laura Kane gazes out of the second floor window	332
President Laura Kane gets stuck into a session	336
Queen Margaret Union Executive 2001-2002	337
Queen Margaret Union Executive 2002-2003	337
Queen Margaret Union Board of Management 2001-2002	338
Queen Margaret Union Board of Management 2003-2004	338
Cover to the 2005 Queen Margaret Union Handbook	341
A gathering of Freshers Helpers in 2006	342
Gill Turnbull and Roslyn Scoular lead Freshers	342
Freshers Week edition of qmunicate	343
Rock band *The Automatic* during Freshers Week 2006	344
Local band *The Dykeenies* at Queen Margaret Union	347
Queen Margaret Union Executive 2003-2004	348
Queen Margaret Union Executive 2004-2005	348
Helpers relax after another successful Kids' Christmas Party	351
Board Member Nicola Clark surveying members	352
Milly the dinosaur on campus	352
President Laura Kane as Santa Claus	354
Gill Turnbull after a visit from Santa Claus	354
One of the many random games at the Union quiz	357
Two volunteers at the Union's quiz	357
Beth Kahn tries to win prizes at the Quiz	358
One of the many random games at the Union quiz	358
A portrait of what members believe matron to look like	362
Gary on election day with Board Member Louisette Baillie	367
Presidents at a gathering in 2006	368
Presidents during a visit in 2006	370

Issue of *qmunicate* magazine featuring the destruction of the
    University of Glasgow's beloved dinosaur – Milly   371
Gathering of Presidents at the Dinner in 2006   374
Queen Margaret Union Executive 2006-2007   376
Glasgow University Union Executive 2007   378
Board of Management meeting in 2008-2009   380
qmunicate, 2005   381
Executive 2008-2009   384
Board of Management 2008-2009   384
Gathering of former Board Members from the 1940s and 2000s   386
The Presidents, in chronological order, from 1894 to 2010   387 to 413
qmunicate, 2008   414

xvii

Students leaders together in the 1940s, Nora in centre

Foreword

E. Nora Beveridge
President
QM Union 1940-1941

I find it hard to believe that it is seventy years since I first joined Queen Margaret Union, at a subscription of one pound, three shillings. It was money well spent!

This was, of course the old Queen Margaret Union, just inside the university gates – full of character, charm and the fairer sex. Men were encouraged to visit but were not eligible for membership.

Many more readers of this book will have memories of the new building which was planned, built and opened in the sixties, however, I think all would agree that Queen Margaret Union was, and is, a friendly, welcoming place, where lifelong friendships were made, romance blossomed, and ended, and the world was put to rights over the coffee cups.

It was there that I gained the confidence to conduct meetings, organise events and deal with people; all skills that were useful to me in later life.

Three of the wartime generation were invited to pay a visit to Queen Margaret Union in June 2007, where we met with past, present and future presidents. I was happy to see that the important features had not changed too much; the welcome, the 'buzz' and the friendly office-bearers. Queen Margaret Union is still, for many students, the focal point of their years at the University of Glasgow.

I congratulate Gary Brown and all the contributors on their hard work in putting this book together and am glad that I am still here and able to enjoy it. I hope you will too.

Gary outside the recently refurbished entrance in 2006

Introduction

Gary R. Brown
President
QM Union 2006-2007

For over one hundred years, Queen Margaret Union has existed as the centre of University life for students at Gilmorehill. This volume is a celebration of its vibrant history. From its humble beginnings as a glorified social club in the basement of the old Queen Margaret College to becoming one of the foremost Student Unions in the country, over fifty contributors will take you on a journey throughout the years.

Queen Margaret Union means something different to everyone who has been a part of it. The contributors in this book are but a small number of the many people who make up its membership. I hope you enjoy each tale and memory as much as I have.

For clarity's sake, all references to Queen Margaret Union are written as either 'The Union' or 'Queen Margaret Union' unless the context determines otherwise. All references to the Glasgow University Union are written as 'Glasgow University Union' or 'the Men's Union'.

This is the kind of text you can dip in and out of. The chapter introductions can be read separately and will give you an overall sense of the history of the Union. The articles in between are collections of memories or experiences from the people who actually lived them.

I'm sure I speak for every contributor when I say thank you for taking an interest in our shared history. Now sit back, put your feet up, make sure your cup of tea is ready and enjoy the history of Queen Margaret Union.

1890

As the nineteenth century was drawing to a close, a revolution of sorts was growing in Glasgow, Scotland. Prevented from entering further education, the women of the city were making their voices heard. Their goal was the establishment of an institution in the city for the higher education of women. In 1883, they got their wish when Queen Margaret College opened its doors. The College was the result of nearly a half-century of tireless effort.

By the end of its first seven years the College was firmly entrenched in the educational life of the city and even saw expansion in 1890. Situated in the picturesque North Park house which would decades later house the BBC - the women students of Glasgow were leaving their mark.

1890 was a significant year for the College. Not only was a medical department added, but also the women students gathered together on 29 March for what would be remembered as a groundbreaking meeting. They had one purpose - the creation of a students union for women at Queen Margaret College.

Queen Margaret Union began essentially as a glorified club or society. It spent much of its early years housed in the basement of the College on what is now Queen Margaret Drive. Social evenings and tea parties were the events of the time. Regardless of how simple the Union may have seemed in comparison to what it became it served its purpose well - to promote the social interaction of the students of Queen Margaret College.

Queen Margaret Herself

Gill Turnbull
Honorary Assistant Secretary
2006-2007

Every year the Queen Margaret Union's Board of Management and their honoured guests raise their glasses in honour of their namesake: Queen M, Queenie, Queen Maggie, or as we should probably address her, Margaret, Queen and Saint of Scotland. It's not an easy toast to make; I know as I did it once. Lifting a glass in honour of the spirit and memories that her title imbues may seem simple enough, but who exactly are we remembering when we do this?

Queen Margaret was born in 1046 and stumbled upon Scotland when her boat to Europe was blown off course. This fortunate twist of fate had a remarkable impact on the country. It seems she is known chiefly for two achievements. The first is bringing learning to Scotland. This is appropriate enough, as she has since given her name to various learning establishments across the country, and I'd like to think that the Union still has a part to play in the education of the University of Glasgow's students.

Queen Margaret Union has become a training ground for those involved with her, as well as a respite from the stresses and pressures that comes with studying for a degree at the University. A handful of members have been recognised by national awards for the journalistic skills that they learned through their time there. Some are taking their experiences of running in elections and assisting in national political campaigns. A recent Freshers' Week Coordinator now runs a business organising kids' parties. Despite the various distractions from learning that Queen Margaret Union is accused of providing, I think the notion of learning is still visible and important to the Union, even if the things we learn are not what Queen Margaret wanted to teach!

Interestingly, Queen Margaret is also remembered, and perhaps blamed, for the decline of the Gaelic language in favour of Latin. The Gaelic language, however, has been very well represented on Queen Margaret Union's Board of Management recently, with Board Members from all over the Highlands, the Western Isles, and the Isle of Skye. In Queen Margaret's spirit of learning, these 'teuchter boardies' managed to teach me a bit of the lingo, although you will need to discover the meanings yourself as Queen Margaret may not have approved of their usage:

Queen Margaret would probably never have needed to use the word 'cliopan' and it would not have been a common feature in the Union until the 1980s, with 'ciochan' being more prominent, and the Union's connection with 'leasbach' culture. 'Teagh' however, is still a favourite in the Union now, as it was back in the early days too, gleaning from the stories of afternoon tea in Queen Margaret Union's parlours. The modern Gaelic word 'bhideo' is perhaps already out of date, but I'm afraid I don't know what the Gaelic for DVD is, perhaps 'DbheaD'?

As well as these two achievements, Queen Margaret is remembered for her saintly personality; piety, virginity and a strict devotion to her religion. It is said that she refused to marry King Malcolm for reasons that the Catholic Church holds dear. No wonder, then, that her title is both Queen and Saint. She did however reportedly have eight children before dying at the age of 47, so the validity of that claim is questionable.

In 2005, the Union's by-laws were completely re-written by the Board of Management. During the discussions over the revision of the Union's discipline policy, one Ordinary Board Member suggested that discipline procedures should exist for those who are caught being 'un-Queen Margarety' in the building. The suggestion was shot down, partly because incident reports from a Friday night would be too much for the Honorary Secretary to deal with, and with all the disciplinary action going on, we'd probably end up with no members. From what I know of what being 'Queen Margarety' might entail, I think I would be a lost cause. Reading some of the stories in the rest of this book, I think you will agree that most of those who have identified themselves with the name of Queen Margaret are also guilty of being 'un-Queen Margarety' at times.

Looking back to Queen Margaret herself provides an inspiration to the Queen Margaret Union ethos of stumbling across somewhere by accident, of activism, femininity, and of generally being a nice bunch of people. It is a good way to start any discussion of the Union's history, as there is probably a (little) bit of the 'Queenie' in us all. I'm sure you'll agree that many of us have turned out okay, and most of us even managed to have a bit of fun along the way. As many a Queen Margaret Union veteran has said… 'We all kind of like it when it's fun'!

View of the West Side of Queen Margaret College

View of Queen Margaret College from Queen Margaret Drive

Queen Margaret College

Frances Melville
Mistress,
Queen Margaret College
from 1909 until it closed in 1935

Queen Margaret College was the outcome, in Glasgow, of the movement for the higher education of women in Britain. The movement had shown signs of its coming in the eighteenth century, and even earlier. The first result was the admission of women to certain university local examinations requiring an improved preliminary education. The next was the improvement of that preliminary education. London founded a 'half-way' College of Higher Education for Governesses, a real pioneer college effort.

In 1867, the 'Edinburgh Ladies' Educational Association' was organised. It continued until 1892 as a 'temporary substitute for University education' and provided courses of lectures, most of them of academic standard conducted by University lecturers. Some of the courses were so exactly correspondent, in subject and order of study and examination, to the Arts curriculum at Edinburgh University that it was possible in 1893 at the first graduation ceremony after the admission of women to the Scottish Universities, to admit seven women to the degree of Master of Arts. St. Andrews and Aberdeen made similar striking contributions to the movement themselves in the following years.

In 1868, a number of ladies in Glasgow, headed by Mrs. Campbell of Tullichewan, organised some occasional 'Lectures for Ladies'. These sporadic lectures, in the words on one who was there, "may be said to have been the introduction to the Higher University education of women in Glasgow".

At a public meeting in 1877, the Association for the Higher Education of Women in Glasgow and the West of Scotland was given formal shape. The objects of the association were clear. Firstly, to systemise and develop the work already begun by offering teaching similar, if possible, to that given to men. Secondly, to generally promote the higher culture and University education of women. In 1883, that is within only six years of the formation of the Glasgow Association and after systematic courses of study had been conducted for six sessions, a momentous step was taken. The Association transformed itself into a College for women. It's aim was to perform for women, work similar to that done by Colleges and Universities for men, and it offered, *inter alia*, a complete curriculum in Arts, and in 1890, a School of Medicine, attached to the College, which was to become the only intramural women's medical school in Britain.

A new governing body, the College Council, was appointed, including men as well as women. Two places on the council were reserved for members of the Senate of the University of Glasgow. In its first moments, when the new College was looking for a local habitation, Mrs Elder, a firm believer in giving opportunities of education to women, presented the College with the most generous and opportune gift of North Park House and grounds.

The College founded in Glasgow in 1883 was, of course, Queen Margaret College, named after Margaret, Queen and Saint, wife of Malcolm Canmore, who brought learning to Scotland. No one need imagine that the foundation of Queen Margaret College was quietly and easily made. The whole question of the higher education of women was furiously debated from around 1860 onward. Somewhat of the furious clash of opinion on the educational question had however passed by 1883. The new institution filled the papers with headlines and columns of news and the leading articles in the Glasgow newspapers treated the project with respect knowing it to be by that time, supported and spoken well of by a considerable group of intellectual and influential people in Glasgow and the West of Scotland.

Principal Caird presided on a memorable occasion and Professor Young's inaugural address looked back on the way by which the movement in Glasgow had arrived. In 1888, the

College was again in the news when it was honoured by a visit from Queen Victoria.

However, by 1889 the affairs of women's higher education were approaching a crisis. The College Council began to discuss the possible incorporation of the College in the University of Glasgow with the University to assume financial responsibility. The day was finally won for the merger after a somewhat lengthy discussion.

On the 4th July 1892, a deed of gift was approved by the College Council, which handed over to the University of Glasgow as the new Women's Department, the whole property and buildings of the College. By this change, neither the College nor its students lost their identity, they were still Queen Margaret Students but, in addition, they were now also matriculated students of the University.

In 1894, the University saw it's first woman graduate in Medicine, who would also hold the coveted President position of the Queen Margaret Union, Marion Gilchrist. Of her time at the College she recalls,

"On the opening day I can remember our speech in the College Library. Speeches of great encouragement and welcome were made, and we all felt we were launched at last on an adventurous course. The newspapers next day reported that we were all there – from the stern female clad in severe navy blue to the little girl with ringlets who ought to have been eating chocolates in the Drawing Room".

With incorporation, lectures and graduating classes, systematic and practical, in the Faculties of Arts, Science and Medicine, continued to be held for women students at Queen Margaret College but gradually lessened in number. Eventually smaller colonies were drafted to Gilmorehill. The most powerful factor for this was the immense number of women desiring to avail themselves of University education overwhelming the limited accommodation of the College. Although the future of the College itself looked bleak, the plight of the Higher Education of women had achieved its goal.

Entrance hall to Queen Margaret College

Pin Badge

First Meeting of Queen Margaret Union

QM Union Members
(28th March 1890)

Every two weeks during the academic year, the Queen Margaret Union Board of Management meets on the third floor of the Union and discusses the business of the fortnight. Presented here is the minute from the very meeting in Queen Margaret College, held on 28 March 1890 that led to the formation of Queen Margaret Union.

Queen Margaret Union Minute Book

Presented to the Students' Union of Queen Margaret College by Janet A. Galloway (Honorary Secretary of Queen Margaret College), with best wishes for the future and success of the Union.

28th March 1890

At a meeting held on the 28th March 1890 in Queen Margaret College, Miss McMillan in the chair, it was decided that a Students' Union should form; the objects of which should be the provision of social intercourse among the students, the representation of the students in matters affecting their interests; to be a means of communication between the students and the college authorities.

Hitherto, no society with those objects had existed among the students.

Mrs Campbell of Tullichewan was elected Honorary President.

The following resolutions were made:

1. 'That the society should be called Queen Margaret Students' Union'

    Proposed - Mrs Robertson

    Seconded - Mrs Jardine

2. 'That all matriculated students of Queen Margaret College should be members of the Union'

Proposed - Miss Watson

Seconded - Miss Robertson

and

'That all matriculated students from the time of entering into the college building in March 1884 be eligible as members'

Proposed - Miss Watson

Seconded - Miss Erskine Murray

3. 'That the Committee of the Union be composed of representatives from each class'

Proposed - Miss Jardine

Seconded - Miss Lang

4. 'That not fewer than two; with the power to add to their number, past students be on the Committee'

Proposed - Miss Gilchrist

Seconded - Miss Norris

5. 'That present students not of first session shall fill the offices of Vice President and Secretary'

Proposed - Miss McMillan

Seconded - Miss McKendrick

6. 'That the Committee shall be appointed at a meeting to be held at the beginning of each session'
Proposed - Miss McMillan
Seconded - Miss Menzies

Miss McMillan and Miss Robertson pointed out the advantages which had followed the formation of such Unions elsewhere and which must follow in this case.

Sixty-five students gave their names as members.

The following class representatives were chosen as a Committee:
History   - Miss Young
German Literature - Miss Watson
German Language - Miss Menzies
German Tutorial - Miss Carrick
French Literature - Miss Story
French Language - Miss Mackay
Chemistry   - Miss Fraser
Natural Philosophy - Miss Gilchrist
Moral Philosophy - Miss McIntosh
Logic   - Miss Black
English Literature 1 - Miss Blacklock
English Literature 2 - Miss Fraser
Art   - Miss Jolly
Latin   - Miss Cumming
Music   - Miss Allen
Past Student 1 - Miss Duguid
Past Student 2 - Miss Robertson

3rd April 1890

The second meeting of the Union was held on the 3rd April 1890 and was composed of the Committee of Class Representatives from among whom the following office-bearers were elected; Miss Watson as Vice President; Miss Cumming as Secretary and by whom Miss McMillan was elected as Acting President.

QUEEN MARGARET'S STUDENTS UNION.

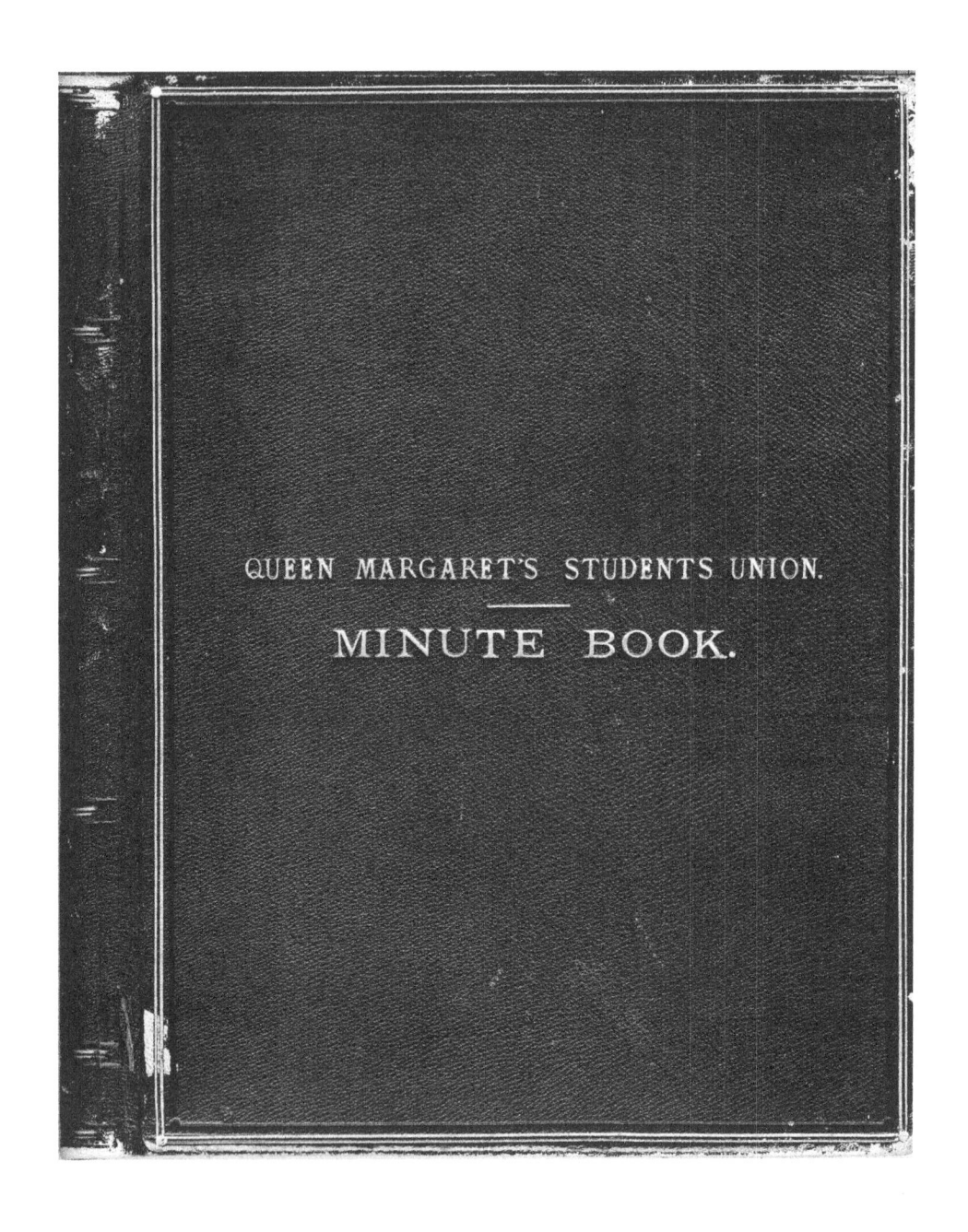

MINUTE BOOK.

Minute Book

1900

With the passing of Queen Victoria, the era sharing her name came to an end. The twentieth century arrived and with it came much change across the country. Far closer to home, Queen Margaret Union was well aware of the need to adapt and was adamant it would not be left behind.

Membership was a fraction of what it would be by the turn of the next millennium at only 150 women students. There were now plans to drastically change Queen Margaret Union. The role of President was one of great honour and prestige (something that has not changed over the years). Every year the membership must carefully elect someone new to lead the Union forward. In 1904 they made possibly their most successful choice in electing Janette R. B. Nelson to the top spot. In the four years she held the coveted position (she would be the last to do so before the constitution was changed to limit Presidential terms to one year) several large steps were taken to allow Queen Margaret Union to obtain its own property.

In 1906 a Bazaar was held in the city to raise the money to find the Union and its members a permanent home. Several similar events would be held over the years (most recently as 1994) but this would be, by far, the most successful. It didn't quite raise enough money to reach the desired goal of a purpose built home but did allow for a new home to eventually be rented.

From its inception through to the opening of the new home, one woman was always a strong supporter of Queen Margaret Union. Janet A. Galloway gave her all for the students of Queen Margaret College and supported them in many endeavours. She would regularly attend events (both as honoured guest and, when necessary, chaperone) and would even host her own events for the women students. She tirelessly served the students until her death. Queen Margaret Union would be a very different place without her efforts.

Queen·Margaret·College
Students' Union.

Bazaar Guide
AND PROGRAMME

7th, 8th, 9th & 10th November, 1906.
St. Andrew's Halls, Glasgow.

PRICE THREEPENCE.

Bizarre Bazaar

Gary R. Brown
President 2006-2007

For over a decade Queen Margaret Union had existed as social relief for the remarkable women of the College bearing the same name. From that fateful day on 28 March 1890 the elected officials of the student body, who were entrusted with the running of the Union, were dedicated to making it everything it could be. Unfortunately, since its creation, the Union had been little more than a glorified club or society, and the College already had several of its own to rival the University of Glasgow's male-dominated groups.

In 1904 the membership elected one of the most dedicated people to the coveted position of President that the Union has ever known. Janette R. B. Nelson had a vision. She saw the hidden potential that was Queen Margaret Union and longed for something greater than a humble Society shut away in the darker recesses of Queen Margaret College at North Park House. The decade prior to her term of office had seen several successful activities run by, or with the help of, the Board of Management. Saturday afternoons were reserved for Afternoon Tea at the house of various members of the Union on a rotating basis. The early minutes of meetings of the Board of Management suggest that these small events were to 'promote sociability' amongst the members, a purpose that has always been the core aim behind any event run by Queen Margaret Union and its dedicated masses.

We must remember when looking back at the early days of Queen Margaret Union and comparing the life of a member in the Victorian era to the life of one circa 2000 that events were very different. Blaring club night music was more than half a century away and besides, even if it were around at the time, it would have been very unbecoming of the so called 'Q-Emmas' to associate with that scene. Tableaux Vivant were de rigueur. Before the days of 'moving pictures' and colour reproductions of images, paintings and other images were 'recreated' on a stage or in a room for the viewing pleasure of those in attendance. Models would appear on stage in elaborate costume, often posed, and carefully lit to give a striking visual feast. Often, one 'image' would be followed by several more, usually to reveal a story or tale.

With around 150 members at this time, the mistress of Queen Margaret College, Janet Galloway would often offer her home as a venue for social events. These so-called 'At Homes' were popular with the students but, in the eyes of President Janette R. B. Nelson, it was still not enough.

From the moment she took over in the top-spot she redefined the role, changing it from the honorary 'back seat' position that it had been to a more 'hands on' job. Queen Margaret Union needed its own home, something separate from the College itself; a place that the membership could be proud to call their own. All they needed was some money.

For two years President Nelson made preparations for the biggest gathering in Queen Margaret Union history since the meeting that founded it in 1890. They created a Bazaar 'obtaining funds for the erection, equipment and endowment of a Union Building for the Women Students and Graduates of the University of Glasgow'. During the preparations, Janette was elected for a third (and would go on to have a fourth) term of office as President. She was also the last President to hold more than one term of office.

The Bazaar itself was held over four days from the 7th until the 10th November 1906. The venue was St. Andrews Halls at Charing Cross in Glasgow. The Halls themselves incidentally were almost completely destroyed in 1962 by a fire and the surviving façade was incorporated into an extension of the Mitchell Library. The event was a huge success, attracting businesses, local traders and other interested parties to rent a stall to sell their wares. Some stalls sold flowers, sweets and confectionery, local and imported produce as well as games, books, parcels and refreshments.

PROSPECTUS.

Queen Margaret College Students' Union Bazaar.

A Bazaar for the purpose of obtaining funds for the erection, equipment, and endowment of a Union Building for the Women Students and Graduates of the University of Glasgow.

The Bazaar will be held in St. Andrew's Halls, Glasgow, on 7th, 8th, 9th, and 10th November, 1906.

Patron.
HER MAJESTY QUEEN ALEXANDRA.

President.
H.R.H. PRINCESS LOUISE, DUCHESS OF ARGYLL.

Vice-Presidents.
LADY STIRLING MAXWELL OF POLLOK. | MRS. CAMPBELL, LL.D., OF TULLICHEWAN.

Vice-Patrons.

THE HON. THE LORD PROVOST OF GLASGOW (WM. BILSLAND, ESQ.)
THE EARL OF HOME, Lord Lieutenant of Lanarkshire.
THE RT. HON. SIR HENRY CAMPBELL-BANNERMAN, M.P.
THE EARL OF ERROL, Hereditary High Constable of Scotland.
THE DUKE OF RICHMOND AND GORDON.
THE DUKE OF HAMILTON AND BRANDON.
THE DUKE OF BUCCLEUCH.
THE DUKE OF ARGYLL.
THE DUKE OF MONTROSE.
THE DUKE OF SUTHERLAND.
THE MARQUIS OF AILSA.
THE MARQUIS OF BREADALBANE.
THE MARQUIS OF LINLITHGOW.
THE MARQUIS OF TULLIBARDINE.
THE MARQUIS OF GRAHAM.
THE EARL OF MAR AND KELLIE.
THE EARL OF ELGIN AND KINCARDINE.
THE EARL OF ABERDEEN.
THE EARL OF STAIR.
THE EARL OF GLASGOW.
THE EARL OF CASSILLIS.
LORD REAY.
LORD BELHAVEN AND STENTON.
LORD HAMILTON of Dalzell.
LORD KELVIN.
LORD BLYTHSWOOD.
THE RT. HON. HERBERT HENRY ASQUITH, M.P.
THE RT. HON. J. PARKER SMITH.
SIR JOHN STIRLING MAXWELL, BART.
SIR ALEXANDER LEITH BUCHANAN, BART.
SIR JAMES COLQUHOUN, BART.
SIR SIMON MACDONALD LOCKHART, BART.
SIR ARCHIBALD ORR-EWING, BART., of Succoth and Garscube.
SIR JAMES KING, BART.
SIR THOMAS GLEN-COATS, BART., M.P.
SIR JAMES BELL, BART.
SIR SAMUEL CHISHOLM, BART.
SIR JOHN URE PRIMROSE, BART.
SIR DONALD CURRIE.
SIR HENRY CRAIK, M.P.
SIR HECTOR C. CAMERON, M.D.
SIR THOMAS M'CALL ANDERSON, M.D.
SIR A. M. TORRANCE, M.P.
SIR W. R. COPLAND.
THE VERY REV. PRINCIPAL STORY.

THE DUCHESS OF HAMILTON AND BRANDON.
THE DUCHESS OF BUCCLEUCH.
THE DUCHESS OF MONTROSE.
THE DUCHESS OF SUTHERLAND.
THE DUCHESS OF ABERCORN.
THE MARCHIONESS OF AILSA.
THE MARCHIONESS OF ZETLAND.
THE MARCHIONESS OF LINLITHGOW.
THE MARCHIONESS OF TULLIBARDINE.
THE MARCHIONESS OF GRAHAM.
THE LADY FRANCES BALFOUR.
THE COUNTESS OF EGLINTON.
ANNA, COUNTESS OF MORAY.
THE COUNTESS OF MAR AND KELLIE.
THE COUNTESS OF HOME.
THE COUNTESS OF ELGIN AND KINCARDINE.
THE COUNTESS OF WEMYSS AND MARCH.
THE COUNTESS OF LEVEN AND MELVILLE.
THE COUNTESS OF ABERDEEN.
THE COUNTESS OF CASSILLIS.
THE LADY ALICE SHAW STEWART.
THE LADY GEORGIANA MURE.
THE LADY BEATRICE DALRYMPLE.
THE LADY MARY HOPE.
THE LADY ANNE SPIERS of Elderslie.
THE LADY EVELYN FARQUHAR.
THE LADY REAY.
THE LADY BELHAVEN AND STENTON.
THE LADY TALBOT DE MALAHIDE.
THE LADY KELVIN.
THE LADY BLYTHSWOOD.
THE HON. LADY ORR-EWING.
THE HON. LADY FARQUHAR.
THE HON. ADELE HAMILTON.
THE HON. MRS. ALGERNON HANBURY TRACY.
LADY LEITH BUCHANAN.
LADY COLQUHOUN.
LADY MACDONALD LOCKHART.
LADY CAMPBELL of Succoth and Garscube.
LADY GLEN-COATS.
LADY BELL.
LADY WATSON.
LADY CHISHOLM.
LADY URE PRIMROSE.
LADY COATS of Auchendrane.
LADY CRAIK.
LADY ROBERTON.
LADY M'CALL ANDERSON.
MRS. BILSLAND.
MRS. PARKER SMITH.
MRS. STORY.

G. N. BARNES, ESQ., M.P.
J. W. CLELAND, ESQ., M.P.
A. CAMERON CORBETT, ESQ., M.P.
ALEXANDER CROSS, ESQ., M.P.
H. A. WATT, ESQ., M.P.
T. M'KINNON WOOD, ESQ., M.P.
PROF. ARCHIBALD BARR, D.Sc.
PROF. LUDWIG BECKER, Ph.D.
PROF. J. H. BILES, LL.D.
PROF. F. O. BOWER, Sc.D., F.R.S.
PROF. JOHN CLELAND, M.D., LL.D., D.Sc., F.R.S.
PROF. JAMES COOPER, D.D.
PROF. W. MACNEILE DIXON, Litt.D.
PROF. J. FERGUSON, M.A., LL.D., F.S.A.
PROF. SAMSON GEMMELL, M.D.
PROF. JOHN GLAISTER, M.D.
PROF. W. M. GLOAG, B.A.
HENRY E. GORDON, ESQ., B.A.
ROBERT GOURLAY, ESQ., LL.D.
PROF. ANDREW GRAY, LL.D., F.R.S.
PROF. JOHN W. GREGORY, D.Sc., F.R.S.
JOHN HUTCHISON, ESQ., LL.D.
PROF. WILLIAM JACK, LL.D.
PROF. HENRY JONES, LL.D.
PROF. J. GRAHAM KERR, M.A.
PROF. ROBERT LATTA, M.A., D.Phil.
W. LORIMER, ESQ.
PROF. J. G. M'KENDRICK, M.D., LL.D., F.R.S.
PROF. DUDLEY JULIUS MEDLEY, M.A.
R. M. MITCHELL, ESQ., D.L.
PROF. ROBERT MUIR, M.A., M.D.
DAVID MURRAY, ESQ., LL.D.
PROF. JOHN S. PHILLIMORE, M.A.
PROF. GEORGE G. RAMSAY, LL.D.
PROF. H. M. B. REID, D.D.
PROF. JAMES ROBERTSON, D.D.
PROF. WILLIAM SMART, D.Phil., LL.D.
PROF. WILLIAM STEWART, D.D.

CONVENERS' COMMITTEE.

Convener— LADY STIRLING MAXWELL, POLLOK HOUSE, POLLOKSHAWS.
Vice-Conveners—MRS. M. PEARCE CAMPBELL, 9 LYNEDOCH CRESCENT.
MISS GALLOWAY, QUEEN MARGARET COLLEGE, HILLHEAD.

THE LADY FRANCES BALFOUR.
THE HON. ADELE HAMILTON.
LADY STIRLING MAXWELL of Pollok.
LADY CAMPBELL of Succoth and Garscube.
LADY M'CALL ANDERSON.
MRS. JAMES A. ALLAN.
MRS. A. MARSHALL BROWN.
MRS. CAMPBELL, LL.D., of Tullichewan.
MRS. ADAIR CAMPBELL of Darleith.
MRS. M. PEARCE CAMPBELL.
MRS. J. T. CARGILL.
MRS. CLELAND.
MRS. WALTER CRUM.
MISS FARQUHAR.
MRS. D. G. FRAME.
MRS. GILL.
MRS. MUNGO GRAHAM.
MISS GALLOWAY.
MISS GRAY.
MISS NELSON.
MRS. ROTTENBURG.
MRS. MUIR SIMPSON.
MRS. STORY.
MRS. STIRLING STUART of Castlemilk.
MISS WHITSON.
MRS. JACK WILSON.
MRS. PATERSON WINGATE.
THE JOINT HON. SECRETARIES (*ex officiis*).
THE HON. TREASURER (*ex officio*).

GENERAL ARRANGEMENTS COMMITTEE.

Convener— MR. A. CAMERON CORBETT, M.P., ROWALLAN, KILMARNOCK.
Vice-Convener—COL. R. C. MACKENZIE, EDINBARNET, DUNTOCHER.

LADY STIRLING MAXWELL, Pollok House, Pollokshaws.
MRS. ADAIR CAMPBELL, of Darleith, Artarman, Row.
MRS. M. PEARCE CAMPBELL, 9 Lynedoch Crescent.
MISS GALLOWAY, Queen Margaret College, Hillhead.
MRS. PATERSON WINGATE, 5 Kelvinside Terrace.
MR. J. ARCHIBALD CAMPBELL, 126 St. Vincent Street.
MR. M. PEARCE CAMPBELL, 137 Ingram Street.
MR. A. CAMERON CORBETT, M.P., Rowallan, Kilmarnock.
COL. R. C. MACKENZIE, Edinbarnet, Duntocher.
MR. JAMES D. ROBERTSON, 1 Park Terrace, East.
THE JOINT HON. SECRETARIES (*ex officiis*).
THE HON. TREASURER (*ex officio*).

Hon. Secretaries.

THOMSON BRODIE, C.A., 156 ST. VINCENT STREET.
MISS AGNES DI C. KERR, 12 OAKFIELD TERRACE, HILLHEAD.

Hon. Treasurer.

T. W. M. WATSON, C.A., 149 ST. VINCENT STREET.

STALLS

I—QUEEN MARGARET STALL.

President—
LADY ROBERTON.

Conveners—
MRS. J. A. ALLAN, Westerton, Milngavie.
MISS GALLOWAY, Queen Margaret College, Hillhead.
MRS. GILL, 47 Kersland Terrace, Hillhead.

Stallholders—
MRS. J. A. ALLAN, Westerton, Milngavie.
MRS. R. S. ALLAN, 15 Woodside Terrace.
MRS. M. PEARCE CAMPBELL, 9 Lynedoch Crescent.
MISS GALLOWAY, Queen Margaret College, Hillhead.
MRS. GILL, 47 Kersland Terrace, Hillhead.
MRS. LINDSAY, 1 Park Gate.
MRS. P. MACLELLAN, 1 Montague Terrace, Kelvinside.
MRS. NELSON, Snowdon, 13 Sherbrooke Avenue, Pollokshields.
MRS. RIDDOCH, 5 Eton Terrace, Hillhead.
MRS. J. HAY WILSON, 6 Park Circus Place.
THE MISSES WINGATE, 4 Rosslyn Terrace, Kelvinside.
MISS WOTHERSPOON, 4 Lynedoch Place.

Receivers of Work—
MISS ALEXANDER, 15 Queen's Crescent.
MRS. ARTHUR, Pruitfield, Airdrie.
MISS BIRRELL, 6 Kelvinside Terrace.
THE MISSES COCHRANE, Crosslee, Strathaven.
MRS. N. P. DONALDSON, 2 Highburgh Terrace, Hyndland.
MISS EWEN, M.A., Craigielea, Bothwell.
THE MISSES KAY, 5 Rosebery Terrace, Kelvinbridge.
THE MISSES KEPPIE, 16 Hamilton Park Terrace, Hillhead.
THE MISSES KER, 1 Windsor Terrace, West, Kelvinside.
MRS. M'CALLUM, M.A., 7 Buto Mansions, Hillhead.
MRS. MACEWEN, 19 Onslow Drive, Dennistoun.
MRS. MACKENDRICK, 44 Hamilton Park Terrace, Hillhead.
MISS MACLAY, 3 Woodlands Terrace.
MRS. MACPHAIL, Calder Villa, Coatbridge.
MRS. MAY, M.A., 15 Athole Gardens, Kelvinside.
MRS. ERSKINE MURRAY, Alva Lodge, Windsor Road, Parkstone, Dorset.
MRS. NAPIER, Schiehallion, Dunblane.
MRS. PARKER, Thornbank, Ann Street, Hillhead.
MRS. RIGG, Lyndholme, St. Andrew's Drive, Pollokshields.
MRS. SPOTTISWOOD RITCHIE, 6 Indale Place, Edinburgh.
MRS. J. H. ROBERTSON, South Edgehill House, Langside.
MRS. G. ROXBURGH, Rosebank, Thorntonhall, Lanarkshire.
MISS RUTHERFORD, M.A., 26 Belmont Gardens, Hillhead.
MRS. SLOAN, 5 Somerset Place.
MRS. J. SPENS, 33 Heriot Row, Edinburgh.
MRS. R. R. STEWART, 25 Athole Gardens, Kelvinside.
MRS. THOMSON, 21 Binnie Place.
MISS THOMSON, 21 Binnie Place.
MRS. WALTER, Greenlodge, Greenhead.
MRS. PATERSON WINGATE, 5 Kelvinside Terrace.
MRS. WYPER, 6 Burnbank Gardens.

Hon. Secretaries—
MISS ANNIE F. KEDIE, 11 Eglinton Drive, Kelvinside.
MISS L. ALLISON RIGG, Lyndholme, St. Andrew's' Drive, Pollokshields.

II—UNIVERSITY STALL.

Presidents—
THE LADY FRANCES BALFOUR.
MRS. STORY.

Conveners—
LADY M'CALL ANDERSON, 9 The University, Hillhead.
MRS. CLELAND, 2 The University, Hillhead.

Stallholders—
LADY M'CALL ANDERSON, 9 The University, Hillhead.
MRS. BARR, Royston, Downhill.
MRS. BECKER, The Observatory, Downhill.
MRS. BILES, 10 University Gardens, Hillhead.
MISS CAMERON, 7 Newton Terrace.
MRS. CLELAND, 2 The University, Hillhead.
MRS. MACNEILE DIXON, 2 South Park Terrace, Hillhead.
MRS. GLAISTER, 3 Newton Place.
MRS. GRAY, 11 The University, Hillhead.
MRS. GREGORY, 4 Park Quadrant.
MR. JACK, 10 The University, Hillhead.
MRS. JONES, 1 The University, Hillhead.
MR. GRAHAM KERR, 12 Oakfield Terrace, Hillhead.
MRS. MOIR, 9 University Gardens, Hillhead.
MISS MUIR, 16 Victoria Crescent, Downhill.
MRS. PHILLIMORE, 5 The University, Hillhead.
MRS. RAMSAY, 6 The University, Hillhead.
MRS. RODGER, 4 The University, Hillhead.
MRS. ROBERTSON, 7 The University, Hillhead.
MRS. SMART, Nunholm, Downhill.

Receivers of Work—
MRS. BAMFORD, 30 Falkland Mansions, Hyndland.
MRS. BARR, 13 Woodside Place.
MRS. BRYDE, 2 Granby Terrace, Hillhead.
MRS. M. CHARTERIS, 4 Queen Margaret Crescent.
MRS. COATS, 8 University Gardens, Hillhead.
MRS. WALKER DOWNIE, 4 Woodside Crescent.
MRS. J. D. HEDDERWICK, 2 Clairmont Gardens.
MRS. W. K. HUTTON, 11 Beaumont Gate, Downhill.
MISS HYSLOP, 2 Endsleigh Gardens.
MRS. JACK, 43 Lansdowne Crescent.
MRS. MUNRO KERR, 7 Clairmont Gardens.
MRS. LANG, 61 Gibson Street, Hillhead.
MRS. M'KECHNIE, Knightswood, Elderslie.
MRS. MACLENNAN, 3 Buckingham Terrace, Hillhead.
MRS. TEACHER, 22 Kingsborough Gardens, Kelvinside.
MRS. SHAW, The Lodge, Dullatur.
MRS. WORKMAN, 5 Woodside Terrace.

Hon. Secretary—
MISS CAMERON, 200 Bath Street.

Hon. Treasurer—
MISS STORY, 13 The University, Hillhead.

Bazaar Prospectus, 1906

The opening ceremony held at 2.30pm on 7th November 1906 featured none other than HRH Princess Louise, Duchess of Argyll. The Princess had been a great supporter of the feminist movement in Britain and was therefore the perfect choice to officially open the festivities. Some of the entertainment over the four days of the Bazaar included an underground casino featuring a rifle range, palmistry and psychic readings, Spanish dancers, dramatic sketches and comedy skits. Of the goods for sale many stalls featured silverware, dolls, clothes, pottery, accessories, embroidery, rugs, needlework, furniture, homemade sweets, cigarettes, ornaments and a litter of deerhound puppies! One of the highlights of the event was a lecture on his Antarctic Expedition by Ernest H. Shackleton, which saw him reach the furthest southern point on earth of any human being at the time.

Perhaps the most fascinating, and beautiful, aspect of the Bazaar was the distribution of a book entitled, 'The Stray Pearls of Queen Margaret'. The text was a 124-page collection of favourite quotes from the many hundred members of the Union, graduates of the College and lecturers of the University of Glasgow. The Bazaar, although successful, did not result immediately in a building for Queen Margaret Union. In fact, the only time the Union would actually have a venue specially commissioned was in the 1960s resulting in the opening of its current home at 22 University Gardens in 1967. Over the course of the next few years however, space was rented for the Union to occupy 12 Buckingham Terrace, near Great Western Road and still within walking distance of the College.

Before moving forward in the history of this great establishment, here are a few quotes from the 'Stray Pearls of Queen Margaret':

The Stray Pearls of Queen Margaret
A collection of favourite quotes and proverbs from the members of
Queen Margaret Union in 1906 – given away at Union Bazaar

Walter Brown
"There may be a good thing and a thing better, but there is nothing better than the best"

Alex W. Donaldson
"Our greatest glory is not in never failing but in rising every time we fall"

J. K. McKell
"Every shadow points to the sun"

A. T.
"It is not how long we live, but how well we live"

George Alexander
"As for women – God bless 'em all I say"

B. H. Lee
"Little things are little things, but to be faithful in little things is to be great"

Janet Galloway

Janet Galloway

*From a speech by
Marion Fraser
President 1953-1954*

Janet Galloway was Honorary Secretary of Queen Margaret College from 1883 until 1909.

Janet Anne Galloway was a strong supporter of the movement that led to the formation of Queen Margaret College. She acted as Honorary Secretary for some time on the Glasgow Association for the Higher Education of Women. In 1883, when the Association became the College, she took on the role as Secretary.

Miss Galloway was a wealthy woman, but it is written of her, "Money's worth is not the standard by which to measure Miss Galloway's devotion and self sacrifice, but it will be seen how large an endowment she contributed to the College when we remember that she rendered services of the most important kind without remuneration for the long period of 32 years". As secretary of the new Queen Margaret College, Janet Galloway was there to be the driving force of the administration. Her task was no sinecure. Everything was being done by, and for, women for the first time and she was determined that no sins of omission or commission on the part of 'her' students should prejudice their cause in the eyes of the University of Glasgow Court or Senate. Many of the Queen Margaret College students were not there for professional training but for the love of learning and it was an extraordinarily united family that inhabited North Park House.

Miss Galloway personally knew every student and brought them all together several times during the sessions at her so-called 'At Homes'. An account about a dance in Miss Galloway's presence at Queen Margaret College states, "We had dances in the large drawing room upstairs. I remember at one of these I was dancing with someone when I was told that Miss Galloway wanted me to speak to her as she sat and watched the dance. In these days, every dance had to be presided over by a chaperone. When I got the message, I wondered if I had been putting my heels down too hard or doing something not quite like a young lady – but to my astonishment, I was given a gold fountain pen which I had won in a raffle".

Miss Galloway's influence was considerable, but not sufficient to win every battle. Another account recalls, "Miss Galloway tried to get me into the men's French class at the University as it would have suited my timetable much better. She applied to the Senatus for permission but 'No' was the answer. Then she suggested that I should sit at the very back of the lecture room behind the men, but this prospect was not accepted either. If I had been a girl of ravishing beauty, one might have understood this rebuff but I was a very ordinary person".

Miss Galloway sat all day in her office, never too busy to see a student, advised as to courses and future careers, encouraged the ambitious, scolded the frivolous, found friends for the solitary, secured posts for those who were ready for them and smothered untrodden paths for many a different beginner. For years she did all this with no paid help. She never spared herself and she had a genius for utilizing the services of untrained but willing volunteers. An untiring worker herself, she inspired willing and cheerful service. Worn out with endless labours, Miss Galloway died, in harness at her desk, as she would have wished.

In 1935, the first women to graduate in Medicine from the University of Glasgow (and a former Queen Margaret Union President herself), Marion Gilchrist wrote of Miss Galloway,

"We can never forget how much we owe to the women who championed our cause and helped us in so many ways. I am glad that there is, in the Bute Hall, a lasting memory of her in that beautiful window by our great artist, Sir Douglas Strachan. Too few of us is given the power of working with such wholehearted selfless devotion for the good of others; too few of us the joy of winning such appreciation and love as she got from her 'old girls', and her memory will be evergreen in the history of Queen Margaret College".

Interior of the office of the Mistress of Queen Margaret College

Miss GALLOWAY

AT HOME

on the Afternoon of Wednesday, 22nd May, 3 till 6.30 p.m.

All Women Students of Queen Margaret College and Gilmorehill of Session 1906-7 and Summer Session 1907, the Graduates, and all members of Queen Margaret College Students' Union, are cordially invited.

Since the annual summer At Home of last year, the Union has had to mourn the death of Mrs. Campbell of Tullichewan, who was its President from the date of its formation in 1890, and to whom the College and the Union owe a deep debt of gratitude. She was a pioneer of the movement for the University education of women from its very early days, and foundress, in 1877, of the Glasgow Association for the Higher Education of Women which became Queen Margaret College in 1883. She was Vice-President of Queen Margaret College from its foundation till its incorporation in the University in 1892; she collected, greatly by her own exertions, the funds for its endowment; and she did much to aid the advancement of education in many other ways. To her enthusiasm for and devotion to the College, and her wise counsels and administration, may be attributed much of the success which has attended its work and progress.

P.T.O.

Invitation from 1906-07 to join Janet Galloway at one of her regular 'At-Home' events where she would host the members of Queen Margaret Union and College

Janet E. Galloway, LL.D.

A Book of Memories

A commemorative book of treasured memories of Janet Galloway
by those who had the privilege of knowing her

With All Good Wishes

for

Christmas and the New Year

From —

The President &

Board of Management

Christmas Card given to members of Queen Margaret Union from the Board of Management

1910

1910 was the beginning of a turbulent period in the history of the world. It was the decade when the legendary ocean liner, the Titanic hit an iceberg and sunk and when the assassination of Archduke Franz Ferdinand would become the catalyst to war in Europe. The twentieth century was showing no signs of slowing down however and Queen Margaret Union was keen to do the same.

Despite the onset of war, Queen Margaret Union went from strength to strength. Six hundred University of Glasgow students fell fighting for peace in Europe and thousands more left their studies to do their part. Following a rousing call from the then Principal the students of the University (of which Queen Margaret Union was firmly associated with as the Women's Department) had newfound enthusiasm to move forward despite wartime conditions still being present.

The ladies of Queen Margaret Union were turning the heads of the men on campus, even managing to make frequent appearances in many University publications at the time. As the decade came to a close it was clear that the demographic at Gilmorehill was forever changed. Women students were firmly entrenched in the corporate life of the University of Glasgow and the city itself.

a "Q-Emma"

A Q-Emma: Drawing depicting the male view of the typical Queen Margaret Union member in the 1910s.

Queen Margaret Types

From **Glasgow University Magazine**
By Tristan

The following article comes from a War Time edition of Glasgow University Magazine (GUM). The stereotypical women observed by the composer of these works, Tristan, may not be as far removed from modern Queen Margaret Union as one would first think.

The Prize-Winner
The face of a Roman Matron, the eyes of a cold sea-trout,
A girl who's jolly clever, and looks it without a doubt,
Who never has time or patience for the butterfly gadabout.
But – I saw her down in Arran a few short months ago,
Sittin' where she shouldn't when the evening sun burned low,
A-whispering mushy nothings to her undistinguished beau.

The Authority
She talks of taste; just note the hues
That shriek out in every direction;
She ought not to air her aesthetic views
Till she knows how to suit her complexion.
The Delicate Female
She potters all day with a scalpel,
Cutting the dead men up,
And potting their brains with the scalp off –
Then she goes home to sup.

The New Woman
An emancipated woman, she tells it aloud in the street,
She worships the Feminist movement, and thinks
    Mrs. Pankhurst sweet;
Men are brutes, and women are glorious, born to be free,
And all her stupid satellites nod their heads and agree;
But we have seen her imbibing wisdom with coffee or tea,
From a man for whom she yearns, as the sea shell longs
    for the sea.
And surely, my lady, if one of the "brutes" for your favour
    is meet,
We old-fashioned women in bondage may claim that our
    men are a treat.

The Super-Idealist
With spiritual eyes and cheeks of flame,
She pleads for the essentials of life –
The soul perfected in sublimest strife,
But then, of course, her body's pretty tame.

The Pillar of Society
She stands for truth and right and honour,
Week after week;
But down at home the urchins call her,
The village sneak.
The Enigmas
Two naughty little Subs. wrote erotic verse
(All the men swore an oath, women are a curse),
Yet are they as cold and chaste I will dare to say,
As snow upon the mountains, or the soul of Archie Tae

[The Editor accepts no responsibility for the above, but offers unlimited quantities of champagne and sultana cake (to be paid for by the Finance Manager) for successful spotting by men.]

Life Before the War

*From a speech by
Marion Fraser
President 1953-1954*

In 1950, as the Fifth Centenary celebrations were about to break on an unsuspecting Fresher population, I came to the University of Glasgow, as an undergraduate in the Arts faculty, where my mother had graduated in 1913. History by anecdote is not ideal, but her reactions to being one of a minority of women students before the Great War enable me to share her memories of that period in the history of Queen Margaret College.

A High School girl with one sister, she found the whole social scene daunting. Her older male cousin was attending medical classes but his skills were more acceptably employed entertaining outstandingly well on the Union piano. He was finally jogged out of that existence by the advent of the First World War. He always viewed his female cousin, even in old age, with slight derision, verging on disbelief, that she had a university education at all – and with a modicum of awe. They were both first generation students and their families were proud of them – well, as proud as a Glasgow family in trade could own up to being! Men were an unknown quantity to my mother and although very pretty, she was shy and proud so she lacked confidence and didn't in fact marry until she was in her fifties. Her time was spent between classes in Queen Margaret College and some in the University itself.

It was a difficult situation for the young women. My mother admitted that she would never have passed her Geography exam had not an obliging African student helped her out. Despite a shapely and academically attuned mind into her nineties, she was deeply ashamed of her third class honours degree but could never be honest enough with herself to admit that it was probably her lack of absorption into university life that denied her academic development.

Yes, she went to dances with her best friend whose attention to sartorial details nearly drove my mother mad (forty minutes to fix properly a brooch at her neck). My mother became an excellent and devoted teacher. She loved teaching; hers was a success story. Her education gave her a rich, satisfying life, serving young people as best she knew how while developing a strong creative bent in her spare time. To her last days she attracted respect. Her younger grandson referred to her, not unkindly, as 'Commander Granny'.

Then came the Great War and those tragic black-bordered reports in the daily newspapers. The walls of the University Chapel tell the story with vivid effect. A complete graduating year of young men perished leaving a strongly unbalanced society. An early memory for me was my mother saying, "Never grudge giving to Poppy Day, you owe them more than you can ever repay.". This was to a small girl from a reticent and undemonstrative woman. "Lest we Forget", was a sharp reality for her generation. No wonder the swing back to what had then become reality – men needing and deserving jobs after the horrors of war – tempered the more strident tones of the suffragette movement.

"Lest We Forget"

Earliest known photo of the Queen Margaret Union Board of Management from 1916

The Great War

Donald MacAlister
Principal
University of Glasgow

The Great War left its mark all across the country. On Gilmorehill, the student publications ceased production during this time. In the years after the war, Prinicpal Donald MacAlister produced the following welcome to the students in the Glasgow University Students' Handbook as a reminder of what we had lost, but also as motivation to push ever onwards.

The War is over, but is not done with. The victory has been won, but it is still to pay. Of the students bred in this University, 3400 fought and 600 fell to save the country, and to set free the student of today for his work here. He owes it to them to resolve that his work shall be worthy of what his freedom cost. The output must match the debt, and each of us is answerable for his share of the whole. The labour will not be light. Steady effort and dauntless courage, such as our comrades put forth to win the War, are needed to fit us for the tasks of peace.

Our students, many of them wise through stern experience, are faced this session with a double duty. They have not merely to enter into and profit by the academic heritage of the past, they have also to refashion it for themselves and their successors. Student organisations and traditions have perforce suffered during the last five years. Whatever in them was helpful to the common life of the University must be revived, and adapted to new conditions, by the present generation. Wise leadership and loyal fellowship were never more needed. They will not be wanting among the soldier-students whom we now welcome back. "Self-reverence, self-knowledge, self-control," these they have learned and practised in the field. They have already proved to us that the lesson is not forgotten in the classroom. If they steadily diffuse this temper among their fellow students, both within and without the classroom, they will enrich the teaching of the University and raise its value as a preparation for the serious work of life.

Without the goodwill of all like-minded men and women, the University will be hard put to it to fulfil its functions under existing conditions. We have recalled a number of distinguished teachers; but we have surrendered a larger number to other universities, and their places are hard to fill. On the other hand, our students are more numerous, and their needs more various, than ever before. Space and equipment are insufficient to meet every claim, and for the time being, money cannot procure them. Building is at a standstill; manufacturers cannot supply furnishings or instruments. Like other schools throughout the country, we are obliged to overcrowd our halls and limit our admissions. War conditions are in fact still with us: their new form calls for the same cheerful forbearance as did the old.

The enterprising spirit of the Students' Council, which has conceived and compassed this handbook in a time of stress, warrants our confidence that a like spirit of comradely helpfulness will prevail to bear us through our difficulties of every kind.

University Chapel
Glasgow

✠

SERVICE

In Commemoration of Members of the University who have fallen in the War

✠

Wednesday, 17th March, 1915

AT 3 P.M.

Order of Service, 1915

Class Room.

Interior of classroom from Queen Margaret College before the classes were moved to Gilmorehill Campus

1920

By 1920, Queen Margaret Union was thirty years young. In three short decades the pioneering women students of Glasgow had managed to transform a small group of like-minded people into a fully-fledged social club that its members could not live without.

In 1922, President Ida Wyllie received news that Queen Margaret Union would be granted a new home at number one University Gardens, right across the street from the Glasgow University Men's Union.

Despite all its recent successes, the Union could not escape the problems of the twenties. As the Great Depression took hold in 1929, the Union saw a drop in membership (which was by subscription). As more and more females sought equality with males it was clear that a women-only club would not appeal to all tastes. The struggle of the Great War had led to a newly empowered generation of women students who had forgotten the struggles of the pioneers who had come before them.

The drop in membership however led to a much closer bond between the various 'Q-Emmas' of the time. Although times may not have been as glamorous as they had been, life at Queen Margaret Union was special, with a newfound emphasis on intimate and meaningful relationships. It was the place where you made your friends for life – one more thing that remains true today.

West Kilbride - self-portrait by Hannah Frank
(Hannah Frank Collection)

Diary Excerpts

*Hannah Frank
Student
University of Glasgow*

Monday 15th [October 1928]
To the University. Wandered about just inside the gates, and inquired of various girls if they know where the Higher English room was. One…[Hannah censored her diaries and some words are missing here] …to her. Meanwhile, the other girl progressed and I was left to find the English room myself.

There was much community singing. The lecturer – I think I shall like him – informs us that (the room being crowded) the ladies shall have to seek another one.

I sat in a basket chair at a window in the Union reading Latin idioms till twenty to one, and then went down to go to Latin. I met Judy, who informs me there is no Latin class till Wednesday.

And so home.

Tuesday 16th [October 1928]
To the University, and filled up a form of enrolment in the English room.

Solly informed me that Belle phoned up, and invited him and me up this afternoon; and also David and Rita. Wondering we went, and discovered that Fay and Lily were having a party. The other guests were younger, and Rita was in her element.

Luckily, we caught the last bus home.

Thursday 18th [October 1928]
To English, and was benched. Would much prefer University life if the personal element entered a little more strongly.

To Q.M. to pay my fees. Met Helen MacAskill. Visited Miss may about French. She was disposed to be amiable and advised me to take out a class ticket and attend some of the lectures.

Monday 22nd [October 1928]
To English.
To the Union. There was I delighted to encounter May Rennie, and, immediately after, Elsa Grieve. Elsa is grown wonderfully tall. We betook ourselves to the drawing room, and sat at a window and talked.
To a Latin Prose exam in the Hunter Hall. It was not difficult, but once or twice my vocabulary failed me.
Mr.Nisbet read out what I take to be our prose sections. Judy is in Mr Nisbet's –A; I am in Mr Austin's – C. I wonder what governs the choice.
May met me coming out, and walked down to the car stp with me.
To the Art School. Life. Ivy has taken to wearing glasses.

Tuesday 23rd [October 1928]
To Q.M. to show the person my certificate of fitness.
To Miss May for an English Syllabus, and was taken for Altie Golombok.
To English. Met Jerry Morris coming out of a class. Anglo-Saxon. Ugh!
Nearly to French, and changed...
[pages removed until sometime during Monday 5th November, 1928]
Till twelve midnight did Latin prose.

Wednesday 7th [November 1928]
To the University and bought a magazine. Idly turned over pages, and turned giddy when I saw 'Night' enthroned in the centre page. Bought another magazine.
Was hardly able to take down Mr Bickersteff's lecture.
French. Elsa greeted me with: saw your drawing in the magazine. Latin. Great interest of bench three in proximity to an artist.

To the union and asked if there was a very big parcel for me. There was. Since I had not claimed it they had sent a postcard to where it came from. But she supposed that now it was alright.

Home.

Found in parcel proof of drawing, and a little note on blue paper which reads: 'My best thanks. You will perhaps allow me to compliment you on one of the most beautiful pieces of work which the G.U.M. has ever had. Please do not stop. G.a.Highet.

Exceedingly pleased.

To the Art School. No Ivy.

Tuesday 13th [November 1928]

Bravely carried a poem and illustration and note to the University. At least the act was brave, though I felt extremely cowardly.

I gave it to the Enquiries man. And now do I live in dread.
[part page removed until Wednesday 14th November 1928]
…therewith. And everything coherent and understandable
To English
To French

Thursday 5th [December 1928]

In exceeding great trepidation to the University. In exceeding great trepidation bought a magazine. My drawing therein, opposite a page of poems, under the heading 'GLAMOUR'. Mine among them. Not over-pleased with drawing.

Handed in our essays. Mine very meagre on 'The forbidding qualities of Wordsworth's poetry'.

To French. Latin.

To the Union, but my drawing not there.

To the Art School. No Ivy.

Friday 7th [December 1928]

To French. Latin.

To the Union, but, the Hall girl not being at hand, and myself seeing no sign of a big parcel, I did not wait.

Monday 14th [January 1929]

Miss May appeared, and informed us that all the lecturers have got influenza.

Reading-room.

Latin. Had only 38/50 for my last prose. I don't see why, for I still think it was rather well done.

Came a letter from Aunt Annie, saying she will be delighted to have me on the date mentioned, and that they are looking forward —

Also came my drawings from the Radio Times. When they have a suitable subject, and enough time for commission by post, they will write again.

To the Art School.

No Ivy.

Tuesday 15th [January 1929]

French. Latin. Have come to the conclusion that 38/50 is quite a good mark.

This was one of my most wretched of days.

Wednesday 16th [January 1929]

Ygorra appeared today.   !!

I paid a visit to dear Professor Martin's cabinet. Miss Ferguson informed me, to my relief, that he was not in.

French. Latin.

Met Zahn and the wee one.

To the Art School.

Saturday 19th [January 1929]

Charities' Day.

Walk with Eva.

At half-past three, as Belle hadn't turned up with the costume, I ran out to 'phone. Lily said Belle had left in the morning, nor did she know where she had gone. Perturbed, I ran home, and then back again, and 'phoned Hochfield's shop. There was no answer. Almost frantic, I ran home once more. To my joy, Belle had arrived with the costume. She had been out collecting in the morning.

So all was well.

I dressed as a French artist, and rouged, and lip-sticked, and powdered, and, in the opinion of all, looked very well.

4W.

Belle accompanied me to Block's, where I found Minnie (in Pyjamas), Moses, Jack Werner, and Solly Goldman.

...boys that I didn't know. Reva and the Golomboks appeared, but they did not join us. We collected the queues, separated to do cars, and returned again. We did the Seamore, Cambridge, and Blythswood Cinemas, and changed our boxes at the Municipal Buildings. On one car I approached a woman, a complete stranger, and she said 'Oh, here's hard-hearted Hannah'.

Jack Werner found time to ask how I was getting on at the [Art School] and at the University,... [pages torn across and removed]

Monday 21st [January 1929]

Postcard from Herta.

Miss May informed us Mr. Wright and Mr. Bickerstaff are not yet returned.

Latin. Mr. Austin off. Our section joined with Mr. Nisbet's. I had the temerity to answer a question which Mr. Nisbet asked thus: Mr. Montague? Wrong. Bench A? B? C? I venture. I was on the whole right.

Paid a visit to Professor Martin. He said rather ominously: Bien, tres bien.

To the Art School.

Found a note from Ivy, addressed to me and Jean. She says she will be back tomorrow.

Queen Margaret College Union
Diary
1923-1924

The Charmed Circle

Jessie Pattie

Originally Printed in
'Twenty-Five'

Women Students' solidarity died during the First World War and the generation that appeared when it was over had forgotten that Queen Margaret College had ever struggled to be recognised by the University of Glasgow. For them there was nothing unique or eloquent in the idea of a purely women's college, and they would listen, half-amused and half-resentful, when they were told, as they were at every party and social function they attended that, "All University women wherever their classes are held are students of Queen Margaret College". What they wanted was to be accepted on equal terms with male students and they planned their curricula of study so that they spent as much of their time as possible in mixed classes within the University.

Their eagerness to work and play alongside, almost to be identified with, men, led to the success of newly inaugurated projects like 'Infirmaries Day' and the 'Students Welfare Scheme', and it helped to light the spark of genius that produced the 'Antigone' of Sophocles in the vast area of Hengler's Circus and set the town talking. But in such an atmosphere a wholly feminine activity like Queen Margaret Union was out of favour: in 1919 no woman from first year medicine had joined, and only about one-fifth of all the women students had become members.

Of course there was lack of money as well as lack of interest. University women were short of money then to a degree that is almost impossible to imagine, and a subscription of 12s 6d a year may well have seemed an unnecessary outlay to people who did not allow themselves a daily cup of coffee and who lunched in a dingy university women's cloakroom off sandwiches brought from home. The only outside financial assistance the average Arts student could hope for at that time was a Carnegie Award of £9 a year, and the principle of taking a holiday job to eke this out had not yet been accepted: in any case there was little hope of obtaining one in a city whose unemployment figures were mounting every day.

There was to be in every generation of women students a large proportion who consider social and corporate activities a waste of valuable time that ought to be devoted to book-learning. The early twenties had more than their share of such, thanks to the post war industrial slump which could not but cast its shadow on the life of a university like Glasgow. Even graduates could be out of work! Fears for the future led to an over-anxiety about getting through examinations and there were too many zealous women students who earnestly noted down a lecturer's every word and were seldom seen outside of classrooms. J. M. Barrie, addressing the students of Edinburgh University, said that the absence of hostels and Unions had "maimed some of us for life". An exaggeration perhaps, but one must concede that there is about a Students' Union, however much it resolves itself into a social club, an atmosphere whose like is not experienced elsewhere; the opportunities found in such a place for the give and take of minds of different interests, attitudes and ancestries never come again.

And so it was to be regretted that so limited a number of the women students of the early 1920's chose to join Queen Margaret Union. It's consequent size, however, led to small group-contacts not to be forgotten; there was about the place an unforced informal air, a fireside quality that will not easily be recaptured. The small Victorian house in Ann Street (with no baths, no bed and breakfast, no smoking) gave to those of us who did become a member almost collegiate corporate life that our daughters and granddaughters will never know.

Co-eds of the 'Twenties'

C.A. Oakley

Originally Printed in
'Twenty-Five'

The year 1919 saw men who had gone to the wars five years earlier, returning to University in sufficient numbers to be able to dictate how student life was to be run. Formerly dances were conducted according to long accepted pattern, with leading women students fluttering about effecting proper introductions; one could, sense the presence in the background of chaperones. But by 1926, the 'palais' and even 'hops' were the order of the day. The 'Charleston' and 'Black Bottom' were the thing.

I was one of that carefree generation that subverted the old way of living. By the mid-1920's my girl-friends were being spoken of as 'Q-Emmas' and even as 'co-eds'. They didn't seem to mind. The conception of Queen Margaret Students as beings apart, with a college of their own, died in those few years in the Roaring Twenties.

The founders of Queen Margaret College, those determined suffragettes who in the 1890's and 1900's wrought so strenuously – and ferociously – for women's rights, should, I suppose, have been pleased, but I doubt if they were. Perhaps these emancipated women students weren't quite the girls their begetters intended them to be.

It is commonly said that the magnificent part played by women in the First World War broke down the old prejudices and that accordingly they gained not only the vote, giving them a say in political affairs for the first time, but also a new sense of independence. And that indeed was a real factor in bringing about Mary Esslemont's election in 1923 as President of the Aberdeen Students Representative Council. But another influence was at work too – the 'Americanisation' of Great Britain and of the rest of the world as well.

Trace, for instance, what happened to student downtown theatrical ventures. Before 1914, there weren't any at all. Then in the early 1920's some spectacular productions of classic plays like 'Antigone' and 'Julius Caesar' were presented at the Henglar's. After that came the Dialectic 'all male' plays. And then in 1925 the first helping of 'College Pudding' was served to a startled public in the Lyric with more women than men in the cast, frisking around in chorus teams and indulging in occasional high kicks. This last development was of course essentially trans-Atlantic in origin. We saw films in the cinemas about collegiate shows. We read monthly magazines with titles like 'College Humour' and 'Student Fun', purporting to be compilations of the best contributions to current university magazines. Perhaps they were the original horror comics.

It would be wrong, of course, to give the impression that the thousand women who were at the University of Glasgow at the time all thought of themselves as co-eds. It is unlikely that many who did not join QM Union – and they were in the majority – entertained any notion about themselves. What, I wonder, has life done to all those diligent class attenders who presumably thought of a university solely as a place for swotting? If they could re-live their undergraduate years over again, would they keep themselves so remote this time?

Glasgow University Magazine cartoons are quite revealing about the attitude of the man to the woman students at different decades. The beginning of the magazine coincided with the founding of the Queen Margaret College and the first cartoonist, William P. Hanks, saw the 'new' women taking classes at Gilmorehill campus as grim, hatchet-faced creatures who aped men in their attire, carried long umbrellas under their arms and were devoted to reading about the descent of men. O. H. Mavor in the Edwardian Age hardly ever included women in his drawings. They scarcely existed as far as he was concerned. Looking back at my sketches of thirty years ago, the girls seem to have been collected from three groups: the vivacious ones, fluffy haired, long legged, full of verve and go; the sensitive aesthetes and intense intellectuals, shingled, with immense horn-rimmed spectacles and short skirts; and the brutal hockey players living up to their reputation in Glasgow for their toughness. It was Ian Phillips who drew the women he looked at in the Arts Quadrangle. He was the only one of us who really saw them and he, a sensitive soul, was much distressed. His cartoon of Alma Mater casting her eye over the new crop of freshers still makes me shudder.

Yet, I suppose that if I were going to develop this theme I would choose a participation in pure athletics – running, jumping and that sort of thing – as the best example of how women have progressively taken a greater share in corporate life. Some of my girl friends 30 years ago could do a soft shoe shuffle with the best, but none of them ever thought of throwing a discus about. The idea of women competing at the annual sports meeting at Westerlands was just unthinkable. Indeed I remember how incredulous we were one day when told that Jean Rankine, the hockey international, had sprinted against some of the rugby club's fastest three-quarters and had beaten them. And she was, no doubt, encumbered by wearing an old-fashioned gym tunic. The modern Queen Margaret Union athlete does not hamper herself in this way. As one of our Rectors remarked to me, "You know, Charles, I shouldn't approve but, truth to tell, I like it".

Frances Melville

Frances Melville

*From a Lecture by
Marion Fraser
President 1953-1954*

Frances Melville was Mistress of Queen Margaret College from 1909 until its closure in 1935. Like Mrs. Janet Galloway before her, she was a champion in the education movement for women. Without her tireless efforts there would be no Queen Margaret Union in the present day University.

It is difficult to recapture a personality of the warmth, dedication and liveliness that was Dr. Frances Melville. An account from one student states, "she gave me good advice, practical yet inspiring. I soon discovered that it was no part of her creed that women should confine themselves to the orthodox byways and sideways of achievement. On the contrary, she encouraged them to step out bravely upon the high road of life, and by so doing, prove their appreciation of the unique opportunities, which the zealous efforts of a previous generation had placed within their reach".

As Mistress of Queen Margaret College, Dr. Melville realised the valuable opportunity afforded the College, when Robertson Hall was gifted to the University. From her personal experience, she knew of the great advantages to be derived from residential life. She determined therefore to develop in Glasgow something in the nature of a residential college hall for women students. She herself superintended personally much of the arrangements for the reconstruction and administration of Robertson Hall, which in 1937 became an annexe of Queen Margaret Hall, which occupied the building that is now Lilybank House. Only those who came into daily contact with Dr. Melville, as I did during this period, can realise the anxious core and thought, which she extended in order to enrich in this way, the life of the women students.

I had the honour of meeting Dr. Melville in 1953 when she was invited by the Board of Management to speak in Queen Margaret Union about our past. There are two things I remember vividly about her visit. One was the appalling instability of the lectern, which we had supplied for this rather elderly lady to speak from and on which she sought to balance. Perhaps that explains my inability to remember what she told us. What I do know is that I have never forgotten her trust in her youthful successors, her genuine care for our problems and concerns and her pride that we were carrying on the traditions and ideals, even in the less complete form of Queen Margaret Union in its historic building on University Avenue.

In 1935, Dr. Melville wrote, "The future is rich with the promise that in thousands of women that have passed through Queen Margaret College in its youth, in its maturity and in its later days, the tradition of the College will continue to live".

In Aid of
Student Welfare Scheme

Goblin Market
Christina Rossetti

**Queen Margaret College
On Friday, 25th May
Saturday, 26th May
at 3 p.m. and 5 p.m.**

Music arranged and played by
Miss Agnes Davidson
Spoken by
Miss Queenie Russell

Produced by
**Miss Muriel Sterling
& Miss Chica Macnab**

Playbill cover from the 1920's for a play in aid of student welfare

Exterior view of Glasgow University Union at the foot of
Gilmorehill after the Men's Union moved to their new home in 1932

1930

Whilst the world was in the throes of economic depression, the troubles at Queen Margaret Union were starting to fix themselves. Having fully adjusted to its new home across from the Men's Union, Queen Margaret Union soon saw further expansion into the ground floor of the neighbouring building. As more and more women students sought to use the facilities of the new building it was clear that space was once again becoming an issue.

By mid-decade, as more and more classes and services for women students were transferred to the main University campus, Queen Margaret College closed its doors. No more would Northpark House be home to the plight of women students in Glasgow. In many ways the original goals of the College had all been achieved and a whole new era was about to begin for the women of the University of Glasgow.

In 1932, Queen Margaret Union was gifted with the Men's Union building to help with its space issues. The men of the University moved to a new purpose built venue at the bottom of Gilmorehill, where they remain today. The wife of the late principal, Sir Hector Hetherington referred to Queen Margaret Union's new home as, "the crown of the hill".

It was a time of great change across the world once again. Despite managing to ride out the problems of the Great Depression; the onset of the Second World War would again change the face of Queen Margaret Union.

Sketch of Queen Margaret Union after it moved into the old Men's Union building at the top of Gilmorehill

Playing with the Big Boys

Gary R. Brown
President 2006-2007

The decades between the two world wars were both difficult and exciting for Queen Margaret Union. The University of Glasgow was ever changing and campus life was becoming increasingly more vibrant. Since moving into its first home after residing for years in the basement of its namesake's College, Queen Margaret Union was on the move again. It would relocate no less than three times between 1912 and 1932.

When the University of Glasgow College Club went into liquidation in 1912, the University Court offered the vacant space at 67 Ann Street to the women of Queen Margaret Union. The letter to President E. R. Thomson was brief,

"Dear Miss Thomson,

The University of Glasgow court offers 67 Ann Street with all grates, furniture, household items and fittings of every description presently within it, with the sole exception of the contents of the billiards room,

Yours sincerely,

University of Glasgow Secretary of Court"

The new Queen Margaret Union quickly became the centre of College and female student life on campus. The removal from 12 Buckingham Terrace to the new premises at Ann Street was described by those present as 'the event of the year'. Suddenly there was space to read in private, the new Union even boasted it's own library. Private rooms were available to clubs and societies that wished to use them and, when vacant, the spaces were available for social purposes to the general membership. To allow for the upkeep of the interior, a cake stall, a far cry for the 1906 Bazaar was held. As the Great War came and went, notably, membership was affected, as entertainment took a step backward, with the Scottish Women's Hospital event being among the few highlights of the period. Another success was the frequent dances in aid of wounded soldiers. The Union however was faced with grave financial prospects (a position it would come to face several times in its existence – each time bouncing back stronger than ever). As always, stringent management and a focus on the core purpose of the Union, its members, paid off and Queen Margaret Union was soon a greater success than it had been before its troubles began.

In 1922 the University Court offered another great opportunity to the Union. A letter from the then Secretary of Court to the current President read,

"Dear Miss Ida Wyllie,

At the suggestion of the Students Welfare Comittee, the University Court has purchased the house at No. 1 University Gardens with the help of a special grant from the Carnegie Trust and now place it at the disposal of your Committee for use as a Women Students Union. In view of certain representations from neighbouring proprietors and occupants the Court would wish to be assured that in the new premises, disturbance by noisy entertainments at late hours of the night will, so far as possible, be avoided.

Yours sincerely,

University of Glasgow Secretary of Court"

Queen Margaret Union soon branched out into the world of debates thanks to the new space it was given. A year into its new existence, the former Principal's wife, Lady McAllister (a women who had the privilege of having held the President's position of Queen Margaret Union before it was a working role) was asked to officially open the venue on 25th May. A bazaar, albeit a much smaller one, was held in 1924 to raise funds for the upkeep of the Union's new home.

With the increased accommodation, membership soared. Space was available for overnight accommodation for members and the new location meant that prominent staff of the University, including the Rector, could stop by to offer support. Perhaps the highlight of the new Union was the elegant grandfather clock that stood as a memorial to the twenty-five years of service offered by the former mistress of

Queen Margaret College, Janet Galloway. A book, entitled, 'Lest We Forget', featuring a series of reminiscences about Miss Galloway was also gifted to the Board of Management of 1924, and to this day it is available for private viewing at the University of Glasgow Archives.

The house at 1 University Gardens quickly became inadequate. As membership grew and the dedicated souls who gave their all to its existence became more involved, the University gifted Queen Margaret Union with the ground floor of the neighbouring 2 University Gardens. A coupon system was used over lunch period to cope with demand, more prominent visits from University officials and MP's continued, events became more extravagant and the Union even hosted the Scottish Universities Debate of 1926. The lack of space was quickly becoming an issue however. As membership approached 650, all of whom frequented the Union building, the Resident Secretary began to supplement the lunch hour by providing so-called 'dainty lunches' to ease the coupon system. The library was proving so popular that getting a seat became a great challenge. By the early 1930's membership was suffering its first drop in a decade due to the overcrowding. Despite the challenges, Queen Margaret Union improved in appearance and its events continued to become more innovative. Teas and dances continued but a Freshers' Social Halloween Party and Dance hosted by the Executive Committee quickly grabbed the attention of everyone on campus. The Union even started to grant its first life-memberships (a tradition that still occurs), reaching 50 people by 1930.

In 1932, the Men's Union, also known as the Glasgow University Union moved into specially built and furnished premises at the bottom of Gilmorehill on University Avenue and their old haunt on University Avenue outside the Gilbert Scott Building was left vacant. Thankfully it was donated to Queen Margaret Union. Sadly, it wasn't left in the greatest state. The men of the University referred to it as the 'rat hole', an apt description considering the condition of it when the women moved in. Thankfully, Queen Margaret College and its mistress Dr. Frances Melville were on hand to help decorate and furnish the new home. On 24th February 1932 Lady

Stirling-Maxwell officially opened the new venue where the Union would remain until 1967.

Membership and activity quickly increased. Debates became a strong point, the large debating hall a great venue for speakers and audience alike. A bright period in the history of Queen Margaret Union was about to begin. Sadly, the renaissance did not last as, in 1939, the University of Glasgow was deeply affected by the onset of the Second World War.

Farewell to
Queen Margaret College

Jean Kelvin

Originally Printed in
'Pass it On'
and in
The Glasgow Herald

Queen Margaret College is no more. When that decision of the University of Glasgow Court became known, thousands of women all over the country must have been assailed by a sudden nostalgia for old college days and a tender regret for the abandonment of the familiar grey house by the River Kelvin.

The older the graduate, the more deeply affected she would be. In it's final years, the College played a decreasing part in the academic life of the student until it became little more than an office. There was however a time when it was the centre of the woman undergraduate's activities. Yet I would be surprised if even those who matriculated in its final year failed to catch something of the tradition and atmosphere of the old building. It belonged so essentially to those days when it was a courageous thing for a woman to identify herself with the 'new-fangled craze' for higher education, and even now, shorn of the great trees which used to screen it from public gaze, it still stands a little aloof from the world surrounding it.

For my part, I shall always associate Queen Margaret College with warm spring days, because my first introduction to it took place in the month of May, when, approaching the end of school days, I came to consult a tutor. Early for the appointment, I wandered into the shady, fragrant garden and immediately seemed to be in a quiet retreat very far distant from the noise and clamour of Great Western Road. It was not difficult to imagine the pioneers, with Miss Galloway, strolling in these secluded walks and talking so earnestly. I had come up undecided about the advisability of having a college education, but before I went to see the tutor I had made up my mind. It is a sad reflection now that after matriculating; I never again sat in the College Gardens.

The most memorable part of Queen Margaret College to most graduates must be the library and secretary's room. It was in the very charming library, which usually had a coal fire burning brightly, that we queued up to matriculate. Oh, those interminable queues! If it was not to matriculate then we were queuing up to enter for examinations or to pay fees. From the library we passed through to the secretary's room, where her minions sat at long desks surrounded by cards of every hue.

I imagine that to most women students who passed through since the Great War, the woman on the staff best known to them was the secretary, Miss Wallace. The Mistress was always approachable but unless one required to, there was no occasion for seeing her, with the result that not a few students have gone through their University course without ever meeting her.

But one could not miss the secretary, quiet and retiring as Miss Wallace was. She, it was, who kept us right in our callow days, and she it was too who could mingle regret and reproof so admirably that we did not quite know which was uppermost when, and if, anything had gone wrong.

As for actual classes at Queen Margaret College, I had only one but it was taken by male lecturers and as it seems that men cannot address an audience of women without being slightly condescending or slightly facetious – either of which is intolerable to the feminine mind – and also, as it was very inconvenient to dash from a lecture at the University over to the College and then back again to Gilmorehill, a transfer to the University class was generally arranged if possible. No doubt it was this, which contributed to some extent to the desertion of Queen Margaret College.

With the new system, the women students ceased to have any cause for complaint against differentiation between themselves and the men; full equality had been obtained. The Queen Margaret Union will help to perpetuate the name of Queen Margaret Students ('Q-Emmas' for short). It will be a pity if the tradition associated with the old college is allowed to lapse.

When next passing along Great Western Road and glimpsing the old College building, dignified in its isolation, do not refrain from the sentimental regret that what was once a pioneer is now left behind in the inevitable march of progress.

The Principal and Lady Hetherington

Memories of Gilmorehill

Lady Hetherington
Printed in
'QM Handbook 1961-1962'

As it happens, I did not see a great deal of Queen Margaret Union in my student days. Its rooms were in or close to the College – now, alas no longer ours. Only my first year classes were in the College but in my second year, most, and in my two finals years, all of my classes were at Gilmorehill, so that except for odd meals and special occasions I was not very often in Queen Margaret Drive. My particular group, the Modern Language Honours student were a lively and cheerful little community, much given to parties at one another's houses, in the Chardon and in the German Club, and especially in the homes of M. Charles Martin (French) and Dr. Herbert Smith (German). Wonderful hosts they were. The French Department occupied Pearce Lodge, and the German Department was high up on one of the staircases of the East quadrangle. You were apt to get there a little late and breathless, to be met, when Herr Brucker was taking the class, with "Spat kommen Sie, Fraulein: doch Sie Kommen".

Our University 'socials' were, I suppose, a good deal more formal than they are today. There were no dances without chaperones, usually some senior member of the College. They must often have been very bored. But we had a good time, and felt no kind of restriction on our gaiety. It was, in fact, at one of these gatherings – fortunately not till my last year so that my Honours work was not seriously interrupted – that I first set eyes on a tall fair-haired student of philosophy who was later to play an important part in my own life, and in the life of the University.

When in December 1924, with two small boys, we returned to No. 1, The Square, Queen Margaret Union was much more prominent in the Gilmorehill scene. It was then just across the Avenue in 1 University Gardens, so that visits were easy, especially in the presidency of Elizabeth Currie, who was one of my husband's students – a very pleasant, though crowded, place to go. But that was a short stay, for in 1927, we moved south again.

In 1936 we finally came home to Gilmorehill. We found the men established in their new fortress at the tram terminus, and Queen Margaret Union in possession of the crown of the hill, in the old Men's Union, more elegantly furnished and made over. It would then move again into more spacious quarters. But it will be Queen Margaret Union as it was then that I shall remember. I always enjoyed going there to meet the Board or the Freshers or the graduates, to a Chapel tea, or to other such parties: and quite often, as the successive generations passed through, I met the daughters (and even lately a few granddaughters) of friends of my student days. I remember looking over the roll of Presidents in the drawing room. There they were – the names of friends of my twenty-five years, beginning with Lorna Tillotson, Carol Bennie, Landa Wingate, and so on right down. They were very different personalities, each with a quality of her own, but together they and their colleagues brought the Union through the troubled days of the war, and the hardly less troubled days of the post-war period. I am sure the good tradition will continue.

Of all the university events of my time, the most memorable, at least to me, was the great celebration in 1951 of the Quincentenary, especially the beginning and the end. First the student celebration in January (which had better weather than the more official part in June), the carrying of the torch by the old road from Bedrule to Gilmorehill, and the river of golden light moving in the darkness along Kelvin Way. Then in June, the first ceremony when the long line of delegates from universities all over the world entered the Bute Hall in solemn procession to hand their scrolls of greeting to the Chancellor, and my husband as Principal gave the short address of welcome. And the last ceremony of all, when the graduates gave me the great privilege of opening for the first time, the commemorative gates, which they had presented to the University. That was a wonderful time, long prepared and beautifully accomplished. But there have been lots of other things too, of a more domestic kind, none more amusing or more to the point than Joanne McNeill's Convention in 1957 – a kind of Jazz Bazaar, when everybody in the Union seemed to be doing her bit in splendid harmony to produce an exciting and profitable show.

Queen Margaret Union, I am sure, can be well content with its achievement. Many notable women have belonged to it, and have set their mark on its doings and its influence. The University of Glasgow would not at all be the same place without it. I am grateful for the memories, which I have, and for the charming Queen Margarert Union brooch, which is one of my mementos. Long may Queen Margaret Union prosper and give to later 'Q-Emmas' the experiences and friendships which it alone can provide.

1940

Once again, Europe was at war and life at the University of Glasgow would be transformed in its wake. On Gilmorehill the student dynamic shifted as most of the male students left for the war (many staff were called up as well). Along with the women, those who remained behind performed their duties with no less honour and determination that those who were on the frontlines.

In between blacking out windows, sandbagging the campus and performing fire duty, life at Queen Margaret Union continued on as best it could. There were fewer social activities in the decade than in previous ones but fun was had whenever possible. A number of vocational lectures and talks were arranged, most notably from the WRNS (Women's Royal Naval Service).

Interestingly, the minutes held in the University of Glasgow Archive Service note that during this period the Board of Management of Queen Margaret Union was gifted with a painting of 'Madonna and Child' by Botticelli. One wonders where this has ended up over the years.

As the world surmised the damage following the end of war it was clear that the University of Glasgow was just as worse off as everywhere else from the horrors of war. Sir Hector Hetherington as Principal however focused on the efforts of the brave staff and students who had given their all (and in many cases including their lives) to allow future generations to steer the University in the right direction.

The vibrancy and atmosphere began to return to Queen Margaret Union in the later half of the forties. As ex-servicemen and ex-bevinboys began to return to the campus it was clear that no one was going to let pessimism take hold of student life. The 'Q-Emmas' of the time note that life was far from easy but each one will no doubt remember all that was achieved with fondness.

Students sandbagging the main Gilbert Scott Building on campus during the Second World War

A World at War

Gary R. Brown
President 2006-2007

In 1938, the world was on the brink of a war with Nazi Germany. Having already seen the damaging effects of such a struggle on the University in the early decades of the century, preparations began for the coming conflict. Beginning with student volunteers constructing air raid defences and building barriers of sandbags to protect the more vulnerable areas of the campus, the University was determined, more than ever, to defend itself. Several areas under the main building were converted into shelters separated by gender for the staff and students of the time. One viewer of these wartime accommodations described a much more luxurious female shelter when compared to the men's one.

Initially, the onset of war in 1939 had little impact on student life as only the campus itself may have appeared slightly different. However, fire duty was arranged both within and outwith the Unions and students with medical expertise were soon helping people across the city in their newly created first aid posts.

The University of Glasgow became somewhat of a refuge for those wishing to continue their studies from all across the country and occupied parts of Europe. However, it was not free from the troubles of war. Bombing raids on the Clydeside of Glasgow saw one mine land in the West End's Kelvingrove Park and the resulting blast shattered nearly every window on the south front of the Gilbert Scott Building.

Student activities across campus were greatly affected during this period. Even long standing publications such as the

Glasgow University Student Handbook (GUSH) and Glasgow University Magazine (GUM) were forced to either produce smaller texts or cease publication completely. Military training was provided across Gilmorehill by the Officer Training Corps, Royal Navy and Royal Air Force to allow students to complete their degrees but also gain the necessary expertise that was so vital for the war effort.

With the re-introduction of conscription in Britain, people signed up in their thousands to the armed forces. The balance of the genders on campus shifted greatly throughout the faculties as more and more men enlisted. Only medics and certain science or engineering students were able to arrange to complete their studies.

By the end of the conflict, nearly four hundred and fifty men and women, staff and students of the University of Glasgow did not return from combat. Sir Hector Hetherington, then current Principal, summed up the state of the University as follows,

"There is no denying that, like everything else in the country, the University is the worse for war – more crowded, shabbier, still short of staff, books, materials and sometimes heat. But the essential things are here…and although the process of recovery will be long and hard and sometimes disappointing, there is no reason for pessimism and gloom". Thanks to the strong and dedicated leadership of Sir Hetherington, the University made great steps towards recovery and growth.

The University Chapel holds nine tablets inscribed with the names of the deceased. Six were presented in 1948 with a further three dedicated in 2003. Without the efforts and sacrifices of those bold men and women, the University and its student body would not be the great success it is now.

G.U.M. - Glasgow University Magazine

Members of Queen Margaret Union taking part in Charities Day in the 1940s

Memories of a Diary

Margaret Sinclair
Board Member

These diary entries were kindly donated by Margaret Sinclair, a former Queen Margaret Union Board Member and belonged to her husband, former Glasgow University Union President, and herself.

>   1941
>   March 13th
>   9pm – Blitz, all clear at 6am.
>   Clydebank, 'terrible havoc'.
>
>   March 14th
>   Fire patrol at QM. Siren's at 8.40pm.
>   All clear 5 ½ hours later.
>   Explosions. Noise (Landmine)
>
>   April 7th
>   9.50pm Raid until 5-10am.
>   Damage +++
>
>   May 5th
>   Blitz on Clydebank
>   12-15, 4-10pm.
>
>   May 8th
>   24 Bombers Down last night!
>
>   May 13th
>   Margaret elected to QM Board!
>   Frequent visits to QM by Union Board Members –
>   most medics (reserved from war service until post-
>   GU qualification).

May 21st
Fire Patrol QM.
Tea in QM, Lemonade mentioned.

November 7th
Reception in QM for Dr and Mrs Benes (President ?)

December 6th
In QM on Duty with Vera Wallace
Daft Friday
Louis Freeman's Band, Home at 6am.

December 31st
Hogmanay Ball

1942
House Convenor of QM
Choice of new curtains for QM.
Mrs Cathcart – Green.
Endorsed at Board Meeting.
Maids Dinner served by both Union and QM Board Members.

25th October
Annual Service at Cathedral – few males!
Many QM Board Members, including Margaret
Saturday 14th November
Margaret Fire Watching in QM

1943
15th January
Margaret on duty at QM – socialisation –bed at 3am.

Friday 29th January
QM Board Dance – bed at 4.30am

12th February
Final Year Dinner in QM. Home at 2.15am.

21st April
Duty at QM – Margaret.

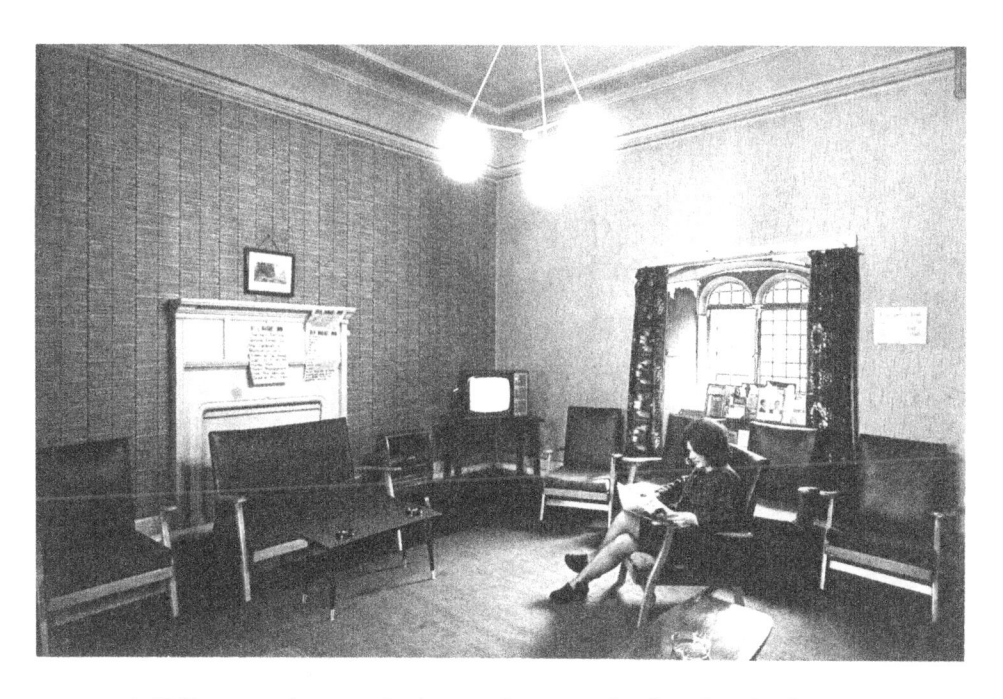

A Q-Emma enjoys a relaxing read next to the fireplace in Queen Margaret Union

A badge given to former Presidents of Queen Margaret Union

Q-Emmas studying in Queen Margaret Union's brand new Study Room

The Post-War Years

Mae Baird
President 1947-1948

I went up to the University of Glasgow (never to be called the 'uni' in those days), in 1944 at the age of 17. My parents suggested a year at university, not being keen for me to go away as my brother had been killed in the Royal Air Force at the age of 21. The war was over by the end of my first year and I went on with my ordinary MA degree (we had to say in our interviews that we would teach or do social work). This was followed by a Diploma in Social Studies. We spent much of our time at the University Settlement in Anderston, lectures in the evenings at university and practical placements in the daytime.

Understandably you may have little idea of what life was like at university in the 1940's. In many ways it seems from what I have been told by youngsters of today to have been quite similar to their experience – working and forging some life-long friendships. We were of course very conscious in 1944 that the war as at a crucial stage and that we were in a privileged position. There were only around three universities in Scotland and Glasgow was one of the best.

We attended each other's Rectorial Elections and balls. The University was small enough for at least the office-bearers to get to know people like Sir John Boyd Orr, Lord Rector and Walter Elliot and his wife. We were encouraged to wear our scarlet gowns and the office-bearers their distinctive gowns on appropriate occasions. We took part in Parliamentary Debates, taken quite seriously, and provided some politicians of the future. After the end of the war, women politicians would come to address us in the Men's Union. In a different vein, there was the weekly Palais on a Saturday night, and many balls. The latter started off quite formally. The women always wore long dresses and the men tails.

O.H. Mavor (James Bridie) of Glasgow University Union fame was up at the same time as me, and as liquor was in short supply, I remember him raid his father's cellar, leaving us feeling rather worse for wear after drinking what I, too late, discovered was rum.

The first chaplain in my time was the Rev. Fraser McClusky, MC and later the Rev. Hamish McIntosh, also an MC and whom I later got to know very well in his retirement in Edinburgh. He died a few years ago but I still keep in touch with his wife.

All our activities took place in a city very different from the Glasgow of today. It was shabby after the war years and we had appalling fog from time to time. But there were few cars to litter University Avenue and it looked elegant with the University buildings, Wellington Church, the Reading Room, Southpark Avenue, and Oakfield Avenue just containing private houses. The old church at the foot of the hill had a wall covered with creepers that glowed in the autumn and always seemed to herald the start of a new university year.

The Professors Quad outside the chapel had professors in all the houses and I regularly stayed overnight after dances in one belonging (or rented) to a friend's family. I seem to remember the period where the number of students rose to five thousand, most of whom lived at home, although there were Halls of Residences for those from further afield. Much of Glasgow was still, in appearance, a Victorian city with many solid houses and overcrowded slums with gas lighting in the closes.

Queen Margaret Union (the old Men's Union) played an important part in most women student's lives. One change from today, no doubt, was the rack of pigeon holes just inside the front door – a quiet and easy place for admirers to leave notes. I should add it was unusual for an Arts student to become President because of the time scale. In my case, the student who was Asst. Secretary resigned after her term of office and I was asked to be Secretary in my 3rd year and

President in my 4th. It was usual at the time to hold all three offices in succession.

In 1946 ex-service men and women started to appear, some to finish degrees they had started 5 years or so before. The mix of ages worked well, I eventually married one of them.

I omitted to mention Charities Week, and probably lots of other things. Many of us worked hard and had a lot of fun in the process. I sometimes wonder how some people graduated when I think of all they achieved in their extra-mural life.

Board of Management of Queen Margaret Union from after the
Second World War

1950

The fifties will always be remembered on Gilmorehill as a renaissance of sorts. Queen Margaret Union remained very active on campus. As the University of Glasgow celebrated its five hundredth year, the Union was on its greatest high yet. Education boomed in the decade after the war and the women students of Queen Margaret Union could often be found gathered together in the lounge areas discussing the finer points of their studies.

The coffee room quickly became the hub of the Union and many a red undergraduate gown would be seen hung in the cloakroom. These were the days when St. Andrews University was not the only place where this tradition was upheld.

In the decades prior to the 1950's, debating had become one of the Union's strong points. This continued unabated – often on very pressing and political issues and themes. After these (any many other events), many a 'Q-Emma' could be heard gathered in the President's Room with their male counterparts singing wholeheartedly.

It really was a golden era in the history of Queen Margaret Union. The interior was used as the set of the 1952 film, *You're Only Young Twice*, which led to many a Board of Management member rubbing shoulders with the stars of the time. Things were about to change yet again in the decade to come as the new guard swept away the old. However the Board of Management and the Union would achieve one more 'first' before leaving the fifties behind – taking on the University of Glasgow court and winning! After managing to remove most of the meddlesome professors' wives from the Board of Management, Queen Margaret Union was left with a newfound freedom - one that would prove very useful in years to come.

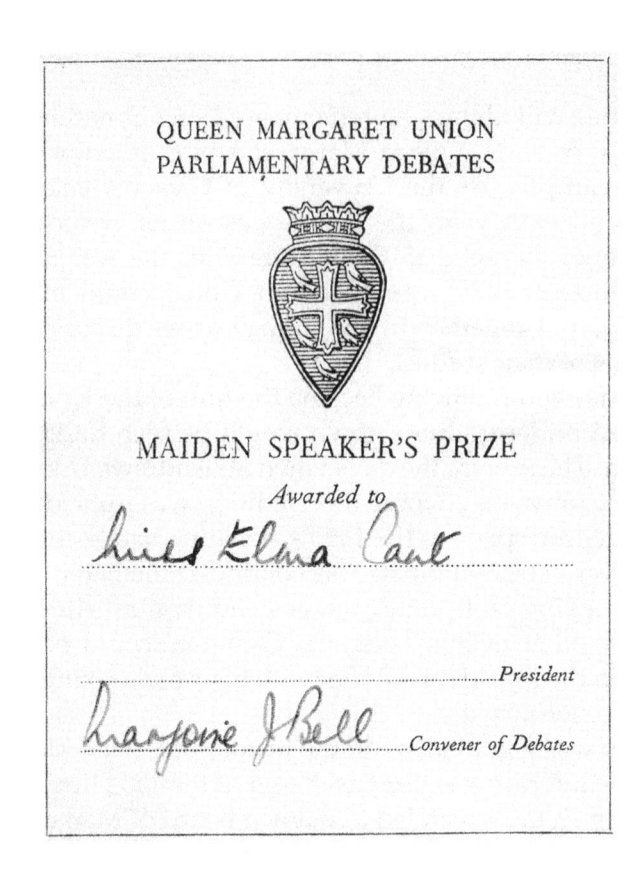

Maiden Speaker's debating prize given to Elma

Presidential Memoirs

Elma Willocks
President 1951-1952

In 1946, immediately after the war had ended, I came off the number three tram, walked up University Avenue, a little bit apprehensive of course, and I suppose a bit timid, but I was excited. As I walked up Gilmorehill, the trees were changing colour and there was a nip in the air. Stepping through the gates of the University was a momentous moment, what a sense of history. The entire place just oozed history. Those quadrangles were, and still are, magnificent.

After matriculating and joining some societies I set off to Queen Margaret Union. My first impression was that it was as near as I could imagine to a marble hall and quite daunting and yet the atmosphere had not arrived. There was a phone box facing me at the top of the steps and to the left there was a wide corridor to be clad, from time to time, with a red carpet for special occasions. Beside the phone box was a row of pigeonholes. This was the way we kept in touch with each other. These pigeonholes were labelled simply with the letters of the alphabet, they had no locks, but I am unaware of any letters going missing. That was how messages or invitations arrived from the various societies - all sent on thick card, often gold edged. Walking past to the right were the kitchens where one would not dare proceed! To the left on the corridor was a cloakroom where coats were left and red gowns donned. Then there was an office.

I walked into the office where two ladies sat dispensing membership cards and accepting money, at that time, all of thirty-five shillings. The lady on the left was fairly formidable with well cut bobbed hair, unusual at the time, elegantly dressed, demure and saving of her smiles. She ran the administration, the staff, the kitchens and lived upstairs on the premises. She was the resident secretary. It became clear as time went on that while she appeared to be responsible to the Board she was really in bed with the University Court and General Advisor of Studies to Women Students. The lady on the right was very homely in an old fashioned way, hair in a bun, and was allowed to smile a little. She looked after the domestic arrangements, like the cubicles (the bedrooms), sat in a sewing room mending linen *ad infinitum* and was clearly kept in her place by her superior. She later married, to our surprise, as we students thought that both ladies were a bit over the hill. However one quickly learns otherwise!

Immediately beyond this office was a large imposing common room complete with a gallery. The wood in this room was oak with some blue applied paintwork. The small stage at the left was used for lunch time speakers of the calibre of Lady Tweedsmuir, de Valera, J. D. Bernal, Sir Walter Elliott et al, lunch time concerts, and debates run on parliamentary lines. These had only been running for about three years when I arrived, but what a wonderful nursery before progressing to the Men's Union debates. In Queen Margaret Union one could utter one's maiden speech before flying up to the Men's Union and making another different one there. Gentlemen were allowed in the gallery but they were only allowed to participate once or twice a year. The common room was also used for afternoon dances, which we called the dansants, choosing a Charities Queen and some evening balls. We had, most of us girls, exploded out of school, out of utility skirts, gym tunics and uniforms and into extravagant ball gowns.

From the common room, I eventually penetrated upstairs to the library and study, for which I was subsequently convenor and responsible for planting and caring for the spring bulbs (now there's refinement). It was a peaceful place and I wish I had had more chance to use it, but science does not permit these luxuries.

The next time I ventured into Queen Margaret Union was a different story, the place was awash with red gowns and students swarming all over the place and the coffee room

QUEEN MARGARET UNION

SECOND PARLIAMENTARY DEBATE

in the QUEEN MARGARET UNION

On FRIDAY, 25th February, 1949,
at 6.30 p.m.

SPEAKER OF THE HOUSE
FRANCES MELROSE
(President of Q. M. Union)

DEPUTY SPEAKER
ELEANOR DEARIE
(Convener of Debates)

Clerk of the House—Janet Bain, M.A.

TIME SCHEDULE

6.30-7.15 p.m.—Opening Period.
7.15-7.45 p.m.—Question Time.   7.45-9.45 p.m.—Open Period.
9.45-10.30 p.m.—Closing Period.

Speakers in the Open Period will be allowed
5 minutes for the completion of their speeches.

DISTINGUISHED STRANGERS IN THE GALLERY MUST OBSERVE STRICT SILENCE

Members of the House are asked to remain on the floor of the House and to refrain from entering or leaving during speeches.
On entering or leaving the House the customary tribute must be paid to the Mace.

CONSERVATIVE GOVERNMENT IN POWER

Members of the House and Distinguished Strangers (including Gentlemen) may obtain refreshments in the Coffee-Room from 7.30-9.0 p.m.

Second Parliamentary Debate, 1949

QUEEN MARGARET UNION

THIRD PARLIAMENTARY DEBATE
in the QUEEN MARGARET UNION

On FRIDAY, 22nd April, 1949,
at 1.15 p.m. and 7 p.m

SPEAKER OF THE HOUSE
FRANCES MELROSE
(President of Q. M. Union)

DEPUTY SPEAKER
ELEANOR DEARIE
(Convener of Debates)

Clerk of the House—Janet M. Bain, M.A.

TIME SCHEDULE
1.15-2.15 p.m.—Opening Period.
7.0-7.30 p.m.—Open Period (1).   7.30-8.0 p.m.—Question Time.
8.-10 p.m.—Open Period (2).   10.0-11.0 p.m.—Closing Period.

Speakers in the Open Period will be allowed
5 minutes for the completion of their speeches.

DISTINGUISHED STRANGERS IN THE GALLERY MUST
OBSERVE STRICT SILENCE

Members of the House are asked to remain on the floor of the House and to refrain from entering or leaving during speeches.
On entering or leaving the House the customary tribute must be paid to the Mace.

SOCIALIST GOVERNMENT IN POWER

Members of the House and Distinguished Strangers (including Gentlemen) may obtain refreshments in the Coffee-Room from 7.30-9.0 p.m.

Third Parliamentary Debate, 1949

was clearly the hub. It was massed with tables, not too many, but girls crowded round them all talking avidly, drinking coffee, which, was no doubt out of a bottle of 'Camp Coffee' (nectar to us), and eating various assorted cakes or biscuits or something. There I learnt the rudiments of other disciplines, what moral philosophy, economics and logic that I know. I got the books, (probably borrowed them), and read them avidly, and then we discussed them. That was an extra mural education for me. We would go next door and get something to eat, probably soup, pie & beans, or sausage roll (chips were rarely on offer). Miss Dawson did very well, as well as she could with austerity. We just did not know it was austerity because the war was over.

Much later I went on through the swing doors and into the cubicles, which were absolute bliss. I can still smell the new wood to this day, hear the University clock chiming through the night (that was only a bad thing if you had an exam the next day). During this time my heart got off lightly but as the song says, "Many a heart was broken after the Ball and many a hope was vanquished"; however many were not.

We lugged our suitcases in on the morning of whatever was going on complete with ball gowns, fur capes, perhaps a mother's fur coat, long gloves, evening bags and loads of makeup. There were a couple of baths and there were calls along the corridor as someone came out of a bath and another one was run and attendant scents began wafting around. There was a flurry of hairdressing going on - the sister of one of the Board Members was a hairdresser and arranged elaborate coiffures for us. Then the corsages started to appear usually followed by some prospective beaux. We descended downstairs, very fragrant, to be escorted down the hill or perhaps to the City Chambers. Many events at that time took place there.

There was a great camaraderie up in the cubicles. We all helped each other, lending makeup or whatever, or finishing off sewing a dress (yours or someone else's). That was certainly one occasion when boyfriends were discussed, joyfully or mournfully. It was bliss not to have to go for the late night bus (I remember them all), from George Square. No one could afford a taxi.

We students did a lot of singing in those days - sometimes after a ball or more often after a debate (Intervarsity debates were full dress affairs, in a dinner gown with sleeves and academic dress). We would repair to a room, perhaps in the Men's Union or to our own President's Room and sing student songs into the small hours. Occasionally we would be talking about metaphysics – I remember doing exactly that with the delegates from Trinity College, Dublin and Galway. The songs were passed down through generations of students but I suspect we learned many from the ex-servicemen. There was often a person 'attached' to a song. I think it was always a man who had a sort of patent on the song, and only he sang it, which confirms that suspicion (I refrain from writing a few well-known names). Alas we may have been the last of that generation, I do not know, but the tradition of singing has gone as students have become much more serious. I did indeed get a full education. We were, I believe, good girls and chaste (as you know from Philip Larkin 'sexual intercourse began in 1963 which was rather late for me'). What a good time we had, and most of us did well academically.

I cannot imagine that another era will dawn just like that time when the boys came home from the war, eager to forget, to get on with their studies, yet also to recapture a lost youth. We had not been to war and yet we benefited. I think in fact both camps did.

Sometimes I and some of my science friends would perch on a windowsill in the corridor on the way in, when there were no seats and watch the Board Members coming down from on high. I don't think I did, but some of the others complained about this difference, this inequality of these Board Members. We saw Queen Margaret Union decked out from time to time, probably just once a year, with red carpet for the Board Ball - what business had they having a Board Ball! But now I realise that in fact those on the Board, did it on top of their studies with no remuneration and so they were probably entitled to the odd perk. Eventually I was elected to the Board myself. I gave up my 'free' time whilst doing a PhD. I was never paid a penny and never expected one. While I was on the Board and Stroma Duncan was President (it was a wonderful time to be there), things were happening. During the fifth centenary of the University we ladies were allowed to take charge. We thought, of redecorating the drawing room, the common room and the President's room and we interviewed people from Heals, Keppie Henderson & Glebe, (the architects of which Charles Rennie Mackintosh was part). These architects kept us informed, or perhaps under control, I know not which. I am jolly sure they were in cahoots with, and were paid for by, the University Court. We got the most beautiful materials. The place looked gorgeous when it was redone. We thought we had done it all ourselves. We learned an awful lot and my parents were duly impressed when I started talking about Parker Knoll chairs. The fabrics were all based on Queen Margaret Union blue. I still think they were splendid.

The celebrations duly went off. They started on a very cold snowy January when there was an epidemic of flu. We had in these days 'King John' McCormack at the beginning of the Scottish National Party revival; his raunchy assessor Robert Gray used to make passes at me and I would run a mile when he was around. It was a great time, the fifth centenary - lots and lots of events, debates (in Queen Margaret Union as well as the Men's Union). The main celebrations started with a torch arriving from Bedrule in the City Centre at the old college site in High Street. Troops of us marched with torches right up to the gate. What an atmosphere; one so great that many of us repeated the march fifty years later. Stroma Duncan (President during this time) was the last of the ladies. I was the first of the awkward squad and on I came as President.

In that year several things happened. One event was that John Grierson and his team from Ealing Studios came up to do a film about students, we thought mainly Queen Margaret students, and they established themselves in the Union - although they were living in the old Beresford Hotel at the bottom of Garnethill Street. I got to know the actors reasonably well. They were especially kind to us and no doubt were used to gawpers. One in particular was very nice; perhaps she was assessing me before playing the part of President. She later appeared as a perfect clone, wearing what I was wearing, it was like looking in a mirror. I soon set about buying a cheeky little urchin cap to look like the stars. Queen Margaret Union became ablaze with cameras and lights. We were involved in nothing much more glamorous than crowd scenes and I remember a friend rushing into the chemistry department calling "Elma, you are on set!" I was having a consultation with my supervisor and it did not go down well when I established my priorities and rushed off. This was important stuff.

We were invited to various parties. My, could those actors drink! We students (apart from the service brigade), rarely drank anything other than orange juice. We went off to the rushes in the Cosmo. We felt we were mingling with the stars, as indeed we really were, but did not know this until the names appeared many later years in neon lights in various other films. The name of the film, black and white of course, was *You're Only Young Twice*. We were suitably impressed. I think I amused the managing director or some such prominent figure by trying to do to a financial deal on behalf of the Union that they had annexed for so long. No doubt the University Court had dealt with that long since. We students had no inferiority complex about dealing with these actors but thought we were on a par with them and possibly even superior.

The next happening that year for me was momentous. The Board of Management up until then had been packed with lady members, professors' wives, put on to make sure that we ladies did not get any ideas below our station. A lot of the girls coming up then (and I was among them) were studying with ex-servicemen who had been away fighting for five years and were mature. We matured, I suppose, along with them and we were minded to alter the Board of Management. We wanted to manage our own Union. All we were doing on the Board was discussing the price of pie and beans, that sort of thing. If someone wanted to book the hall for a twenty-first birthday as a lot of us did, including me, it came up before the Board of Management and we had to wait for the lady members. The Board meetings had been held around four o'clock or maybe earlier. The time did not suit us students very well. We changed the times to later in the afternoon and eventually evening, which suited us fine, but it did not suit the lady members. The professors' wives were not pleased. I'm

Queen Margaret Union students on campus at the University

Cover of QMU Constitution

not saying they were unpleasant people; they were extremely nice but they were just there to keep an eye on us along with the General Advisor of Women Students who was responsible to the Court.

We wanted equality so we put our heads together. We took to scouring the constitution with a toothcomb and we discovered that there was a clause or clauses in it saying that the court would have to look at any alterations in the constitution and say 'yay' or 'nay' within a certain time period. So someone, just by chance of course, from the body of the Union got a petition up that the lady members should come off the Board. We duly had a Board meeting and decided that it would have to go to an Extraordinary General Meeting, which we organised. We gave the adequate notice. We did everything according to the law and the members of the Union agreed that the constitution should be changed. Now, surprisingly, the Advisor to Women Students just happened not to know about this. She had not been turning up at Board meetings and it went through the Court; we were in very bad books. I had been having trouble for sometime from the Advisor. At the Board meetings she was telling us what to do and when that did not work she took to writing to me personally. I took to reading the letters out to the Board and having them minuted. The motion went through, and most of the lady members came off the Board but not all of them so we set up an Advisory Committee who met separately (we still had graduates on the Board). The result of all this was that I was summoned up before the Clerk of Senate and the Principal. The Clerk of Senate told me that if I would tell him who had got up the petition I would not be sent down. I refused; so I was *persona* very *non grata* but I did get my PhD. And I may tell you that the Advisor to Women Students did not help me one little bit with jobs. I remember her suggesting South Australia. So I promptly went to the male advisor. I had been working with males anyway all the time apart from Queen Margaret Union, which was an absolute haven. I got my job in Courtaulds in Coventry, not South Australia, and did well. Crossing swords with the Court and Senate is never recommended as a good career move. An old 'Q Emma' and Board Member said to me recently that I must have been pretty intrepid. Honestly I did not think about that too much; the job got done and I kept my integrity. I have no regrets.

Once we were autonomous Queen Margaret Union remained open longer in the day; meals became available in the evening and we got down to much more important business. We had entered the feminist age. We women wanted equal rights but still not men within our walls. We valued our sanctuary far too much and we spun ideas off each other.

About a year later when food restrictions were easing and some of us, like me, had hitch hiked on the continent and seen other food, someone suggested a buffet party to be called the 'Fork and Glass'. We got the Board Room table ready and heaped it with goodies of the time. Salads and cold meat were rustled up and someone produced a large slab of butter. We had Vienna rolls to heap the butter on. Another produced a huge wedge of cheese and Miss Dawson produced trifles and other delicacies. As there was a glass in the title, we had wine and someone must have been liberated enough to buy it. As far as we were concerned it was a buffet fit for a queen (perhaps Queen Margaret). More such events followed. One in particular was held in one of the University halls on the occasion of Sir William Gray's honorary doctorate. On that occasion we were formally invited to a champagne breakfast. We all supported them in force and the breakfast consisted of Bucks Fizz. I can't remember the accompanying food, I was too taken aback by Bucks Fizz, something I had never had in my life. It is not a breakfast I would recommend. I certainly did not have much and will never have it again, but it was a good time.

I have the happiest memories of Queen Margaret Union as a sanctuary and an extra-mural education. I went up as a timid student and emerged as a much more confident and happy woman.

The Professors' Wives

Jean Reid
President 1952-1953

In the annals of Queen Margaret Union, my main claim to distinction must be as the President who almost never was. At the time in 1952 when I took over the chair the whole Board of Management was out of favour with the powers that be: I still have a letter from the Principal addressed to 'The President's Office' rather than the President.

What, you may ask, had this group of generally compliant young women done to call down the wrath of the University Court and Senate? Was the noise from late-night parties (mainly piano and hearty singing – I don't remember any electronic music) disturbing professors who still lived in their quad? Was participation in political parades causing concern? Perhaps, but these were permanent parts of student life. What caused the real 'stushie' was the fact that Queen Margaret Union had pulled a fast one over the University authorities.

For years, the Board of Management had chafed under the restraints imposed by a clause in their approved constitution. At some early stage it had been decided that a gaggle of girls could not be expected to have the experience or common sense to run a club of this size without the moderating advice of more mature women of the world. Besides the dozen plus elected by their fellow students, the Board of Management included a strong group of senate appointees – five wives (or sisters) of professors, plus the formidable General Adviser to Women Students, Miss Barbara Napier, who had herself been Queen Margaret Union President in 1932. In her official capacity, she had an influence not only on a student's choice of course but also on her subsequent career. It was commonly believed, no doubt mistakenly, that the best jobs were allocated to those in her favour.

At meetings in the bright Board Room to the south of the building, these women could be counted on to support the steward in all her preferences for the day-to-day running of the Union. Miss Dawson (typically she was never called by her first name, which I don't remember ever knowing) was an elegant lady of uncetain age who ran a fairly smooth ship but kept her distance from the generally rowdy rabble of students, including most of the Board of Management.

When, as happened from time to time, she disapproved of a student proposal, she expected the 'lady members' to support her in turning it down with no particularly telling reason given. This reached a crunch point in her refusal to serve chips more than twice a week in the dining room. There were logistical reasons for this stand, arguments of staff time and equipment, but none that convinced the hungry students or that had anything to do with healthy eating!

Growing resentment of this official interference, so different from the easy-going responsibility of the men down the road, led to attempts to amend the constitution. A proposal to reduce the number of lady members to two was passed at an Annual General Meeting and duly submitted to the University Court – which, after some delay, replied that this was simply not acceptable [see Elma Willocks article for the details].

It was only when a friend of the Board of Management was reading the constitution in detail that a loophole was discovered; any proposed amendment should be rejected within a three-month period, or it would be deemed to have been accepted. With the tacit support of other student bodies, the Queen Margaret Union Board of Management sent in another proposed amendment, then sat back and waited with fingers crossed. As they had hoped, the court merely acknowledged the receipt of the proposal. By the end of the three months no refusal had been received, so a letter was sent off to the clerk of court to point out that the amendment had been accepted by default.

That was when, (as fifties students would not have said), the excrement hit the air conditioning. Leaders were called in for interviews by the authorities, letters shuttled back and forth, and in the midst of the melee the annual elections were held and I found myself chair of an outlawed body.

Of course it didn't last. Many members of the University Court and Senate had some sympathy with our cause and even the hardliners had no wish to create martyrs out of 'not-irresponsible' young women. After a month of going back and forth the new set-up was generally accepted, a mere two lady members were appointed to the Board of Management, and life went on much as before although with rather more chips on the plates and fewer on the shoulders.

The position of student unions was set to change anyway. Our Queen Margaret Union was a voluntary club supported by subscriptions: soon unions were accepted and subsidised as an essential part of university life. Queen Margaret Union itself was shortly on the move, and its women-only status was soon to go. Such modernisations left our own small victory in the shade – but it was fun while it lasted.

Board of Management of Queen Margaret Union from 1950s

Board of Management of Queen Margaret Union from 1950s

The Late Fifties

Margo Pitt
President 1958-1959

Life in the late fifties for those of us involved in university life and Queen Margaret Union in particular had not changed unduly in the decade. What did change however were the personalities.

One should remember that the university sector was so much smaller, consisting of Oxbridge, Durham, the Scottish universities and the great English civic redbrick universities. We saw the founding of the new universities like Keele, Lancaster and Sussex and perhaps envied their rural settings. I recall being invited to the opening of the new Students' Union at Keele and marvelled at the black swans. I attended the opening of the then new Union Building in Manchester and was astounded at the facilities available but life in our modest building on the campus at Gilmorehill provided for what we thought at the time was all that we needed. Membership was wholly voluntary and I doubt if more than half of the women students were actually members despite (if my memory serves me right) the cost of annual membership being equal to three pounds per annum.

The universities themselves were so much smaller. Glasgow probably had at the most, five thousand students. Barely a quarter of that number would have been women. As a result, and in percentage terms, we were likely to have known many more of the university community than could be possible today, and I suspect that we may have known our lecturers and professors so much better.

One of the first memories of my university days was being summoned along with all the other Freshers to the Bute Hall by the venerable Sir Hector Hetherington, the Principal to listen to some wisdom on how we should conduct our university years. The one message that stayed with me was that apart from the inevitable suggestion that our studies were important, our life outside the lecture halls (but still within the university), was just as, if not more, important. It was a message that many of us took on board happily.

The explosion in provision of student halls of residence had not then taken place and most students still lived at home. Personalities were there in profusion. Some of them were introduced at the Fresher's camps, held at Auchendennan and Gilmorehill. These camps were run by the Students Representative Council, and for me, were the first introduction to the characters of the student world. There were few ex-servicemen other than those who had been called up for National Service as eighteen year olds, or perhaps had messed up their studies sufficiently to receive their call up papers. Some of the latter were lucky enough to be readmitted to their studies later if their professors had reasonable recollections of them.

Clothes were so much more formal. Trousers for women were unknown. The men almost always wore ties and jackets and red gowns were still seen around Gilmorehill. We wore them to Queen Margaret Union Board Meetings whilst the Executive office-bearers wore the silver and blue gowns. Professors and lecturers also wore gowns. Grants were unknown. Some of us were lucky enough to win scholarships that helped pay the fees but the cost of my Arts course was equal to fourteen pounds per annum and my Law course, nineteen pounds per annum. It seemed a lot at the time.

Of course we thought that we owned the world, and student life was not too serious, though we still did expect to pass our exams. I suspect that we had a proper respect for most of our professors and lecturers. We were a generation still respectful of our elders. The only time that I recall some truly appalling behaviour was at Rectorial Installations. My memory is of sitting on the platform at the Installation Ceremony of the Rt. Hon. Rab Butler and seeing him covered in flour. Sir Hector Hetherington, the Principal and Vice Chancellor, sat solemnly through it all.

Queen Margaret Union was a wholly female organisation. Though there were graduate members and professors' wives on the Board of Management, we very much ran the place as a personal fiefdom. We appointed the staff and the accountants and we balanced the books by surviving on member subscriptions and the income from Saturday night dances, the coffee and dining rooms and the bedrooms. From my years as Honorary Secretary and then as President I have no recollection of any involvement from the University authorities. By the later fifties, the Union was beginning to look somewhat worn, and the then President, Joanne McNeill, decided to raise money to refurbish the library by holding a convention. This was to be a gathering for past members and a celebration of twenty-five years in our then building, which had originally been handed to the women students with the description of the Rector, Stanley Baldwin, as a 'rat hole'. We had originally refurbished it before being handed the keys, but over the years we were very conscious that we were responsible for the state of the internal fabric of the building and that it needed our attention.

That 'rat hole' was the focus of our lives. Placed so wonderfully close to the two quadrangles where most of us went for lectures (apart from those scientists, engineers and medics who needed laboratory space) it was where every women student passed through on a daily basis.

The University of Glasgow's great debating tradition was at its height. During this period we regularly won the Observer Mace, which was awarded to the most talented debating team in the university sector, inevitably from the Men's Union. Queen Margaret Union had its effective debaters but probably none on the level or the conviction of the Men's Union team; John Smith, Donald Dewar, Menzies Campbell, Jimmy Gordon (Lord Gordon of Strathblane), the McCormick family, to name but a few.

We were a generation who are still breaking moulds. Lady Marion Fraser (née Forbes) became the first female Lord High Commissioner of the General Assembly; Joanne McNeill was one of the first women graduates taken on by Rolls Royce on the management trainee scheme and was also an interviewer on television (still then much in its infancy); Deirdre Brown must have been one of the early women lecturers in the Law

Department; Meta Ramsey became one of the government whips in the House of Lords as Baroness Ramsey of Cartvale; Rona Davidson, now Lady Black, is one of the foremost cancer specialists in the country. I became the first woman Chairman of Council and Pro-Chancellor of the University of Manchester Institute of Science and Technology.

I am sure that many more names could have been added to this list. But most sadly several of my fellow Presidents died too young: Jean Livingston, Mary Rodgers, Joanne McNeill, Margaret McNamara, and Deirdre Brown - otherwise they could have added their recollections of the past.

What special years they were and how privileged we were. I suspect however, that every generation probably feels much the same.

Students gathered in the reception area of Queen Margaret Union

Members of Queen Margaret Union Board of Management in a meeting

Queen Margaret Union Ball decorations

Annual Ball

Alasdair Gray
Writer in Residence
University of Glasgow

In the middle 1950s a medical student became editor of *Ygorra*, the University of Glasgow charities day magazine. Wanting to make it less amateurish than usual he produced, with the help of Art School students, two numbers for which collectors today would pay good money, if any survive. I was one of those art students. I cannot remember the name of the medic. He became a doctor in Yorkhill Hospital, but before that was on the board of the Men's Union, and got me also to paint a large Daft Friday decoration. This led to the Board of Management at Queen Margaret Union asking me to decorate the ballroom for their Union's annual dance. The ballroom was the upstairs chamber in what is now the Macintyre Building on University Avenue, with its splendid open-beamed ceiling. Two other art students (Malcolm Hood and Anne Rogers) helped with the decorations, but only I caused trouble.

The Board of Management had given us sheets of cardboard roughly four feet by three. I joined several in a strip one yard wide and at least as high as the ceiling. Laying it flat on the floor I outlined a giant naked female figure, then cut two disks and a triangle out of silver paper and stuck them on for nipples and pubic hair. I threw ropes over the centre of a beam, pulled up the figure to hang from it and fixed the base to the wall behind a platform where the band would play. Probably the tallest nude in Britain, if not the world, would now overhang the dancers. I did this thinking it great fun, had no thought of shocking anybody, for though 21 year old I was unusually naïve. So I was terribly shocked when a member of the Board of Management told me she and others wanted my decoration taken down. I could not imagine it should be disliked, said that if it were removed I would give the story to newspapers. Shortly after Joanne and Greta, also Board Members, cheerfully told me they didn't know what the fuss was about, so my decoration remained. These two Board Members became my life-long friends.

Board of Management of Queen Margaret Union 1958-1959

Queen Margaret Union Board Members gather together for a meeting

Memories of Student Days

Rona Mackie
President 1961

In Autumn 1957 I was a keen but very raw young Fresher anticipating Freshers' camp at Loch Lomond Youth hostel. There was however a setback, an outbreak of Asian flu meant the camp was cancelled. Plan B was dreamt up on the spur of the moment allowing us to celebrate independence and go hitch hiking and youth hostelling. I think our parents were only told of the latter half of this plan. Off we went to hitch on the M8, then the A8, near Barlinnie. We travelled to Scotch Corner, then to Hull and Goole because this was where the lifts were going. It was mad. My good friend of fifty years who did this with me was staying over recently and we laughed at our innocence. Not a trip I would have liked my daughter to do, but life was safer fifty years ago.

Back at Glasgow as a first year medical student, I was, academically, probably 'over ready', having done a very comprehensive sixth year, but I was also, socially, very naïve. In 1957, first year medicine was not stimulating for those who had done a sixth year or A-level sciences; it was just physics, chemistry, botany, and zoology, all of which could very easily be mugged up the night before an exam. There was no introduction to people and patients, the reason for doing medicine in the first place, until the end of your third year. This was probably the reason for my drift towards Queen Margaret Union and student union politics, combined with the fact that at that time medical students had no base on campus. How much things have improved thanks to the former Dean of Medicine, Brian Whiting, who deserves much credit both for altering the medical curriculum so that students meet patients and their families in the first week of their course, and also for being an integral force in fundraising for the Wolfson Medical School Building.

In 1957 there were four outlets for student politics, using politics in a fairly broad sense. These were Queen Margaret Union and the Men's Union, both then strictly segregated, the Glasgow University Athletic Club (GUAC), and Students Representative Council (SRC). The choice of Queen Margaret Union for my student activities was stimulated by an older student, who was active on the Entertainments Committee, and who introduced me to the ritual of Sunday afternoons spent making astonishingly ornate decorations for the Christmas ball. I am sure that those attending the ball and who had not participated in the detailed construction plans had no idea of the number of woman hours that went into such transient fripperies.

The President's room within the Building, (now the John Mcintyre Building), was a natural meeting place in the afternoons for tea. Life was very innocent, with tea being the strong drink on offer. Beer was for the Men's Union 'Beer Bar' and for the occasions when Queen Margaret Union had a Saturday dance with a licence. We were also pre-cannabis and other substances, although cigarette smoking was almost the norm and, at the time, was a sign of sophistication. Men were not officially allowed through the doors until the afternoon, but were then tolerated if chaperoned by a female. Friends and opposite numbers from the Men's Union would drop in for tea and lengthy repetitive gossip, mainly of relevance to those who were law or arts students. My memory of these afternoons, which I usually dropped into briefly after a lab or lecture, was one of astonishment at how much free time my friends doing languages or English seemed to have to sit around. For them tea seemed to begin at lunchtime and continue through to the early evening.

An important part of this lifestyle was of course the Men's Union and Queen Margaret Union debates. The late 1950s were a very rich time for the debating societies, with John Smith, Donald Dewar, the McCormick brothers and cousins, Menzies Campbell, Jimmy Gordon and many others at their peak. One of the few female debaters who made an impact and is remembered fifty years on was Winnie Woodburn (later Ewing) who brought intelligence, information, and conviction to the debating chamber. Debates began on a Friday at lunchtime, stuttered slowly through a weary afternoon, and came to life in the evening with a usually exciting end to a debate full of sound and fury, and culminating in a post debate party which went on into the small hours, ending with a few stalwarts insisting on a rubber or two of bridge.

Rectorial elections were very messy affairs at this period-literally. The student body was going through a conservative phase and both Rab Butler and then Lord Hailsham were elected. They were treated at their rectorial addresses with astonishing rudeness; shouts, jeers, flour bombs and more. It is difficult to understand why this was tolerated or indeed why it was considered the done thing, as often students who had campaigned hardest were the most disruptive on rectorial installation day.

At this time, those who were elected to senior union positions did not have a sabbatical year, and in retrospect it is difficult to see how or why they took on a heavy administrative post at such an early stage in their life. My memory is of many re-sits among those working in and for both the Men's Union and Queen Margaret Union. There may have been some fields such as business or public relations work in which such activities were useful on a CV, but not many. For medical students such as myself, the main bonus was a feeling of being part of the main university, and thus of mixing with a wider circle of students than would otherwise have been likely. However, when I entered fourth year medicine and the real life of a medical student began with long hours in hospital wards and clinics it was time to move on and substitute the afternoon tea sessions in Queen Margaret Union for talking to patients, an aspect of my work I enjoy to this day.

Students taking part in a debate

1960

Across the world the 'swinging sixties' were all about change. At Queen Margaret Union the changes were slow in coming but certainly left their mark. The Board of Management began the decade with a very conservative attitude in what is now the John McIntyre Building at the top of Gilmorehill and ended it in a much more liberal manner in its new home at 22 University Gardens – where it remains to this day (its sixth home).

Membership was on the rise with almost ninety percent of all women students joining as members at one point. The diehard volunteers who made up the Board of Management continued to give their all to the Union – often to the detriment of their degrees. The staff were playing an increasingly more important role and were seen by the members as both life guru and provider.

In 1967 a purpose built venue was created at 22 University Gardens. The new Union was larger, featuring facilities such as catering, dormitories, dance floor and debating hall, reading rooms and lounges over three floors. Debating continued to be a Union strong point and dances and balls provided the much needed entertainment to supplement studies.

Great Queen Margaret Union traditions were taken to new levels. The Annual Fork and Glass evening was awaited by all with much excitement. The spacious new venue meant that new ventures could be taken on including live acts from comedian Billy Connelly and The Who. Along with many others, these acts graced Queen Margaret Union's stage with sell out crowds.

The difficult times of the first half of the century seemed a distant memory and things certainly were looking up. The 'winds of change' were starting to blow and Queen Margaret Union was certainly moving with the times.

Students at the Freshers' Camp with some staff members, in the early 1960s

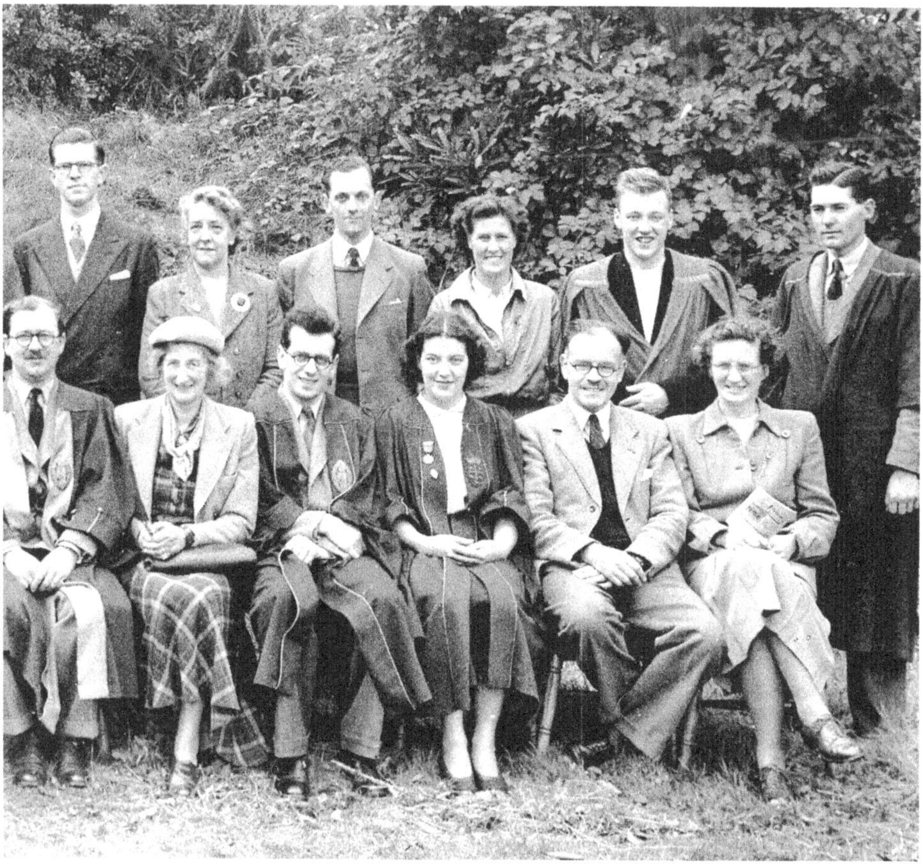

Queen Margaret Union members relaxing in the 1960s

Group of Queen Margaret Union Board of Management members in a meeting in the 1960s

A Past President Reflects

Marcia Pirie
President 1962-1963

When I came up to the University of Glasgow in 1960 the 'Old Order' was firmly in place. When I left in 1964 the 'winds of change' were blowing, not only through the university but also through every establishment and institution in the country. However, we student leaders did not see ourselves as harbingers of the storm that was to engulf education in the later sixties. We were a mere breeze, ruffling the surface of institutional correctness.

'Correctness' – a socially approved way of behaving permeated every aspect of middle class life in the 1950s and none more so than the upbringing of middle class girls. University education for women had been hard won and there was still a widespread belief that tertiary education for women was a waste of money. Those girls who made it to university were not only overwhelmingly middle class, (which also applied to male students) but more often from families with an enlightened attitude to education. This combination of 'social correctness' and 'enlightened feminism' was a powerful mix, to be found in concentrated form in the Queen Margaret Union Board of Management.

I came into contact with the Board of Management as a 'fresher' and newly recruited member of the Entertainments Committee. I was struck by how much the mores of the girls' private school still affected the tone of behaviour. 'Twee' was how some of the less conventional of us described such behaviour and indeed the male students used to refer to our Board of Management as the 'Twee Club'. It befitted an establishment that was run as a private club, which in effect, both unions were in those days.

Membership was entirely by choice, funded by the student. However, as both unions were the major providers of social and physical student needs, membership was a basic element in student life. Out of a women student population of around one thousand in 1962; over nine hundred were Queen Margaret Union members.

The Board of Management was elected annually and with the invaluable assistance of the legal and financial skills of several co-opted members, not to mention the ubiquitous 'Professors' wives', was entirely responsible for running the place.

The University provided a rent-free building – the rest was up to us, to run the 'club' for the sole benefit of the members. The President was the chief executive, the Secretary and the Assistant Secretary did the 'donkeywork', and the office staff and the Catering Manageress carried out the actual day-to-day running of the place. 'Respect for authority' was the mortar which held up institutions in those days, and it hadn't quite started to crumble. Everyone was very deferential to those 'above' and the staff addressed Board Members as 'Miss'!

I was projected prematurely into the position of Secretary at the start of my second year, along with Liz MacKinlay as President, due to the sudden resignation of the previous incumbents. It was a definite 'regime change' which was physically evidenced by numerous small updates of the fabric and furnishings. At the time they were a little radical in their way, but laughably so now.

Not only did we have the paintwork changed in the ladies toilets from 'lavatory green' to more voguish pastel shades, but had each loo door painted a different colour. There was even greater apoplexy among some when we decided that the other set of toilets, which doubled as the gents from two pm onwards, were not coping (to put it politely) with the heavy traffic of the Friday and Saturday dances and that urinals would have to be installed. After much discussion they were installed with ceremony and a write-up in the University's newspaper, the *Glasgow University Guardian*.

Other nods to modernity were made. Relaxing chairs and low-level coffee tables were installed in the 'lounging' areas.

The pitiful wages of the cleaning and catering staff (whom we referred to as 'maids') were raised. The practice of phoning down to the kitchen from the President's room to have tea brought up followed by replies of, "Will that be all, miss?", was phased out.

In such small ways we were changing things without being duly aware of any groundswell. We had been brought up in a post-war world very different from that of the generation who were running the established institutions and it seems obvious now that the two were bound to clash. However, in 1962 it was still a brave person who 'stepped outside the box', and most of us edged only very tentatively towards change.

Our concerns were much more with the day-to-day business of running a solvent Queen Margaret Union. For the Executive Committee this was fairly time-consuming and there was a strong temptation to make it all consuming. The University authorities made no allowances for student leaders and appeared to treat their activities with an air of disapproval. If such students failed to graduate, it served them right! Some student leaders did fall by the wayside and it was a constantly nagging concern of mine that I was not doing enough work to scrape through. Scraping through was all that mattered for a great many of us – an ordinary degree was quite acceptable and the majority of students opted for that. A few were scholarly, and a few even had strong career ambitions, but most of us felt that just getting to university privileged us enough and would ensure some sort of professional-type job for life. Although student grants were modest they seemed to be readily available, even for 'extra' years. Students who lived at home were cheap to maintain as our material needs were very basic. Life as a student was, for most of us, fairly relaxed and non-competitive, which allowed for a great deal of fun and socialising.

Queen Margaret Union was fortuitously sited on a main thoroughfare of the University, and was a lively and busy place. The mock gothic interior layout, designed around the idea of a House of Commons style debating hall, was far from functional but it encouraged an intimate, collegiate atmosphere.

Powerful memories still linger: the pervasive smell of floor polish and cigarette smoke; the queues snaking out of the coffee and dining rooms; plates of haggis or chips and mutton pies; the continuous din of female chatter, frequently over-ridden by the precisely intoned announcement from the tannoy that Miss so-and-so is 'wanted at the hall box'. Upstairs, the elegant library with its cosy open fire would be full of studying students (there were some) In the little corridor room, others, their be-rollered heads encased in huge hair dryers, would be submitting themselves to the weekly hairdresser. Further along, in the hallowed Board Room with its beautiful oval table, a Board Member might be seeking quiet for a last minute essay. In the bedroom corridor, overnight stayers might be using the ironing board or even having a bath.

We even had a television room although viewing did not then impact much on students' lives – except for one new, and daringly subversive show. Once a week the little room up the turret was packed with students, both male and female, being hugely entertained by *That Was The Week That Was*. The established order being debunked and on Auntie BBC? It was a whiff of promise that change was in the air.

Above the television room in the attic turret, lived Mary, the cook. Years ago she had come 'down from The Highlands', as girls of her generation did, in search of domestic work and had lived in Queen Margaret Union ever since, a last remnant of generations of institutional live-in maids. She had an unnervingly wild look about her. As the Union was her only home we accepted her use of the place as such, even when we discovered her underwear soaking in the capacious pans of the kitchen Bain Marie.

The most comfortably appointed rooms of all, originally designed for a live-in steward, were for the exclusive use of the Board of Management. Here, on comfortable sofas in front of an open fire, we lounged, played bridge, entertained favoured guests, listened to records, exchanged confidences and generally enjoyed a privileged existence. It was all for the benefit of the members, we reminded ourselves.

Another significant privilege was the existence of the Board dormitory (the President had her own private cubicle, complete with dressing table). In addition to the Duty Board Member who stayed overnight during her duty week, the dorm was used regularly by other board members. For most of us living at home, this facility allowed us to enjoy a social life free from parental constrictions. For those women living away from home and in a hall of residence the 'in loco parentis' constrictions were draconian - male guests had to be out of the building before ten pm. Student flat sharing as an alternative to lodging with a landlady was just beginning to gain ground and for girls it was a significantly liberating move. Many parents and authorities were still fearful of what might 'happen' to girls if they were let loose at night.

For the majority without access to a flat or a car, amorous contact depended on the opportunity afforded by dark corners, the back row of the cinema, and dimly lit rooms set aside at parties and dances. This opportunity probably accounted for the popularity of the weekly Queen Margaret Union and Men's Union dances.

Union dances were organised by the Entertainments Convener and they were an important source of income. On dance nights the Duty Board Member had the daunting responsibility of being in overall charge of the building. She had to be constantly alert to pre-empt disorderly behaviour by drunken male students (drunk women were rare and usually retired to the loo or passed out quietly). Admittance to the dance closed at nine twenty pm – ten minutes before all pubs and bars had, by law, to eject their clientele from their premises. We could hear the revellers advancing up the hill as we closed the massive oak door of Queen Margaret Union and slid the heavy bolts into place – often to angry hammering of fists and feet on the outside. We learned to nip rowdy behaviour in the bud and at the first sign offenders were forcibly ejected, usually with the help of Board Members' boyfriends. These occasions could be quite lively – I once found myself outside the shut door in the middle of a crowded punch-up, attempting to separate the protagonists.

The more up-market social scene was punctuated by a succession of Annual Balls. These were glamorous black tie affairs where we swished around in long dresses and long gloves and smoked cocktail cigarettes. Most major student societies held an annual ball as did the Unions. The Queen Margaret Union Christmas Ball and the Board Ball were highly acclaimed and a great deal of work went into running them. Each weekend throughout the winter, members and friends of the Entertainments Committee toiled away converting huge swathes of cardboard and paper into 'decorations'. On ball nights these would encase the interior of the building, transforming it into grottoes, woods, lunar landscapes, the Kremlin, or whatever was appropriate to the theme.

The fire hazard aspect of this did cross my mind and I remember putting up notices in the loo cautioning against careless use of cigarettes. However there was never any mention or discussion among us about the risk. These were pre-litigious times and we never thought about public accountability.

Unlike most balls, which were fund raising activities, the Queen Margaret Union Board Ball was 'by invitation only'. Its purpose, apart from boosting the profile of the President and Board, was to repay hospitality and favours and ensure their continuance. The guest list was wide and sweeping and included some professors (who often came in white tie and tails) and university staff. Some guests were more favoured than others and they were invited to the more exclusive reception and buffet in the Library. Among these were student leaders from universities all over the UK and such was the reputation of the Board Ball that few were deterred by long distance travel. They were greeted grandly at the entrance to the Library by the President arrayed in her blue gown of office (over a ball dress probably only hours previously released from someone's sewing machine.)

It was always a very grand affair and we justified the cost by believing that its acclaimed reputation somehow reflected on the ordinary members to their benefit. 'It's for the good of the members in the long run' (I have ever since recognized this as a basic construct which drives the strategies of business and politics, doubtless bolstered by the same delusions).

We were small fry but as student leaders we were introduced to a little world where the power of influence and patronage and other people's money could be very seductive. We, the Queen Margaret Union Board of Management, of course saw ourselves as occupying the high moral ground. Everything had to be accounted for and justified, but I could see how easily, in high stake situations the boundaries might blur and how slippery could be the slide into 'dubious practices'.

All student leaders received invitations to far more functions than they could ever attend and in Queen Margaret Union we passed these around the Board of Management – after the President had 'picked the plums'. As Secretary and then President I attended a black tie function at least once a week throughout most of the winter for two years. Fortunately, I had an accommodating boyfriend with a dinner suit (who stuck it out, eventually becoming my husband six years later.) Unattached Board Members generally had little problem finding escorts for free functions, as there were usually plenty of spare and willing males hanging around.

Relations between the Board of Management of the Men's Union and Queen Margaret Union were friendly and although there was a historical tradition of making fun of women students we weren't conscious of any real animosity. Men's Union Board Members often dropped into the Presidents Room for tea (and gossip) in the afternoons.

I was fortunate to have Donald Dewar as the Men's Union President during my term, and Menzies Campbell towards the end of it. Menzies I knew from my schooldays but Donald at first seemed a daunting figure to get to know. He affected a dismissive and bluff front, especially with women, which belied his surprisingly gregarious nature. As we shared many top tables together and had friends in common, I eventually got know him as a valued and respected friend.

All this might give the misleading impression that all students led a busy social life. The vast majority returned home every evening, went to one of the dances or to the cinema on Saturday night, the Union bar or an occasional debate on a Friday and perhaps splurged out on a ball once a year.

For those more involved in corporate life the hub of activity centred on the political debates, held alternately in the Men's Union and Queen Margaret Union. The parliamentary form of these was so strong and historically rooted that the main hall of each union building had been designed to accommodate the procedures. We students were well aware that the standard of debating at the University of Glasgow was very high. The Glasgow team had consistently won the Observer National Debating Trophy, beating the Oxbridge Unions. By the early sixties these debaters were in their student prime, most of them maturing into their second degrees (some degrees, like law, had to be preceded by a first degree) It was a wonderful training ground for those with political aspirations and it has been no surprise to us that such luminaries as Donald Dewar, John Smith and Menzies Campbell should have made it to the top of their political tree. There were others too, with less earnest political leanings who could deliver brilliantly entertaining performances.

Although there were no women debaters of quite the same stature, there were a number of feisty women in the front benches of the political clubs who could hold their own. The Queen Margaret Union Debates Convener was responsible for organising the debates. They were run on exactly the same Parliamentary lines as in the Mens' Union. The President and the Debates Convener, attired in their gowns of office and gavel in hand, shared the role of Speaker of the House. Set out below the Speaker's raised chair was the Clerks' Table complete with mace, dividing the cross benches. The process would start at two pm on a Friday and run on, often until the small hours of Saturday morning. By the evening the hall was usually packed. The political club members occupied seats on the floor of the 'House' and the 'public' crammed into the gallery or squeezed in around the edges of the Floor. Some nights were utterly memorable, not only for the brilliance of the oratory but the hugely entertaining nature of the skits and parodies, which occupied the slot known as 'Question Time'.

There were of course, moments of seriousness and boredom as well as awe and drama. Of the latter, one memory remains especially vivid. It was during the Cuban Missile Crisis when it looked like we might be on the verge of a Third World War. The Crisis was at its height and a debate was in progress that evening in Queen Margaret Union. Someone rushing in with a radio and placing it on the Clerks' Table interrupted the debate. For the next twenty minutes a packed and hushed hall strained to hear a BBC voice describe the seemingly inexorable final progress of the Russian missile ships towards Cuba. Hundreds of hearts missed a beat when the voice, in the same detached tone, announced that the ships had stopped and were turning around. I can remember the cheering and stamping, which followed, but the rest of the night remains a blur.

It was also during a debating function that we learned of the assassination of President Kennedy; at the Inter-Varsities Debate, hosted annually by the Men's Union. We were seated at the rather grand black-tie dinner which preceded it when a lackey came in and walking down the central aisle to the top table whispered in the President's ear. We heard the subsequent announcement in shocked disbelief, but it says something for the quality of debating which followed that we could put the tragedy to the back of our minds for the rest of the evening.

These were the glory days for the Debating Tradition and we vaguely imagined they'd last forever. Signs of the changes to come were already around us. Bulldozers and pile drivers were at work and 'University expansion' was the new national buzz. In 1961 the retiring Vice Chancellor, Sir Hector Hetherington, had forecast that the then existing student population of five thousand five hundred might conceivably expand by one thousand by the end of the decade. By 1964 it had already happened.

Among the proposed new buildings was a new Queen Margaret Union and the Executive Committee and I were invited by the Senate Planning Committee to view the plans. There was no question that the traditions of the past would be safe in the hands of a Senate Committee – which reassured us as there were several traditions we hoped would continue. We were pleased to note that there would be a debating hall and a Presidential Suite. However one tradition that was no longer relevant was that of a large dining hall and a small coffee room. We pointed out to the Committee that students no longer sat down to three course lunches and that the vast majority now frequented the coffee room for snacks and 'pie-and-chip' type meals. None of us round that table thought much further in terms of the needs of the student of the future or the likely knock-on effect of other major changes.

As we came out of the meeting I remember speculating to my colleagues that students in the not-too-distant future might think single sex unions an anachronism. This was greeted with a dismissive snort of 'not in our lifetime'.

The summer of 1964 was my last at University and I spent it getting down to some serious study. Between me and my BSc degree stood the little matter of a pass in Natural Philosophy (Physics) and I would be joining the other four hundred or so candidates in September at the annual re-sit for this compulsory subject. I had already been accepted for a place on the Personnel Management Diploma Course at the LSE, provided I graduated. I had rather taken this for granted at the time; as in my parochial way I was unaware of how prestigious an institution it was. I knew it wasn't the quality of my degree that had impressed my interviewers, but my activities in running Queen Margaret Union, which I felt rather mitigated my woeful neglect of my studies.

So I got down to work and studied daily, not in the University Library that, in four years I'm ashamed to say I had never visited, nor in the Reading Room that I'd only rarely visited, but in one of the little committee rooms in Queen Margaret Union, free from all distractions. There were many of us scattered around the University, each in our chosen corner, preparing for the re-sits, so it was also a companionable time. For those of us on the last-chance run it was also a slightly manic time. I remember a group of us, wandering around the University grounds dressed in an outlandish assortment of attire, looking for solemn sculptural symbols of 'academe' to perch upon while I photographed the disrespectful act. That was about as much a protest against the old order that we could muster. It is interesting on reflection to note that it was through dress that we expressed this little debunking of the Establishment. In 1964 our regular attire was still the uniform of correctness – pleated skirts and V-necked sweaters, blazers and grey flannels for the boys. We wore trousers only at the weekends, tailored 'slacks' with a side–entry zip.

To the wave of 'Baby Boomers' about to sweep in we must have seemed as conventional and smug in our elitism as the 'Twee club' of the fifties. We would say we helped to dust away the cobwebs but we could never deny that as members of the Queen Margaret Union Board of Management we enjoyed a unique and privileged time, for which I have been ever grateful.

Decorations from Queen Margaret Union in the 1960s

Staff members from Queen Margaret Union in the 1960s

Board Meeting, 1965-66

The Staff: Backbone of Queen Margaret Union

Elisabeth Greene
President 1963-1964

No reminiscence about Queen Margaret Union in the sixties would be complete without a fond tribute to the long-serving, and long-suffering staff. After all, Boards of Management and Presidents came and went but the staff was constant and made provision for what most 'Q-Emmas' wanted – socialising, sustenance and shelter.

There were the 'maids', who addressed the members as 'Miss'. In the Coffee Room they served snacks; hot orange was a favourite in the mornings, and Bovril in the afternoons. Most were local to Clydeside, which may have prompted their rallying to the cause of higher wages when led by May, stalwart of the Coffee Room, to down tools and go out on strike one busy morning; all was eventually resolved. They lit the coal fires each morning; a seat by the fire in the library was especially favoured by members although with it went responsibility for 'stoking up'. They manned the tannoy from the kiosk at the front door and ensured that no male proceeded any further into the building until after two pm.

The kitchen was presided over by Mary. She had her good days and her bad days and her cooking had good days and bad days too. The one tended to reflect the other; if she was crossed, the cuisine suffered. For many years Mary had compiled menus and supervised cooking on the strength of past experience. Hers was a live-in position, with her room in the turret whence she came and went via the door opposite the Porters lodge. Security of tenure, terms of service and suchlike were all hazy; she seemed to have just always 'been there'. What a shock for Mary then, when a 'new broom', Board of

Management and Executive, decided to engage a Catering Manageress and Mrs. Jamieson was appointed.

At the behest of the Board of Management – in the words of the President, "We are not a charitable organisation", Mrs. Jamieson brought a structured business-like approach to Queen Margaret Union's catering management, which was to ease the transition to the extended requirements of the new building.

The Office Staff, Mrs. Halliday and Mrs. Cairns, administered day-to-day activities for the members. Their role however extended well beyond the formalities of club bookings, hairdressing appointments, selling tickets, processing posters or notices and making overnight bed bookings. They were party to the joys, the heartbreaks and the intrigue behind these formalities. Mrs. Halliday's reserved, non-committal responses always implied sympathy for predicaments whatever might have been her opinion. She would say that her youthful regrets about her childlessness were matched in later years when working in Queen Margaret Union's office by her relief at being spared maternal involvement in students' crises and traumas. Discretion was assured for any confidence shared with Mrs. Halliday. On the other hand, the widest dissemination could be assured for any information imparted to Mrs. Cairns. They complemented each other perfectly. Mrs. Cairns bubbled with enthusiasm about a 'Q-Emma's' student life. She could be relied on for the hoped for response to any personal news, for updating on current gossip and for an informative chat or a good laugh when some light relief was necessary.

Such were the people who made much of what we remember Queen Margaret Union to have been in the 1960's. Fond thanks to them all.

Freshers Camp Staff, October 1965.
The front row includes
extreme left Sheila Crawford (President, 1965-1966) and
third from right Maren Hunter (President 1968-1969)

MARGARET FAIRLIE

In the final of the 'Scotsman' debate in the Union on 27th February, the first Q.M. team (Mila Rocho and Margaret Fairlie) took an impressive second place behind the Strathclyde first team. Also in the final was the Q.M. team of Moira McBride and Gillian Smith.

From *Glasgow University Guardian*, 14 March 1967

QM Memories

*Margaret Fairlie
President 1966-1967*

I grew up in a sheltered world, attending a small convent school, so I was more than ready to sample all the experiences 'the Uni' had to offer, beginning with Auchendennan Fresher Camp in September 1962. That was my introduction to what was called the "corporate life" of the university and I dreamt someday of becoming a member of the Students Representative Council and returning to Auchendennan; at least until I set foot in Queen Margaret Union.

It was love at first sight. Being right inside the gates of the University, it was the perfect place to meet friends outside of class, to (occasionally) study in the splendid upstairs library, to have lunch or a coffee, or to summon friends via the tannoy system at the entrance booth. The wood lined debating chamber that doubled as a dance hall and ballroom, the glorious drawing room with blazing coal fire, the tiny upstairs rooms that you could rent for a night rather than leave an event too early to catch the last bus home — the memories are still fresh.

I joined Queen Margaret Union, proudly paying my seven shillings and sixpence and receiving my diary as proof of membership, opening the path to a host of new friends and experiences. That fall was the quadrennial Rectorial election, and rivalry was intense between supporters of Albert Lutuli and those of Lord Rosebery. Donald Dewar, President of the Men's' Union and a big Lutuli supporter, had previously been involved in heated debates with Rosebery supporters. Tempers were running high and on election day a little yellow Volkswagen Beetle was driving up and down University Avenue, blaring

debates report - Q.M. Sec

Although not of course up to the standard of Jordanhill Freshers' Debates, GARY McLAUCHLIN (Conservative) opened the debate with what was, for Glasgow University Debating, an excellent speech—in fact the best speech of the debate. He dealt clearly with all three clauses, refused to let himself be sidetracked by information. His major faults, shared by almost every speaker in the opening round, was that of over-running his time.

KEN LITTLE (Labour) opening for the opposition, made a good, fighting, debating speech, but spent far too long on the first clause. The whole of the debate was marred by the over-emphasis on the details of the first clause, rather than the principles underlying the bill.

If any member of the house suspected that the clerk's table was not functioning with its usual efficiency during the opening round they were probably right. **Linda Baird** (Liberal), **Margaret Logan** (Ind. Soc.) and **Gillian Smith** (Scot. Nat.) were all opening the debate for their clubs. All made competent, reasonable speeches.

Carelessly and nonchalantly, **Gerry Somers** (Distrib.) opened the debate for his his club, amusing the house if not exactly holding it rapt!

After the excellent quality of the Maiden Speakers in the last Q.M. debate, the House was delighted, if a little surprised to see this trend continuing. **Ian Robertson** (Tory), **Alistair Beaton** (Ind. Soc.) **Paddy O'Donnell** (Distrib.), and **Richard Moore** (Tory) all made very fine speeches.

There was also an unusually good crop of lady maidens. **Greer Chadwick** (Tory), **Rosemary McDonell** (Distrib.) and **Ailsa Campbell** (Scot. Nat.) all showed great promise. Miss Campbell let herself to be flummoxed by a point of information from that arch-enemy of maidens, Gary McLauchlin. But she is certainly one of the most promising new woman speakers for some time.

The Maiden Speaker's Prize was finally awarded to **DAVID WALSH** (Labour) who made a speech worthy of a debater of long experience.

The first four speeches of the pointed round were of exceptionally high quality. **Michael Hirst** (Tory) made about his best speech to date, **Alasdair Smith** (Labour) had a good, reasoned approach and **Alan Rodger** (Liberal) made a lively, fighting effort that held the attention of the House. **John Harrison** (Ind. Soc.) continued to show great promise.

Mila Rocho (Distrib.) and **Janice Purdon** (Scot. Nat.) both gave sensible but uninspiring contributions.

Other noteworthy contributions were from **Gerald Warner** (Tory), who made an excellent speech, and **Nancy Robertson** (Labour), who told Alan Rodger, in the nicest possible way that she wasn't interested.

RSITY GUARDIAN Tuesday, 29th November, 1966

retary's - debates report

On the whole, the beginning of the evening session was disappointing until **Maeve McDonald** (Scot. Nat.) quietly but forcibly put before the House some of the practical issues involved in the Bill. **Sylvia Sayle** (Lab.) and **Elissa Dawson** (Tory) both made good, sensible if not very lively speeches.

Colin Mackay (Liberal) told the House that "if you rave for long enough, you can fill up 10 minutes terribly easily," and proved that he was right. Anyone who calls the Labour Party "a kill-joy organisation" in Mr. MacKay's inimitable style deserves (and he got!) the acclaim of the House. **Matt McQueen** (Distrib.) also made an exceptionally good speech, his attack on the Opposition on the 3rd clause making a pleasant change from comprehensive education.

Alastair McLaughlin (Tory) made his usual excellent speech, which we loved at first but which we are getting now to know practically off by heart. **Irene Christie** (Tory) despite difficult conditions, made a good speech. **Norman Bissell** (Ind. Soc.) then gave us some superb Marxism — arousing if not convincing.

MOIRA McBRIDE

The Closing Round was of a reasonable standard. GEORGEANNA PHILIPS (Scot. Nat.), JOAN SHAW (Distrib.), CAROL CRAWFORD (Ind. Soc.) and PATSY HAMILTON (Liberal) all made run-of-the mill competent speeches. The new Labour Club convener, FLORA SULLIVAN, made her debut in the closing round with a really excellent speech, confident, forceful, and interesting. MOIRA McBRIDE in her Prime Ministerial speech, covered the bill well, debating each clause fully and competently.

If not in itself outstanding, this debate augured well for the future of debating, since in the afternoon session the inexperienced speakers showed that they could give contributions in many cases far better than those of the more practised speakers in the Evening Session.

From *Glasgow University Guardian*, 29 November 1966

THIRD Q.M. DEBATE

In the third Q.M. Debate, held on Friday, 3rd February, a Labour Government sought to introduce a national minimum wage, equal pay for equal work, and greater social security benfits.

KEN LITTLE (Lab.), opening for the Government, gave a good statement of his principles and his economic views. In reply, GARY McLAUGHLIN (Cons.) attacked in an outstanding and fiery speech. GEORGE BEATON (Ind. Soc.) brought in a welcome touch of humour, whilst BILLY McLACHLAN (Scot. Nat.) was enjoyably extreme in a misogynistic way. Most of the allusions made by IAN FORRESTER (Lib.) were too unfamiliar to the House to make much impact. Finally, GERRY SOMERS (Distrib.) spoke so quietly that he produced almost a hypnotic effect.

The rest of the afternoon session was marked by maidens ranging from the disastrous to such as ALEX. MACKAY (Scot. Nat.), whose fine content and presentation deservedly gained him the Maiden Speaker's Prize. The House also acquired a most attractive Continental flavour from JEAN PIERRE CATTELAIN (Ind. Soc.) and JAARL AAGEDAL (Distrib.). In the pointed round, passion was the order of the day, notably in the speeches of NANCY ROBERTSON (Lab.), AILSA CAMPBELL (Scot. Nat) and GILLIAN SMITH (Ind. Soc.). However, the star of the round, and probably of the afternoon, was undoubtedly MICHAEL HIRST (Cons.), who fell on the House like a Tory bombshell.

The evening session opened in quieter vein with competent statements of their respective cases from IAIN SMITH (Lab.) and DAVID ROSS (Cons.). JOHN TRAVERS (Ind. Soc.) did very well for one who only made his maiden speech in the first debate. KEN CAMPBELL (Scot. Nat.) produced an incredible performance. JIM FORREST (Lib.) continues to improve, but MILA ROCHO (Distrib.) was obviously nervous. The mid-evening round was of a high standard. GORDON HEWITT (Lab.), in all his sartorial splendour, combined wit with solid content. ALAN RODGER (Lib.) made his usual fine speech. IAIN VALENTINE (Distrib.) was as amusing and irrelevant as ever.

Question Time taxed the House's patience with two written questions. There were no less than four stunts, of which the Tory Stunt was the most striking visually and the Labour one the best written. Of the independent speakers, the most outstanding was an amazingly clear and reasonable MARGARET FAIRLIE, who achieved the impossible of bringing in new arguments even at this late hour.

In the closing round, a sincere JOAN SHAW (Distrib.) was unfortunately hampered by points of order from her own club, PATSY HAMILTON (Lib.) also made a very attractive effect, and CAROL CRAWFORD (Ind. Soc.) succeeded in debating instead of lecturing. GEORGEANNA PHILLIPS (Scot. Nat.), having alienated every member of her club except for the President, wisely returned to the protection of the hon. member for Merryflatts. MOIRA McBRIDE (Cons.) was well received, though at the risk of an irreparable breach with the member of the Nineteenth.

In her Prime Ministerial speech, FLORA SULLIVAN (Lab.) covered the bill very competently, and with admirable brevity. On a vote by acclamation, the motion was carried.

The Clerk's and Convener's Reports were given, and the prizes presented. Maiden Speaker's Prizes were gained by JOHN HARRISON (Ind. Soc.), DAVID WALSH (Lab.), and ALEX. MACKAY (Scot. NAT.). The Best Speaker's Prize went to GARY McLAUGHLIN, the best Woman Speaker's Prize to MARGARET FAIRLIE, and the Most Promising Woman Speaker's Prize to FLORA SULLIVAN. The Debates Trophy was won by the Labour Club, who defeated the Conservative Club by half a point.

In conclusion, the Speaker thanked the House for a most enjoyable session, and declared it adjourned.

● To bring it into line with tradition in a neighbouring House, Q.M. Debates Report should, of course, have awarded a 'G' mark to Miss Rocho and Miss Logan.

From *Glasgow University Guardian*, 28 February 1967

SECOND Q.M. DEBATE:

TRANSPORT BILL UNDER ATTACK
QUESTION TIME BELOW STANDARD

Transport was debated both in Q.M. and Westminster last week and the arguments followed much the same lines in both Houses with the Conservatives opposing Mrs. Barbara Castle's plans.

In Q.M. opening for the Tory Government, Gary McLauchlan stated that there had been an air of confidence about transport during the latter years of Conservative but this confidence has been shattered since the Labour Party came to power. Moving on from this he explained that Tory Club policy was to regard transport as an industry. This aroused the hostility of the Opposition who regarded transport as a social service to which profit was unimportant. And these two conflicting viewpoints formed the basis of the debate. The Tories also advocated regional control and co-ordination but stressed that the latter should be brought about by persuasion of private enterprise companies rather than nationalisation. This "persuasion" was unfortunately left to the interpretation of the rest of the House.

The Opposition case put first by Philip McGhee, of the Independent Socialists, was that there should be integration of the transport system, thus eliminating competition between road and rail.

The debate continued with much repetition of these arguments although different aspects were introduced by a few speakers. One maiden speaker, William McCarthy (Ind. Soc.) dealt exclusively with the question of civil aviation and advocated total nationalisation in order that higher standards of safety could be enforced. At this stage the Distributist Club's main grouse was that nationalisation of the railways had resulted in dirty compartments.

In the evening, "the balding and ruggedly handsome" Brian Gibb, just managing to forget sex for ten minutes, attacked the White Paper on Railway Policy and argued that management was insecure under the Labour government.

Drastic measures for relief of the congestion in cities due to the increase of the number of private cars was suggested by Barbara Hoare (Lib.).

The Labour Club continued arguing that the transport system should be dealt with in connection with development areas and economic growth, indeed all aspects of community life and after question time Gordon Hewitt gave an excellent account of what was needed to be done.

"People before profit and Scotland first" was the Scottish Nationalists theme while the Independent Socialists still cried for complete nationalisation.

The least said about question time the better.

The arguments of the day were summed up for each club by their respective leaders and the Prime Minister, Pat Wright again detailed her club's policy, but the bill was defeated when the House moved to a division.

From *Glasgow University Guardian*, 30 November 1967

pro-Rosebery messages through a loudspeaker. Bystanders were heckling back, and then someone had the bright idea of making flour bombs and bombing the Beetle. Things quickly degenerated from there to bombing buses and private cars, 'the polis' came out in force and arrested thirty two students, and the Daily Record headline the next day was "oh thae Students". It was all great fun and quite exciting, if not perhaps as meaningful as the student riots at Berkeley, California!

The Men's Union had six parliamentary debates a year, Queen Margaret Union had three, and they were extremely well attended, especially around ten pm for question time, when humour was the order of the day. The President was the 'Speaker of the House' when hosting debates at the Union. I had been an avid debater and President of the Distributist Club, but it was a truly special moment when I first became Speaker. Some were not quite so impressed as I, since the debate review once referred to me thusly, "She banged her little hammer in a most determined manner"!

Saturday night dances at Queen Margaret Union were highly popular, as were the two or three formal balls annually. The Entertainments Convener and her committee worked tirelessly for weeks to make all the decorations for the balls, creating a different theme for each one, and they were always a sell-out.

One of the perks of being a Board Member was access to the Board flat and the Board dorm. The flat was a good-sized sitting room with fireplace, at the top of a flight of stairs. Coffee was strong, black and unlimited and you could always find a fourth for bridge. If any regular members had rented a cubicle for the night, a Board Member was required to be on duty, sleeping over in the Board Dorm. Board Members were also responsible for checking that the premises (including the men's room) were vacated before locking the building down for the night.

Two of the more distinguished visitors to the Board flat were Lord Reith and Malcolm Muggeridge. As President, I had attended Lord Reith's installation as Rector in 1967 and we got along exceptionally well. He was a giant of a man, both literally and figuratively (as Chairman of the BBC during the war years, he had the nerve to stand up to Winston Churchill on issues of censorship). He was a friend with Muggeridge, who also attended his installation, so I invited both of them for coffee after the ceremony. The next two hours were full of highly entertaining and wickedly challenging conversation, particularly in areas of politics and religion.

My University experience would not have been half so valuable, enjoyable or rewarding had it not been for my involvement with Queen Margaret Union. The social and leadership skills I learned and the friends I made have been even more important than the excellent education I received. Kudos to the current 'Q-Emmas' who are carrying on the best traditions of the 'corporate life'.

Queen Margaret Union Ball

Tuesday, 24th January, 1967

WHAT TO DO WITH Q. M. ?

Next October, the new Queen Margaret Union is scheduled to be opened and the occupants of the present building will move there. Naturally this raises the question "What happens to the present Q.M. Building?" Although perhaps the building itself is rather drab, it is still serviceable and whoever gains the building, gains with it some other advantages.

Certainly, the central position of Q.M. is an asset for any organisation and it is undeniable that the building has a character of its own, being the former Men's Union as well as the present Women's Union. These advantages, added to the constant demand from practically every organisation for more accommodation suggests that the requests for Q.M. will come in from many quarters.

Rumours are rife about the possible contenders, with the S.R.C. and the College Club the favourites. Pearce Lodge is anything but commodious and one would think the S.R.C. could usefully acquire another building. Although, no doubt, the College Club needs more accommodation, like everyone else, the present quarters of the Club are palatial compared to those of the S.R.C. However, little was to be elicited from either group about their intentions although the S.R.C. admitted to being interested.

Despite conjecture, the University authorities will make their decision unaided and, until that happens, no definite statement is possible. However, it would be a loss to University tradition and history, if the Q.M. Building, the centre of student activity for so long, was to cease functioning as an integral part of the University.

From *Glasgow University Guardian*, 24 January 1967

Battle for Q.M.

The end of this session should see a tremendous scrap for the old Q.M. When the women move to their new premises in University Gardens, just who is going to take over the vacant building?

At the moment, it looks like being a tug o' war between the S.R.C. and the College Club. The Arts Faculty are also rumoured to be looking for temporary accommodation, but it doesn't seem likely that their claim will receive a favourable hearing. On the face of it, S.R.C. would appear to have the best claim, but it seems likely that the Staff Club have more strings to pull.

Certainly the S.R.C. has raised its standing since the Jack Murray era and the unfortunate scandals that preceded his Presidential year. But how far can S.R.C. improve its services to the student, when it is couped up in Pearce Lodge? Anyone will testify that Pearce Lodge is so hopelessly inadequate that enthusiasm is bound to ebb, the surroundings are depressing. It is a sad reflection that the Union has better facilities and yet S.R.C. is allegedly the Student Representative Body.

A move to the vacant Q.M. Building would give S.R.C. the shot in the arm that it badly needs. Once installed, the possibilities are endless. The S.R.C. Building would become the focal point of student life that it should be.

ADVANTAGES FOR S.R.C.

Facilities could be provided for Clubs to meet, but more importantly, S.R.C. could fulfill its obligations to the student more adequately. Meetings of Council would no longer be the cloistered affairs that they are at the moment. They would provide a forum of debate that could be witnessed by all interested students.

The right of the College Club's claims to the Building are more questionable. This is particularly true when it is considered that the ruling is that no matriculated student is allowed into the College Club, not even when accompanied by a member of staff. In these circumstances, why should the teaching staff be allowed to take up more space in what is essentially a student building?

All our conjecture, of course, might be wrong. The Senate may well be planning to pull the Building down. And that undoubtedly would be in very bad taste.

From *Glasgow University Guardian*, October 1967

MOIRA MACBRIDE SLAMS UNION
"INDIFFERENT TO OXFAM"

●

The Glasgow University Oxfam Bihar Appeal, thanks to the efforts of Q.M. Members and University Staff has got off to a reasonable start. Considering the size of this University a reasonable start is just not good enough — we ought to be ashamed of the lack of response. This does not mean that individual members are to blame — the fault lies with the student bodies of the University

Q.M. Union did as much as possible to appeal to its members for help; numerous posters were put up and a senior member of Staff addressed a lunch time meeting which recruited twenty-five volunteers to help staff the Gift Shop. The response of the Men's Union has been entirely negative — the Board of Management, weighed down as they are with all their pressing problems, somehow could not find the time to have anything to do with the Appeal, thus displaying their reluctance to come out of their own little world to participate in anything where they would not be the king-pins. They were not asked to do all that much! Advertising the Appeal would have been no more trouble to them than advertising their own dances; but, let's not forget, the Union had nothing to gain from the Oxfam Appeal . . . . Their apathy is all the more frustrating for those who have helped with the Appeal, e.g. Q.M., the International Club, the Catholic Society, when one considers the vast number of people who could have been contacted through the Men's Union.

The S.R.C. began by considering the Bihar Appeal a worthy cause, which they were willing to support. But did they do anything about it? No — all words and no action. To be fair, the Appeal was launched at roughly the same time as the S.R.C. elections with a resulting change in personnel, but this does not excuse them completely. More use could have been made of "Guardian" to publicise the Appeal.

The Oxfam Shop in Buchanan Street is to be open for the next month. All you men can still help — bring in your gifts to Q.M. or George Service House. You still have time to make up for the selfish attitude of your governing body, and you can contribute to this deserving cause.

The Oxfam Bihar Appeal can still be a success if you all help. Anything is taken, so bring in you odds and ends — it all helps to save lives.

From *Glasgow University Guardian*, 30 November 1967

The New Union

Moira McQueen
President 1967-1968

My year as President turned out to be eventful, since 'the new QM' was opened during my year in office. Our Board of Management spent countless hours at committee meetings with members of the University Senate, administrators, building contractors, architects, engineers and so forth, all of whom were involved in the planning and construction of the new Women's Union. Considering our relative youth and inexperience, I have to say that the professionals took a great deal of care to make sure we were aware of what was involved. We had a lot to contribute to the design and use of space in the building. We knew what students wanted, since we had several open meetings with the members to discuss that. It was still a Women's Union at that point, and so, apart from deciding on the location of men's washrooms, we did not have to consider male requirements much further.

My memory is that the plans looked wonderful. The space available seemed immense after the tiny size of the old building, interesting though the latter was architecturally. For those who remember the old building when it was in use as our home, it consisted of the cafeteria (haggis and chips), which was rather small, with the lounge and general area adding some seating space at busy times. The library upstairs, though attractive, was akin to a school library, and a small school at that. Still, the parties we had there; post-debate gatherings, and the like. The debating chamber (my favourite, since I became Convenor of Debates at age nineteen) was used as a general 'hangout' during the day, although it was not designed for that. The Board Room, the Board of Management offices and the guest rooms were barely adequate, since they were so small and a little bit like a doll's house.

The new building offered space, and the drawings and plans looked inspiring. Choosing colours, selecting furniture, working within a budget - all this was good training for the future for those of us involved, and that would sometimes be the entire Board of Management. I suspect now that we were not as wise about some of the choices as we thought. Even then, though, I had reservations about the look of the concrete used in constructing the place. Granted it has staying power, but I must say that the last time I saw the building I was disappointed. It looked scuffed and rundown, and, as for the state of the outside walls; let's just say that they have been no match for the 'guid auld' Scottish granite of the original building. Anyway, it's not only aesthetics that matter. What goes on in the building is a lot more important than how it looks (a bit like relationships), and the place looked busy and thriving.

The official opening was quite a celebration, with television cameras whirring, and the University top brass making the necessary speeches, as well as one from me as President. My Board of Management worked hard that year. We had so many extra meetings, over and above the regular union business, that I am amazed I passed any examinations. I learned the importance of details and organization, not to mention the need to be clear about proposals and specifications. I had thought I was already quite well organized, but the experience of planning and consulting was helpful for my later career plans in law, and now in academia. One snag was that I had a major row with my boyfriend at one point because there were so many meetings, and I had had to cancel a few arrangements with him. It turned out well, nonetheless, because we married about a year later.

I was fortunate to have been Convenor of Debates and Secretary before becoming President and was able to follow the plans for the new Queen Margaret Union over a good period of time. I would like to thank the University of Glasgow Senate, (rather belatedly), for including the student body as much as possible in the planning and suggesting stages, and for consulting with us and explaining construction problems when those conflicted with what we had requested for the building. My memory is that the Senate members involved were very accommodating, and took our suggestions very seriously. After all, the University was the real client: we were just the current student representatives, and the money being spent was not ours. Farquar Gillanders, on the University side, and David Leslie, on the architectural side, were very easy to work with, even although they must have known that we were amateurs at the construction game. I hope we thanked them adequately at the time

It was a very good year. We had our usual Parliamentary debates, the Christmas Ball, the 'Fork and Glass' dinner, and the usual dances and events. I was fortunate to become a little part of Queen Margaret Union history through being President in that transition year, and I am grateful for that experience, as well as for the chance to develop the skills so essential in later life. In retrospect, I am especially grateful for the opportunity to have met so many interesting and talented people, both on the Board itself, and through the 'town and gown' aspects of creating 'the new QM'.

Freshers Camp at Auchendennan in the late 1960s.
Maren Hunter, President 1968-1969, *fourth from the right in the front row*, is three seats away from the Principal, Sir Charles Wilson.

153

Glasgow University Guardian lead story, 11 February, 1968

View of the new Union at 22 University Gardens

Lounge area of the new Union at 22 University Gardens

The Late Sixties

Jane Hook
President 1969-1970

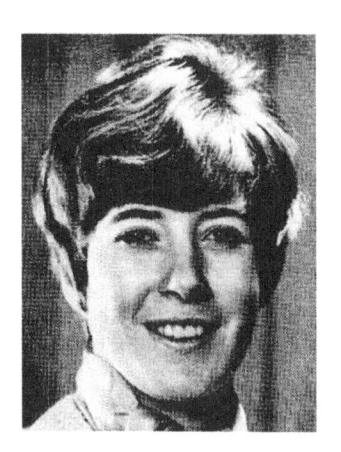

Having come to the University of Glasgow from Lerwick in Shetland and knowing no one on my arrival, becoming President of Queen Margaret Union was very exciting. The biggest event during my time as President was the introduction of the first permanent bar. I remember spending a large part of the summer break supervising workmen, re-organising plans, dealing with a whole range of fire, health and safety issues.

This all had to be completed before we got around to the interviews for new bar staff. We were lucky enough to have the help and support of Scottish and Newcastle to do so. One post was to be a live-in position with use of one of the small flats on the top of the building and this meant that we had a vast number of applicants. However when the experts reviewed them it soon whittled itself down. Even when we finally found someone, that was not without its troubles and I suspect that this continued after my time.

The opening of the bar changed so many things within Queen Margaret Union. We were able to launch into a whole range of exciting social events and compete with the Men's Union and Strathclyde University. This was the start of big events. We had a whole range of gigs. It is impossible to remember them all but some of the most memorable included Dave Berry whose rendition of the 'Crying Game' brought the place to a stand still; I think he is still wowing audiences with this. We also had a very new young group called 'The Who'. I remember a very spaced out Rodger Daltry arrived at Queen Margaret Union at six pm and I had to take him to join his mates who were at

Catering area of new Union shortly after opening

Strathclyde University where they were to play first. It was an immense relief to see them all arrive at Queen Margaret Union for our turn. They also brought the place to a halt.

The biggest memory of all is reserved for Marsha Hunt whose arrival suddenly turned Queen Margaret Union into a besieged building and for the first time in our lives we had to limit tickets. The queue for admission snaked its way well down University Avenue. We almost had a riot and it took all of our skills to calm things down and have Marsha do her turn. A very excited member of the audience came up to me after what was amazing performance and asked if I would like to touch his hankie which apparently had a large range of famous pop stars sweat on it not only Marsha but also Mick Jagger! That was one piece of excitement I declined.

Another fond memory of these great social evenings was how we paid most of the group's roadies in cash. It was not unusual for Board Members to be carrying one thousand pounds in cash on their person over their Duty evening. We were very lucky never to lose a penny.

As well as the big gigs in the huge hall at weekends we often had folk groups during the week and the most memorable would of course be the 'Humble Bums' with a young Billy Connolly already reducing everyone to tears of laughter.

The debating scene at Queen Margaret Union was a very important part of my time, not just as President, but also as a very active debater. The bar also livened up the Union debating scene but meant we were able to hold special events with some well-known characters. The guest speakers at this time included Donald Dewar, John Smith, Menzies Campbell and Nicky Fairbairn all of whom attracted a large audience. The debaters of my time included Anne Long, our Debates Convenor, (now Anne Maguire MP), Andy Neil who became, well, Andy Neil, Gerry Malone - who came and went as an MP - and lots of others whose careers took off and are now in a range of significant posts. The importance of the debating scene at the University of Glasgow at this time is often forgotten but it really did produce some excellent speakers as well as an incredibly lively social scene. Many of us who met at this time have remained firm friends over the years.

The social scene included a large number of formal

functions and I remember having a considerable number of long dresses. Fashion was interesting ranging from floral patterns from Laura Ashley to plunging necklines, which were particularly admired by the Gallery audience during debates! The hairdos were hysterical for these events. Those of us who had short hair owned hairpieces, which were deposited at the hairdresser on the Tuesday or Wednesday before an event, and we went on the Friday to have our individual concoction perched on or attached to our heads by enough pins to fill several buckets. These pins gradually loosened themselves over the evening and with vigorous dancing were often fairly odd looking by the end of the night. Those of our friends who had long hair spent vast amounts of time crouched over ironing boards with brown paper while we short haired pals help iron and straighten their hair. Hair straighteners would have been a blessing but, alas, did not exist, although the electric roller did, but that is enough on the topic.

We were at the end of the 'swinging sixties', but most of us at the University of Glasgow were still very conservative. I remember the Board of Management arguing about permitting visits from a health professional to discuss contraception as many felt that lots of our members would be offended. The talks went ahead amid some controversy and were well attended.

Drugs may well have been part of the scene but for most Queen Margaret Union ladies our only contact was an odd pong at some parties. I think if memory serves me someone was sacked from the Biology department for having LSD in the fridge but booze was still too exciting for us to be interested in another scene.

My year as President was busy, happy and full of fun although not much academic activity. It must have been a huge relief to my parents that I did actually get my degree. The experiences I gained at this time have been so useful to me in later life when I discovered my daughter had autism and introduced a campaign for better, or even any, appropriate services. At the time none of us quite realised that these experiences would impact on our futures. Debating honed my ability to think on my feet and being thrust into a management job at an early age taught me skills I have never forgotten. Time seemed a great deal slower than it does now and the memories still last and are very vivid.

1970

A great many movements sprung out of the seventies. One of the most powerful promoted women's rights. Nowhere in Glasgow was the feminist movement making its mark more strongly felt than at Queen Margaret Union.

There had always existed a very obvious sexual divide at the University of Glasgow. With the incorporation of the College it seemed that equality with men had been achieved in all aspects – with one exception. By 1970 both Queen Margaret Union and Glasgow University Union were among the last (if not the only) single sex students unions left in the United Kingdom.

Several times in the decade, members of Queen Margaret Union put proposals to allow men to join. By 1979 they would get their wish. The changes came fast and furious. In 1975 the Union was granted funding for a sabbatical officer. This meant that the President could take a paid year break from their studies to focus on the running of the Union without jeopardising their degree.

The Annual Fork and Glass Evening spawned another tradition – the 'Strawberry Tea' which was a social afternoon shared between the student Boards of Management at each Student Union on campus.

It was the so-called 'Mixing Debate' that really took centre stage however with demonstrations against the sexist views of Glasgow University Union and organised events that would lead to large groups of students storming the male-only bastion that was the Beer Bar at the Men's Union. It would only take until 1979 for Queen Margaret Union to allow men to join. Glasgow University Union would not mix its membership for a further two years.

History had been made yet again by Queen Margaret Union. All members were now equal and the radical views and opinions of its membership had once again kept the Union moving with the times. Queen Margaret Union would become a social haven for all social groups with no exceptions on campus and this idea of integration is at the heart of the Union even today.

GLASGOW UNIVERSITY GUARDI[AN]

STOP THINK
Steer clear of alcoholic drink
SCOTTISH TEMPERANCE ALLIANCE

Vol. 17. No. 6. Tuesday, 24th January, 1967.

71% SAY 'YES' TO MIXED UNION

A "GUARDIAN" OPINION POLL HAS REVEALED THAT OVER 70% OF G.U. UNDERGRADUATES WANT A MIXED UNION.

Last week "Guardian" reporters conducted a poll around the University, trying to discover the feelings of Glasgow students on the subject of a Mixed Union. They found that 70% of men and 72% of women approved in principle of a Mixed Union. It would seem many students feel their unions are not adequately fulfilling their functions as social centres.

Many more women than men wanted to see the Men's Union open to all students. First year men applauded the idea on the whole, but most older male students were not in favour. Men only were asked if they would like to see the Union Extension become mixed — 63% said "Yes". The Poll made no provision for "Don't Knows", but their numbers were not found to be significant.

The results of the poll, involving almost 1,000 students, generally confirm the current opinions on mixed unions — "We agree in principle ..." people have been saying — "but the practical difficulties are too overwhelming". There was considerable confusion about the advantages and disadvantakes of the various proposals for the establishment of a Mixed Union.

INSIDE: "Guardian" analyses the detailed results of the opinion poll, and examines the feasible suggestions for a Mixed Union.

Its open at last! The Adam Smith Building started in March, 1964, whose outside structure was completed 15 months ago, has since been almost completed inside. All will be finished in five weeks time, it is hoped. "Delays are due to the long wait for essential supplies, a problem which afflicts British Industry in general and the building trade in particular."

Of course, friction between procrastinating professors and construction workers is only natural — after all it's a part of the game. One professor said to a workman, "If you leave that door stop there I shall only fall over it". Needpartment, convinced as they are that half their students are borderline cases who would just love to throw themselves off.

There will be no comments like 'are we angels?' about this building; for it is equipped

From *Glasgow University Guardian*, 24 January 1967

WHO WANTS MIXED UNIONS?

ANALYSIS OF THE RESULTS

1. The fact that such a large majority of the random sample were in favour of the idea of a Mixed Union strongly suggests that the existing facilities for sexually-integrated activities are found unsatisfactory by most students.

At present, the Men's Union allows women entrance only to attend meetings and recognised functions: men are admitted to the Q.M. coffee-room from 2.30 p.m. each day. Apart from week-end dances in both unions, students are segregated. Incidentally, the segregation policy extends even further into some classes, especially in the Science faculty, where men and women are required to sit in separate parts of the lecture-hall.

2. A majority of men disliked the idea of their union becoming a mixed one. Their reasons were twofold. Some say they wish to preserve the "status quo": other declare: "Things are very well as they are — why change anything?" Some students talk about the traditions surrounding Glasgow's unions without being very specific about what these are.

A number of male students seem to feel that their union (perhaps because of its red leather armchairs) is rather like an exclusive men's club. And like Englishmen of the 18th and 19th century who retired there to escape their wives and mistresses they feel the need of a refuge from women. It is not clear how many Glasgow students have wives, or, for that matter, mistresses as well.

The large number of "Noes" in reply to this question were probably based on the mistaken assumption that a Mixed Union would mean there were no male preserves whatsoever in what is at present their building. This is not so. All proposals for any type of mixed union include the proviso that lounges for men and women exclusively would be set aside: as well as e.g. a hairdressing room and possibly a coffee-room for women, snooker rooms and the indispensable beer-bar (on their present premises) would remain for men alone.

The last two questions in the poll referred to alternative suggestions for the formation of a mixed union. Most students agree that there is no possibility within the forseeable future of a new building being provided to house a Mixed Union: in any case, one building to serve over 7,000 students might turn out to be rather an unwieldy proposition.

3. 65% of men and 61% of women liked the idea of turning the old Q.M. building into a mixed union, with the existing buildings remaining as they are. This is a most attractive first step towards integration, and would provide a trial period for the Mixed Union principle.

However, two main difficulties face this idea — University authorities are thought to have ear-marked the building for the College (Staff) Club. Secondly, no-one knows who could run the building as an efficient union, though S.R.C. has been suggested.

4. Most men approved the integration of the Union Extension, but the existing facilities there (a small coffee-room, hall and committee rooms) would do little to satisfy the desire for a mixed union.

It seems then that the only workable solution is that the new Q.M. and the Men's Union should become two mixed unions.

"WHERE GOETH?— GOD KNOWETH."

IN the Board Room of the QM on Wednesday, 14th December at 1.30 p.m. The first meeting of the mixed Union Society took place in an atmosphere somewhere between that of a funeral parlour and that of Intervarsities Question Time. The advertisement in Guardian had specified "all interested" and amongst those who claimed to be so were sizeable portions of the Union and QM Boards who all but outnumbered others who considered themselves to have more altruistic reasons for attending.

GUARDIAN POLL RESULTS

DETAILED RESULTS
QUESTION 1. Do you approve in principle of a Mixed Union?
	YES	NO
Men	70%	30%
Women	72%	28%

TOTAL 71% in favour

QUESTION 2. Do you want the present Union to become mixed?
	YES	NO
Men	38%	62%
Women	50%	50%

TOTAL 44% in favour

QUESTION 3. Do you want the PRESENT Q.M. building to become mixed?*
	YES	NO
Men	65%	35%
Women	61%	39%

TOTAL 63% in favour

QUESTION 4. (men only) Do you want the Union Extension to become mixed?
	YES	NO
Men	67%	33%

TOTAL 67% in favour
* i.e. When new building taken over.

The one fact which emerged from a very lively meeting full of thrust, counterthrust, re-crimination, counter-recrimination and Jim Bogan (with his own brand of impeccable logic) was that however full of intent the society was, they were devoid of ideas about how to approach their task. Even the most fanatical mixed unionite must admit that the ideas which they are putting into practice were those suggested by members of both boards.

The Gallup Poll was suggested by the Union Board with the proviso that it should present not only percentages for and against but also a breakdown of those asked, whether they thought present facilities were sufficient and whether the idea was feasible. (It is to be hoped for the sake of validity and accuracy that their poll includes this breakdown).

OBJECTIVES

Not only were they unsure of the methods they could use; they were also unsure of their objectives. The need for a mixed union was contested on the grounds that facilities in QM and the Refectory were adequate at present and that the whole idea of a mixed union was not feasible.

As streams of questions about where? who would run it? who would pay for its upkeep? what about the people who didn't want one?—came forward Judith White (chairman by divine right) and her companions were forced more and more to talk about theory, as it applied to other universities and not about Glasgow. Moreover to try and argue about the position in both unions when they didn't know that they could call a Special General Meeting in either union (on the production of 20 signatures) to discuss the matter, struck many people as showing little knowledge of what they were trying to do, or how to go about it.

The general impression of some of the non-aligned persons present (and there were some) was that the mixed union society would have to concern itself more with the practicalities of what they are attempting and less both with the theory of a mixed union, and the unquestioning faith they have in mixed unions elsewhere.

View of the new Union at 22 University Gardens

Extract from *Toast to Queen Margaret Union,* June 2005

Christine Hamilton
President 1974

It is a real honour to be invited tonight and to propose the toast to Queen Margaret Union. It is an act of some bravery on your part, Madame President, to allow a President from thirty years ago a platform for their reminiscences. It did strike me that had I been so brave in 1975 I would have been welcoming a past president who had student memories of VE day.

So on embarking on this I had to remind myself that nothing sounds so last century than the good old days. In proposing this toast what I do want to reflect on is what Queen Margaret Union means then and now, and to suggest that the spirit of Queen Margaret Union may take new forms but it lives on in the radical tradition of student politics. While we know that there are other institutions on this campus and elsewhere whose role it is to fight for student rights and engage with wider political movements, it is here in Queen Margaret Union that the real heart, soul and let's face it the sheer fun of being a student activist really lies.

Let's just be clear, however, that I talk not of this monument to the brutalism movement in architecture. The building is not Queen Margaret Union – it is its members and in particular, its Board of Management, its Executive, and, tonight especially, its President.

I make no apology for introducing politics into my speech. I come from that generation for whom politics was deeply personal. Sitting as we were between the generation of post-war reconstruction and the generation of post-industrial re-structuring – we were, in contrast, the children of the revolution. Paris 1968, anti-Vietnam demonstrations, that

Queen Margaret Union Board of Management

other 11 September in 1973 when a CIA backed coup overthrew Allende in Chile: these global events might all seem very far away – particularly then when there was no internet or 24 hour news. But the repercussions were felt on this campus and in this union and for me personally.

On the face of it, Queen Margaret Union in the early 1970s was not very radical. The perception was it was run by a lot of nice girls from Hutchie – which indeed it was. We, myself and some friends, shocked them by organising ourselves into a slate of candidates to get elected and in some way change the Board. Indeed we wanted to fundamentally change the Union – but more of that later. We swept the elections, stormed the Board Flat and cleared the bottles of Estée Lauder perfume off the shelves while removing the long evening gowns from the wardrobes. Gosh, we were bold.

Of course, the first invitation to a formal function had us crawling back to them asking to borrow their cast offs. In fact we came to an accommodation – we listened to their tips on the best buys in the Jaeger sale, and they politely put up with lectures from our more politically active comrades on fifty ways to cook mince and how ironing jeans was bourgeois. I have to say since I had never introduced an iron to any of my clothes – not least my jeans. I was very pleased that I was heading to be a fully paid up member of the revolutionary vanguard – even if I found the 'Socialist Worker' a bit too earnest for my taste.

But there was some evidence that Queen Margaret Union was not as it appeared. When clearing out the Board Flat one day, I came across an old diary which had belonged to a former Board Member who was known to have been active in a previous rectorial campaign. The diary contained the home and office numbers in Paris of Daniel Cohn Bendit – Red Danny, leader of the student revolt in 1968. Indeed it appeared that the attempt to promote Red Danny as a candidate had been devised from here in Queen Margaret Union. This campaign floundered when the then home secretary Jim Callaghan refused Cohn Bendit a visa to enter the UK – *plus ça change, plus c'est la même chose*.

In Queen Margaret Union spirit, however, our politics had to be about fun. I am pleased to say we introduced lunchtime theatre – long before Oran Mor; we organised all day festivals which celebrated left leaning politics – with satirical performances, poetry, song and – I seem to remember the first and largest inflatable I have ever seen which filled Qudos – formerly known as the Common Room.

We pushed the boundaries of the licensing laws and got ourselves an all day license for these one off events. These were very old days in terms of licensing but I am also pleased to say we organised all the student unions in Scotland to respond to proposed changes in the licensing laws at that time.

Today I see that QM is involved in an even greater number of social events and promotes and develops the new as well as the old favourites. But I particularly want to applaud now the campaign on Fair Trade and the role Queen Margaret Union has played in ensuring the whole of the University has taken up the cause.

But Queen Margaret Union is – as I have suggested – about the people it shapes.

Madame President, we know that we, and our fellow past-presidents, are people of gravitas who command respect. Entertainments Convenors, however, are the stuff of legends. In this I suspect nothing has changed. We had two in my time on the Board.

I suppose Marion was the more conservative – with the very small 'c'. After all, she and her jeans had to be surgically separated on graduation. This was reflected also in her programming. Once a band had made its mark, they got invited back again and again. Which is why Freddie Mercury did quip that Queen had performed at Queen Margaret Union so often that perhaps next time we could go to their place.

Ruth on the other hand was of different stuff. Variety was undoubtedly the spice of her life. It was she who coined the mantra of Entertainments Convenors:

Rule number one, never touch the boys in the band; rule number two, never pine after them, there is another lot along next week.

While eyebrows are raised about just how far Ruth kept to her rule, it is no doubt good advice for many walks of life. And I suspect one that my young academic colleagues chant to themselves all the time.

There is however one area of our time at Queen Margaret

Union which is very different to today and that is we were an all woman organisation. Although men were admitted as guests to the Union – not until after lunch time. Indeed many of the members were adamant that they did not want men in the building before 2.30pm clogging up lunch queues and being around before the girls had time to apply their make-up. I have to say once the men were allowed in the afternoon, we, the Board, had to put up posters asking diners to desist from coupling over their afternoon tea.

We would have none of this separate nonsense. We were fighting male chauvinism and for equal rights. We did not need our own Union – we could play with the big boys and pity help any man who gainsaid us.

Remember even the personal was political. And we had our own guru. She may be a failed Big Brother celeb to you, but to us, Germaine Greer, author of the Female Eunuch, was (and still is) a heroine.

We failed to persuade the membership and the battle was left to be fought another day. But I don't suppose any of us really thought we had failed. We secretly liked having our own Union. There are certain things which I am sure are missing now – not least the romps in the Board dorm – but perhaps it is better that I say no more on that this early in the evening. I am delighted to see, however, that woman have continued to play a key and equal role in the development of Queen Margaret Union.

During my time as President, I received an invitation from the Lady Provost, to a lunch at the City Chambers to which she had invited women from all walks of life who in some way were making a contribution to the city. A flattering invitation indeed – and a very pleasant event altogether.

I met there a woman who had preceded me as a Board Member and President who shared with me her memories. Then she looked at me wistfully and said, "Enjoy it! You have the chance to exercise more power now you will have throughout the rest of your life".

As you can tell, these words have haunted me across the decades. How true was this? Was this it? I did not think at the time; and I certainly don't think now that she was referring just to the chance to organise an all day festival or chair a Board Meeting. No, this woman was talking about power in the sense of personal liberation. Is it the case that nothing matches up again?

Well of course not.

The Queen Margaret Union experience sits alongside all those other 'firsts' which student days offer. For me, they included – first time living away from home, first time travelling on my own or with friends, first introduction to a seeming endless world of learning and really clever and creative people, first overdraft and most memorably, first love. These are all experiences that go on developing across one's life – although perhaps in mine so far there is too much of the overdraft and not enough of the falling in love bit as I might like.

Last year I had a big birthday party and among the souvenirs of the day I have a wonderful photo of eight slightly sozzled fifty something women who were all on the Board of Management together united in a friendship which has lasted thirty years – and not looking a day older. But precious though these women are to me, they are not my only friends. It did not all stop when I left University.

So the legacy of Queen Margaret Union – politically and personally – is the gift of comradeship and friendship; the courage to try and make things better while having fun; and the belief that sometimes anything is possible. It shapes your future, it does not determine it.

Ladies and Gentlemen, I give you, Queen Margaret Union.

Debating in the Early Seventies

Irena Brichta
Debates Convener 1973–1974

Debating was particularly strong in the early seventies at the University of Glasgow, especially parliamentary debating along the lines of the House of Commons. These were held both in the Glasgow University Union (the Men's Union) and Queen Margaret Union (the Women's Union). The only other University in the world at that time which also had separate Unions was Sydney University, in Australia.

Some thirty years later, the world seemed very different from when we entertained 'Thin Lizzy' (of 'Whiskey in the Jar' fame) upstairs in the Board Room before and after their concert downstairs in the hall.

Today, so many of us are living and working in foreign parts with packed chests stored with memorabilia and have nothing to jog our much older and more worn out brains. Some memories have dimmed, others have gone altogether and maybe what has been remembered is only half the story.

I was persuaded to stand for Queen Margaret Union Board of Management by my good friend, Christine Hamilton (we were at Queen Margaret Hall of Residence together in our first year), who then became President afterwards. I became Debates Convener as I had thrown myself into political debating very enthusiastically, never missing a debate if I could help it.

In the early seventies, debates took place every two weeks; on a Friday and alternating at each Union venue during term time. Someone took the role of Mr. Speaker (usually the President of the host Union presiding, with the Honorary Secretary) and clerks (all officials dressed in gowns). The political debating clubs aligned themselves on each side of a long table running down the middle. The debates were very well attended with a crowded public gallery though they looked more authentic in the grand House of Commons style hall of the Glasgow University Union.

Each political club and hue was represented at these debates; Labour Club, Conservative Club, Independent Socialist Club, Scottish National Party, Distributists' Club, Dialectic Society and more. Each club took it in turn to be the government of the day and put forward their 'manifesto' (the topic for debate).

Debates began at one pm with an opening speaker for the government of the day. There would also be an official opposition party with a leader of the opposition (President of the club chosen to oppose the government of the day); an order paper was also printed (giving the parties, clubs and alignments for the debate and the individuals who would be speaking). The government gave notice in advance of the subject for debate (the order paper stating, 'The government of the day states that...').

Opening speakers in the afternoon (from one pm to five pm), were followed by more for the evening session (seven pm onwards, usually until nearly midnight) usually known speakers, either ex-University debaters or politicians. There would be strictly timed sessions (by the bell) for 'virgin' debaters and their maiden speeches. The final speech of the day was given by the Prime Minister of the government (President of the club); only their speech was not timed. I believe I spoke for fifty-two minutes when my club was in government. I was a long time member of the Distributists' Club (the vision that every inhabitant of the United Kingdom should have 'three acres and a cow', and this would lead to a fairer and more equitable society) which was essentially a club of those who did not wish to be defined as either 'right' or 'left'; though we were mostly 'right of centre', and we could freely decide whether we would support the government or oppose them once we had heard which club was to be the government and what they wished to put forward

Each debater and club had a 'political constituency'; mine was 'Free Czechoslovakia' because at that time the

Czech Republic was still together with Slovakia and under communist rule (behind the 'Iron Curtain'). Given my background (my parents were originally Czech and had come to England in the early fifties), I was a fervent supporter of the return of democracy to Czechoslovakia. I mentioned 'free Czechoslovakia' whenever I stood up to speak – this was my 'leit motif'.

These debating sessions lasted some ten hours in two sessions, afternoon and evening, with lots of hot air, arguments and points of order. Anyone in the debating chamber, usually the opposing side, could raise their order paper in the air and ask a question of the debater holding the floor and it was up to the debater if they took the question and answered it. There was sometimes a lot of quick thinking and repartee as well as heated debate. Madame or Mr. Speaker had to intervene if any rude words were used or any 'ungentlemanly' behaviour was exhibited. Debaters could be expelled from the chamber, although this happened rarely. Points of order could be asked of the speaker, if it was felt that 'rules' of debating were being 'bent', or someone wanted to slow down the pace of the debating.

As to Queen Margaret Union debating; it had a very strong tradition and both Brenda Dowd and I were very proud to be the debating team representing the Union at The Observer Mace Universities Debating Competition (this was an annual UK debating competition). We were quite successful as we beat the Glasgow University Union team, and in fact came second (we were robbed) to, I believe, the Irish Dublin team in the finals. It was a great achievement for Queen Margaret Union.

Finally apparently there was much discussion, teasing and ribbing during Board Meetings as to my new Debates Convener gown (minutes if not hours were spent on the colour of the piping around the gown) and the minutes were peppered with comments on the proposed new frock, dark blue gown with blue Russell Cord piping. I wonder where that gown is now, and come to think of it where have all the debaters gone as well?

Speaker at the main debating chair at debate

The Mid-Seventies

Jane McMinn
President 1975-1976

My predecessors had worked hard to justify a paid sabbatical year for the President, and I was honoured to be the first. In those days there was a President's bedroom, which along with the Board dormitory, was the scene of many a late night shenanigan. I stayed there more often than my flat. My election campaign was based on cleaner toilets, cheaper food, but not really on any 'hot potato' political issues. I remember the campaigning, however my main opponent fell ill at the time of the election; I had quite a majority.

The Board meetings that used to go on for hours on a Wednesday evening were dramatically reduced when I first starting chairing the meetings. I think I was one of the very few Presidents to ever post a profit, or certainly not a loss at the end of the financial year. The Presidency ran for sixteen months to align it with the academic year. My successor, Moira Corrigan, really took over and shared these extra months. One topical decision was to put a 'one armed bandit machine' in the bar, with many objections in principle, but the vote ended up being in favour. My argument was that students were intelligent beings and could make up their own mind whether to use the machine or not. I certainly spent a lot of my time in the bar, but these were very sociable times. I used to chair debates at the Union and that was a new experience for me. Tradition has it that you were dragged into the debating chamber reluctantly. There was all the traditional set-up of a parliamentary debate, I must confess that I used to knit to while away the hours of the sessions.

Queen Margaret Union had a 'trendy lefty' political bias compared to the ultra conservative Men's Union, and as

Queen Margaret Union Board of Management, 1974-1975

Queen Margaret Union Board of Management 1975-1976

President I took part in a few demonstrations, some more memorable than others, like picketing the Men's Union the day they had strippers performing at an event.

Our entertainment was legendary, and being on duty at these popular events was never dull. Some neighbours objected to the noise partygoers made on the way home, and for a while we were under police scrutiny to conform to our licensing agreements. Queen Margaret Union was run as a licensed club and a member could sign in up to six guests. One time I remember very well was when a young man drew a knife on me, nothing too dangerous, just an old kitchen knife. He had broken in during the gig, and I had found him. I was so annoyed with him, and about a foot taller, so I lifted him off the ground by his shirt and held him against the wall until re-enforcements arrived. Another time we were actually raided by the police (this was very exciting really) to make sure we were complying and, perhaps, to check for drugs. There were no major issues, but I had to go to the police station in Partick next morning for a review of the situation.

We had fairly good relations with both the Students Representative Council and Glasgow University Union, and I remember John Bell and Brian MacBride fondly as Presidents respectively during my tenure. As President you got invited to all the other University Balls in Scotland and treated like a queen. There were many formal occasions to attend to in the University itself, readings in the chapel, dinners and luncheons, Freshers Week and Daft Friday. What a universal education the Presidency gave me, including licensing laws and authorities, lawyers, police, accountants, building maintenance, business management, personnel management, club constitutions, parliamentary constitution, public speaking, politics, University senate et al., and I even confounded the University Senate members who said I would never finish my degree.

QMU diary, 1979-1980

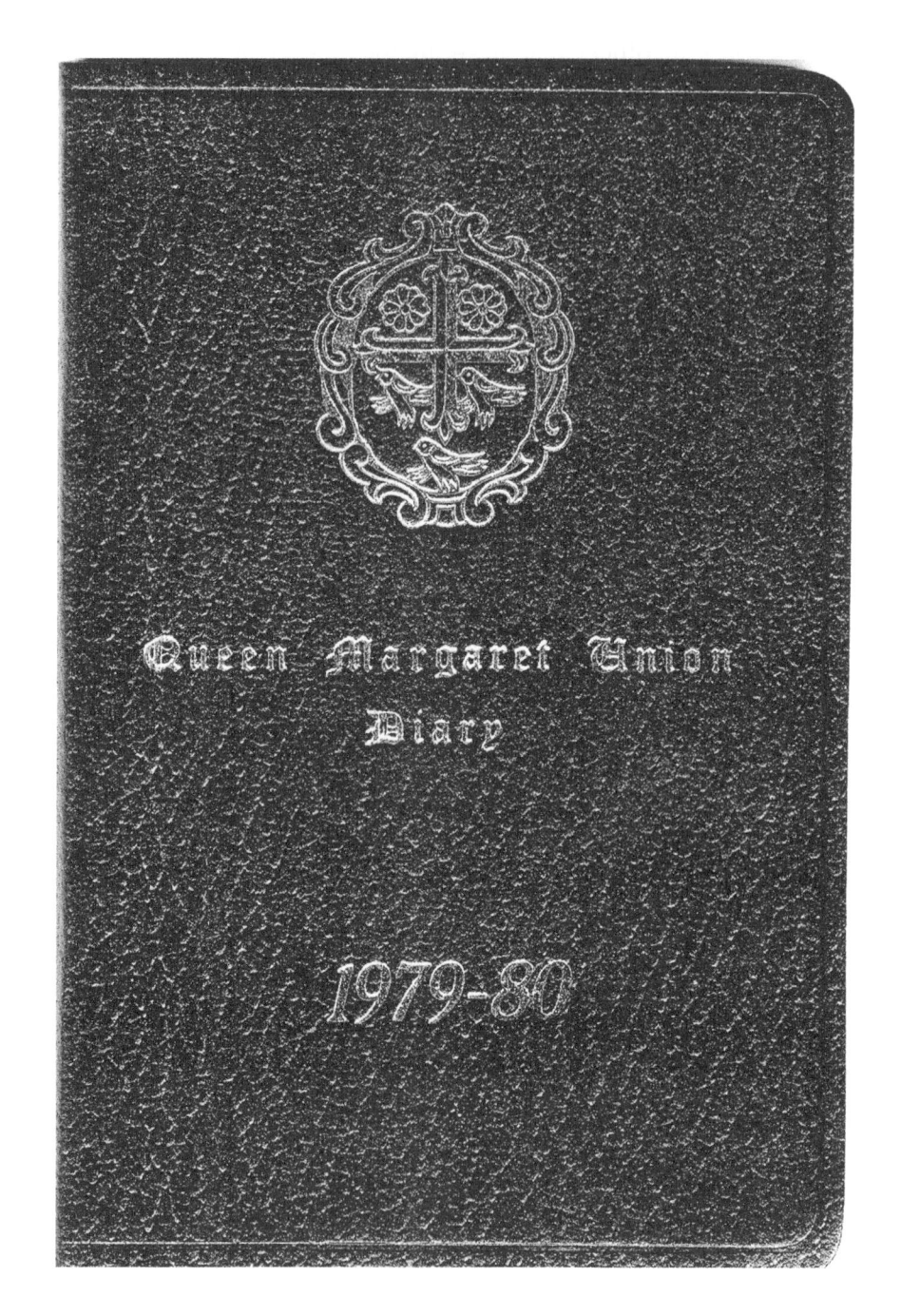

One of the several overnight rooms in Queen Margaret Union

Jane McMinn at protest on University campus

The Fire That Never Went Out

Moira Corrigan, President, and Liz McSkeane Debates Convenor 1976-1977

Moira Corrigan

They told us we'd be 'Tories' before the age of thirty; they said that our manners might improve with age and they were absolutely sure that one day, when life had left its mark on us, we'd mellow. We're not, they haven't and we didn't.

'They' were the opposition, or the government, depending on which side you were on, in the mammoth parliamentary debates that made up one half of the debating universe of the University of Glasgow up until the early eighties (the other half being held in that quaintly, but at the time, accurately-named, 'Men's Union'). These debates would be on a Friday afternoon, starting at lunch time, breaking for tea and then carrying on throughout the evening and the long, Friday night into Saturday morning, when the political clubs (Labour, Conservative, Liberal, Scot Nationalist and a peculiar entity call the Distributists) lined up in favour of, or against, a motion drafted by the 'Government' of the week. Let us not forget the Independent Socialists, (with an emphasis on Independent), which was the spiritual home of the Right Honourable Member for Fishwife (don't ask) and the Right Honourable Member for Aviemore, also known as wee Moira Corrigan and slightly less wee Liz McSkeane.

A 'Right Hon' was an elevated personage, (except in the Independent Socialists, where all were equal), who had had the distinction, in their role as chair of their club and therefore leader of the government of the day. They led their

Liz McSkeane

'government' in the presentation of a motion to the House. Ours was a Clause Four bill (if it moves, nationalise it and also if it doesn't. Everything; including banks, building societies, insurance companies and multinationals). Those were the days when lots of things, such as the railways, already were nationalised, so we had a bit less convincing to do than you might think. We also had a clause banning the private motorcar, for all the right reasons. Clearly, we were ahead of our time.

Our triumphs were almost as dramatic in style as in substance. In spite of the liberated ambience of the 1970s, which, if our antediluvian arrangements for single-sex student unions were anything to go by, had not quite made it to Gilmorehill; women debaters were expected to be fairly polite. Which meant that Liz and Moira, Moira and Liz were really up against it, especially when we proudly represented Queen Margaret Union at inter-university debates. There you could hear young ladies from Edinburgh University who would 'venture to suggest'. Moira and Liz never ventured a suggestion in their lives. Instead, we smashed the non-sequitur; we took a scalpel to the logical inconsistency; we showed the begged question no mercy; we were unimpressed, (and certainly not flattered), by the compliment from one well-meaning, but foolish, Distributist that we were the best female debaters of our generation; and we did not forgive – especially not the judges in the intervarsity competition who said plainly that yes, Queen Margaret Union were the true winners but they were giving it to Jordanhill because they had a team of chaps; the prize was a magnum of whisky.

Judges, chaps; your names have disappeared into the mists of memory (*où sont les neiges d'antan?*) but two things we do not forget; firstly, that was our magnum and secondly, 'we wiz robbed'! We were the best and still are, bar none.

Tales from the Seventies

Catherine Savage
President 1977-1978

The Queen Margaret Union played an integral part in student life at the University of Glasgow. The year was 1977 and membership was then open only to women. For men there was Glasgow University Union (or the Men's Union), but all that was about to change.

Much heated debate was taking place on the subject of such segregation and when I stood for the office of President in 1977, it was the big issue. You were either for or against the mixing of the Unions. I was pro-mixing, and got elected on that platform. The rest, they say, is history.

Taking a subsequent trip down memory lane, I noted that the Board of Management was at that time comprised of comparatively very few women members.

It is still the case now, as it was then, that a disproportionately large number of students, in comparison to other UK Universities, live at home and commute, on a daily basis, to University. The campus, being in the heart of the west end of the city, was easily accessible by public transport. Once there, outwith lectures and tutorials, both Unions provided their members with a venue to meet their, largely non-academic, needs.

In the seventies, Queen Margaret Union had a library, which doubled as a study room, showers and bathrooms, a utility room, music room, committee rooms and television room along with a cafe area, restaurant and a 'totally ace' salad bar that many non-members could also enjoy when signed in as a guest of a member.

Thankfully, for those of us who hadn't yet flown the nest, you could stay overnight. If you wanted to 'hang out' on campus late at night or 'hit the city centre' and couldn't crash somewhere, you could always book a room or a 'horsebox' as they were affectionately known as then.

By way of explanation, the thin walls of these partitioned rooms were suspended above the floor and didn't extend to the ceiling, so privacy was impossible, or as they say in Glasgow, 'oot the windae', even though there were no windows. I daresay, no doubt other former horsebox dwellers could tell a tale or two of the shenanigans that went on inside.

Enjoying much deserved success as a music venue, Queen Margaret Union in 1977-1978 was host to artists as diverse as Cliff Richard and The Sex Pistols, both of which were sell-outs. I remember Sir Cliff ensconced in the board flat, conversing amiably and looking as markedly orange-skinned as Tommy Sheridan, before the advent of 'Sunny D'.

The Entertainments Convener, at the time, was Grace Maxwell and thanks to her efforts along with those of her predecessors and successors, Queen Margaret Union became well established in this field. Grace is still much involved in the music business along with her husband Edwyn Collins.

During my time in office, the writer in residence was Alasdair Gray and he held that post until 1979.

"Freshers" were issued a copy of the Students' Handbook by the S.R.C. and the '77-'78 one had a pink elephant on the front cover.

I'd love to trace it as it included an introduction to Queen Margaret Union in the form of a poem. I asked Alasdair if he had a copy, as I'd wanted to include it in this article, and it is missing from the Student Representative Council archives. Ah, the importance of being an archivist.

Sisters are doing it for themselves

Marie Kimmins
Entertainments Convenor
1978-1979

Ironically, sisterhood and brotherhood was strong in the seventies at Gilmorehill. Every other month, Board Members from both Queen Margaret Union and Glasgow University Union would get together for what was known as the 'Strawberry Tea'. This occasion was not as the name would suggest: a polite and tentative meeting of the minds *à la* Jane Austen. Rather, it involved the host union providing food, of any description; and the guests, wine or beer - or both in great quantities. It often descended into an all-day drinking session where a few people let their hair down, along with their guard, making a right fool of themselves. I'm ashamed to say that on one of these occasions I was indeed the fool. However all had a great time.

A certain silvery-tongued young woman who would later became a Labour politician in Bristol was admiring the trousers of a rather hunky young Glasgow University Union board member (B for brevity) whose company I happened to be enjoying. To me, this was obviously blatant and downright shameless flattery and flirting with 'my man'. Moreover, it offended the principle of truth and honesty, which I have always cherished – and I suspected might have been inspired by his connection to a minor 'Scottish soft-drinks empire'. The trousers were after all chequered and belonged on a fifty-year old on a golf course, not on a teenage student stud. The drink got the better of me when I dramatically quipped in with, "Do you want to know what I think of your trousers, they are f***ng awful".

Seeing that poor bloke turn bright red made me realise my fatal error. Perhaps I had gone too far in delivering the line.

You can understand the reasons why I chose to stop drinking alcohol around twelve years ago. Not that I was ever a heavy imbiber of the demon drink: it's just that I've always been sensitive to the toxic!

I did try to make it up to 'B' by being gushingly positive the next time I saw him: seeing his green canvas tackle bag, not to mention the headgear, I greeted him with, "Oh, hi, have you just been fishing?" only to be told he hadn't, with just a hint of surprise expressed at the question.

I had one more chance to make it up to 'B', at the most glamorous event of the year, Glasgow University Union's Daft Friday Ball. As a perk of the Queen Margaret Union job, you might say, I was partnered with the guest speaker – now columnist on one of Scotland's finest broadsheets. After I'd done my duty: enjoying the most decadent eight-course dinner (accompanied by a different drink with every course), I was just about still standing and looking forward to dancing the night away with 'B'. However karma caught up with me, for politician girl and her beau (who'd been the recipient of the most awful coffee concoction prepared by me and the girls in the board flat late one night) decided to match make. Laying for me an emotional guilt trap – sorry trip – they decided that their friend who'd just broken up with her long-term boyfriend was just the person for him, and I ran off into the night. Ah, now I can say good times: and yes, some of best times of my life.

A More Perfect Union

Gillian Govan
President 1979-1980

As I watched Barack Obama's impassioned speech in Philadelphia during the 2008 United States presidential election, I experienced the same feelings of hope and optimism that I did back in 1979 in the Queen Margaret Union Debating Hall when the vote 'to mix' the Union took place. Sure it was a smaller venue and a highly localised issue but the principles of equality, fairness and the spectre of discrimination were just as real and pertinent. Much of Mr. Obama's word choice echoed, and ours was an election issue too.

Unbelievable as it seems now, there was a time when student union membership at the University of Glasgow was discriminated on gender. Glasgow University Union (the men's Union), took the lion's share of the per capita budget and firmly closed off three-quarters of its facilities to females. Just along the road, like a poor relation, the smaller, more aesthetically challenged Queen Margaret Union happily shared its facilities (albeit not membership) with all, with the exception of the third floor overnight accommodation or 'horse boxes', which could be rented out at the Porter's Box. Though many would attest that this too was mutually enjoyed.

Tensions had been building during the summer term. The Glasgow University Union had recently opened a state of the art extension to its building, paid for from bar takings and membership funds. To us 'weekend pass visitors' it was a 'Studio 54' with a highly exclusive door policy. Stories started to spread that the weekly 'Quimbies' – ostensibly cartoon film shows of the innocuous Fred Quimby variety - were now featuring live strip shows too.

Students during a debate in Queen Margaret Union

Students during a debate in Queen Margaret Union

188

It seemed as if a testosterone shot had been administered and the Beer Bar, which we could smell as we passed (and glimpse the unloading of keg after keg), became the focus of a misogynistic mystique. Women were never allowed in, ever. And the *Glasgow University Guardian* carried weekly Men's Union President pieces proclaiming a die-hard challenge to 'mixers' that would make Bruce Willis rethink his motivation. I truly don't recall how the idea to storm the Beer Bar began. I think it was a bit like the first Glastonbury Festival; if you remember it you weren't really there.

But soon a monstrous regiment of gallus besoms and friends were charging down University Avenue (thank God for the male friends as we didn't even know where it was in the building) surrounding the bar demanding drinks. They served us and then they threw us out.

The actual vote to mix Queen Margaret Union, took place during an Extraordinary General Meeting, chaired by President Rosemary Nugent in the final term of 1979. I was President-Elect, and like many in the hall, believed wholeheartedly that not only did things have to change, but also that Queen Margaret Union should take the leadership and mix first. Sadly, the Men's Union had resolutely decided to remain just that.

The prospect was of two Unions, one with men and women signed up and the other only males. I'd love to say that we moved everyone with our rhetoric but there was fierce opposition, and fear. Many argued an all female Union was positive discrimination and we would be 'swamped' by a male hierarchy; essentially colonised by the Men's Union.

There were light hearted concerns too; would there still be Carmen heated rollers for rent (this was, after all, the era of 'Big Hair')? Would our much-enjoyed Salad bar make way for the 'who ate all the pies' brigade (our spies in the camp told us that the Men's Union was awash with saturated fats)?

However, the motion was carried – and I looked forward to the coming October and a matriculation period that would become a contest for membership. Most of all, I looked forward to a 'mixed' board; how weird the very wording seems now. The first challenge was rather more prosaic - how many membership diaries to order, how to guess the numbers of males who would forsake the Beer Bar, the Billiard Room and the Smoking Room. We know the results, the success that swept all before it, the campaigns at Senate and the University Court to persuade that both Unions required to be open to both sexes. There were long and smoke-filled caucuses. Tim Heath of the Students Representative Council and I became rent-a-speakers, threatening to get tour jackets as we drummed up support across Scottish Universities and dodged the Men's Union at closing time when Beer Bar stalwarts were looking for trouble. We nearly had a European leg of our tour with an appeal to the European Court of Human Rights.

It wasn't all po-faced. Suddenly we could book bands that previously rejected playing at Victorian single sex establishments. Queen Margaret Union Entertainments had always been good, often booking bands before they reached what we now call the tipping point. I look back now at what was an empty gig for an unknown band called The Stranglers and remember the Entertainments Convener tearfully saying, "They're going to be huge".

We were now able to negotiate on a bigger scale with the brewers, and we quickly built a rather plush disco area and bar in our previously 'school- gym' style hall. There was a royal visit and an exhibition. Yes, it was contentious, the debate and protests were lively, but you couldn't mistake that Queen Margaret Union was on the map, stealing the headlines and was loud and proud. At least it got a much-needed makeover from the authorities. In the end, it was a more perfect Union because of it.

A View from the Staff

Ann Ingleston
House Manager and
Honorary Life Member

I first started working in Queen Margaret Union in September 1971, as far as I can remember. In those days it was referred simply as the Womens' Union, a far cry from today. It was a female staff, mostly in catering with a few exceptions who doubled as cleaners and catering assistants. As most of us had children, it suited us because it closed down for most of the school holidays. The bar was manned using part-time staff made up mostly of male students who worked in the evenings.

The only other male staff were the porters who worked reception and the caretaker who lived in one of the flats on the roof, the other flat being reserved for the Catering Manageress as the living quarters came with the job.

Queen Margaret Union was mainly run as a catering establishment. Even in those days it was still the place to go for the majority of male and female students who liked their food and service with a smile. We were always packed out every day of the week. On weekends, the Coffee Bar opened from eight am until three pm allowing us to cater all seven days.

Every weekday, the Board of Management, wearing their gowns came around the building reminding non-members that they had to leave the building. This meant that they (mostly male students) had to vacate the Union around three pm each day.

Although the Catering Area has always been situated on the Second Floor, there have been a number of changes throughout the years elsewhere. The Ground Floor used to be the home to the General Office and Managers Office (around where the current reception desk is) and the present day Shop area was regarded as a lounge until the decision was made to put in a snooker table. The Porter's Box was situated to the left just as you entered through the front doors in the area that became the shop display window and office. Qudos itself was known then as the 'Common Room' and, many moons ago, was used frequently by the debating society as Queen Margaret Union had a great debating membership at one time. The room also doubled as a venue for the Saturday Night Palais featuring a live band and, if memory serves me well, our first resident DJ who was none other than Paul Coia of television fame. The windowed area on the right hand side of Qudos used to function as a Reading Room, separate from the main venue with armchairs and tables running the length of it for students to simply relax and chill out. The area hosting the coffee bar and gent's toilets was once a custom built cloakroom.

The shop of old featured a very limited stock. The serving area was accessed by the raising of a wooden hatch and also doubled as a dry cleaners counter and storage area. The first floor has always been home to the bar area and has remained the same (redesigns notwithstanding): however we did once have a hairdressing salon. Opposite the bar, the Games Room was originally a Library named after the mistress of Queen Margaret College, Frances Melville. The current bar was established in the room in 2003; before this the room was simply as it appeared in the name, a Games Room with slot machines, games and pool tables.

The third floor has undergone the most changes. The staff General Office was once the Board Lounge complete with fitted kitchen; the General Manager's Office was once the domain of the Executive Committee (the Executive Office was the Convenors Office), the Staff Room was the Television Room where students could catch all their favourite shows; the Convenors Office was the Music Room and the Board Lounge was the Board Dormitory. With the exception of the Laundry Room and toilets, all other rooms were at one point dormitories. These rooms were rented out to students and, for the most part, were cheap accommodation for many postgraduate students who were either researching or having to attend the University simply for seminars and the like. The

Q.M. CLOSED TILL MAY AFTER FIRE

The Queen Margaret Union will not reopen before 10th May, because of damage resulting from the fire at the end of last term. However, the Board of Management does not believe that the enforced closure will damage the Union's financial viability.

Dominic d'Angelo, President of QMU, explained, 'Financially both Unions will be better off in the short term: GUU, together with the refectory, should be kept busier than usual because of the students who are unable to use the QMU, while the Union itself normally sees a downturn in the business in the third term. The insurers cover us against any loss in profits while we're closed and also should cover the wages which we must pay for fixed-term employees under the 'loss of profits' section of our insurance policy. Ultimately, the QMU shouldn't lose money as a result of the fire'.

The blaze was discovered around 8pm on 11th March. Smoke was spotted coming out of the service duct on the third floor. The fire alarm went off almost simultaneously and the building was duly emptied. The Group 4 security alarm had also gone off, alerting the police who arrived in a matter of minutes and radioed for the Fire Service. Within a short time the fire was under control and the damaged assessed.

It had originated in the basement of the building, though how and when is a matter for conjecture. The Strathclyde Region Fire Department think it may have been started by a burning cigarette end, which could have been smouldering for some time.

The damage to the building is fairly serious. The entire basement area needs renovation and there is extensive smoke damage throughout the building. The area worst affected is the service duct, which carries plumbing

Continued Page 4

From *Glasgow University Guardian*, 1982

Group of Students in the 1970s

Board Dormitories were mainly used by the on-duty Board Members who worked through the evening and early morning but there was also a dorm set aside for the sole use of the President with en-suite facilities no less! That particular area is now the male toilet.

The Board of Management invited all the staff to an annual Christmas party in the Union where they prepared the three-course meal and served the food. They even did all the washing up afterwards. They also provided us with limited entertainment; a few songs, some poetry and some comedy skits. They then left us to our own devices. We had a record player and some records and we provided our own booze then danced the night away. We had a similar party at the end of every term, which we dubbed a 'Cookie Shine'; we always had the time of our lives.

There are a few memorable moments from over the years; one that springs to mind was the official opening of the new building by Princess Margaret. The exact date escapes me but I remember all the fuss, the free buffet, and the bar as well as all sorts of wannabies and self-appointed dignitaries. There were even fur covered loo seats. My claim to fame was serving the Princess with drinks, which she declined; and there was me all done up in my best black and whites. The only thing Queen Margaret Union provided us with for the occasion was white gloves with which to serve the drinks. You can imagine what we would all have been thinking if eBay had been around at that time; we could have made a fortune.

The Games Room was used on a regular basis for special occasions; for instance the Presidents' Dinner was held there every year and I'm sure Jimmy Reid attended a do, possibly concerning the University Rector, but it could have simply been a left-wing political thing as students in the 1970's and 1980's were a lot more politically oriented. The Medics held their ball in Queen Margaret Union also but they caused so much damage when they trashed the place that they ended up with a ban. I have no idea whether it's still in force or not. Then there was the fork and glass experience before the end of term around May of each year. The Board of Management invited past Board Members and guests including the Rector and his wife and residents of Hillhead as well as various people deemed important enough to enjoy sampling the cheeses, strawberries and cream and champagne, although it could possibly have simply been 'bubbly' to lull them into a false sense of security that these people were well brought up, modern young ladies of etiquette!

The only major disaster at Queen Margaret Union that springs to mind was when we had a serious fire in March 1982. The fire started in the basement by someone either deliberately or accidentally throwing a lit cigarette onto a pile of chairs outside the goods lift. Luckily the alarm was raised and everyone was evacuated safely from the building; no one was injured. The one thing that sticks out in my mind was that although the fire started in the basement, it was someone on the third floor who raised the alarm as the smoke travelled up the shafts connecting the electrical cupboards. The building was closed and did not reopen until Freshers' Week in September. Most of the staff were laid off apart from myself, the General Manager, Office Manageress, Bar Manager and our handyman. The fire damaged the main service cupboards and it was a nightmare trying to salvage as much as we could with no electricity, no heating and no lighting. There was hardly any daylight either but we survived to tell the tale. The new Executive Committee under President Abdul Ibrahim (male Presidents would eventually grace the Union) brought in contracted catering staff in order to get Queen Margaret Union back to some kind of financial stability.

As for other tales; there is a rumour that the balcony in Qudos is haunted but I believe that may simply be a myth as the Night Porter who created the story was on the balcony one evening when he discovered that in one area that had been rather busy the night before some students had dropped a lot of coins on the floor. Then there either was too much money or he simply couldn't find it all in the dark and made a small fortune by telling the ghost story to prevent the cleaning staff getting there before he did.

There are plenty more tales but let's just say that some of them would not be fit for putting in writing. Queen Margaret Union has given me a great many memories over the years and I am glad to have been a part of its history.

1980

Depending on who you speak to the 1980s can bring up countless memories of joy or endless memories of anguish. It really is the decade that you either love or hate. For Queen Margaret Union it would prove to be another decade of great change.

Following on from the 'Mixing Debate' of the 1970s it would take only two years for Queen Margaret Union to elect its first male President. After editing the *Glasgow University Guardian* newspaper, Dominic d'Angelo made history by taking the top spot in 1981. The women students would have to wait until 1984 before a woman would next hold the Presidency.

In 1982 the Union began its darkest period yet. A fire which started in the basement of the new building meant that the Union would close for around six months. The demise of business saw huge financial losses from which the Union would not recover until the 1990s.

Despite the problems, live acts became more common at Queen Margaret Union and the student volunteers took more control than ever before in running the Union.

In 1989 it was clear that things were incredibly serious at Queen Margaret Union. The financial problems were so great that rumours started to be heard around campus that Queen Margaret Union was only twenty-four hours away from closing its doors for good and that the President had eloped with the Unions cash. As it turned out the Union was in fact close to closure but no one had vanished to the Caribbean. Stringent financial controls and a complete overhaul of the internal workings of the Union would eventually bring financial stability in the decade to come.

Cartoon published after the 1982 fire

198

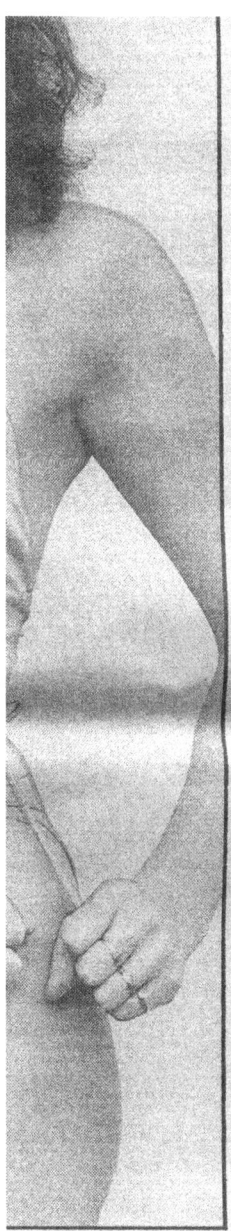

STUDENTS IN ROW OVER BOOZY STRIP

By DICK TEMPEST

A **DRUNKEN** frolic has landed student leaders' in hot water.

For they have been accused of allowing an impromptu strip to get out of hand.

And Glasgow University's Queen Margaret Union has been rocked by the affair. Students' council board member Maria McInneny, has resigned in protest after claimimg that fellow board members condoned the strip.

The high jinks happened at a festive party when students were egged on to strip off.

But things hotted up when some girl students tried to take down their male colleagues' underpants.

Miss McInneny (18) said: "It was disgusting. Four girls tried to get a man's underpants off.

"If it had been a girl who had been at the centre of the strip all hell would have broken loose.

"I know many others share my view that this is not the sort of thing that should have gone on at a student's council party."

But Queen Margaret Union president Richard Gass said: "Okay, things did get out of hand and some students did get carried away with drink.

"But they meant no harm, I think Miss McInneny is over-reacting."

Meanwhile, Miss McInneny contends that what is good for the boys is good for the girls. She said: "Those male students were forcibly stripped. The girls pulled their pants off.

DIVIDED . . . Richard Gass and maria McInneny who share a different viewpoint over the impromptu strip at a festive party.

"How would people feel if it had been a girl student with boys doing the samething."

Miss McInneny is now finished with student political life at Glasgow University.

She said: "After the failure of the board to condemn such behaviour I want no part in helping to run the union.

Writing in the University's newspaper, The Guardian, Miss McInneny said: "If several women had been stripped by a group of men, those self same people who thought that it was a "good laugh" would have been the first to condemn such actions.

"Several board members had the opinion that the men did not mind their clothes being taken off in front of 70 people, because the men were drunk.

But is it fair to take advantage of someone's drunkenness?"

Both Miss McInneny and Mr Gass were not prepared to name the four strippers.

National newspaper report from mid-1980s

D'ANGELO ELECTED

DOMINIC D'ANGELO Is the new President of the Queen Margaret Union. The former 'Guardian' Editor beat Charles O'Neill and Anne Jordan to be the first male president of the Union. In the first count Mr d'Angelo had 204 votes with Mr O'Neill and Miss Jordan getting 202 and 158 respectively. But, when Ms Jordan's votes were split, they gave the new President a majority of over a hundred.

The poor showing of Anne Jordan who is this year's Honorary Secretary is seen by many as a vote of no confidence in those running the Union this year. It seems that Dominic d'Angelo benefitted most from the strongly critical campaign of Charles O'Neill who now has only his finals to worry about. The new President, however, has to tackle the dire financial position of the QM. He will be assisted by the new Honorary Secretary Abdul Ibrahem and the new Assistant Honorary Secretary Maureen Blackwell. The new Conveners are: Publicity—Douglas Finnegan (who beat Jill Simmons), Social—John Ewing, Entertainments—Jane Harris. Gavin McBurnie beat Joe McCroy for the honour of being the Union's last Debates Convener.

Ordinary Board Members elected were Janice Edgar, Billy Garret, Angela Kerr, Jane McKenzie, Lorraine Wright, Nick Thomas, Anne Dawis and Keith MacDonald.

Mungo Bov

Dominic d'Angelo, qmu's first male President.

From *Glasgow University Guardian*

First Male President

Dominic d'Angelo
President 1981-1982

I didn't expect to win. The previous year's Honorary Secretary usually wins when he or she stands for President of a student union, so it was something of a surprise when I, as a short-lived Debates Convener, was elected. I had originally stood to split the vote and stop another (arguably less politically *simpatico*) male candidate from winning, but that's politics: sometimes you get what you wish for.

By the following morning, the *Evening Times* was on the case. "What we need," they said, "is a photo of you surrounded by smiling supporters". And so it was that that afternoon's edition carried a photo of me perched on a concrete bollard outside Queen Margaret Union surrounded by a number of cheerful women all of whom were supposed to have voted for me as their first male President – and none of whom actually had. At least we hadn't been asked to dance the conga, a photographic fate that seems to have befallen more lottery-winning chairwomen (and always in George Square) than I can remember.

To business, and a first glance at the account books suggested something was lop-sided; in this case, the entries. About eighty per cent of the entries appeared to congregate in the far right-hand column of the ledger book under 'Other Expenditure'. Apparently, no one had updated the bookkeeping system since the days when Queen Margaret Union occupied what is now the John McIntyre Building and the Board of Management largely appeared to concern itself with male student conduct at the weekend 'squeezies'.

One whole (and at the time, empty) column was headed

'Dress Allowance'. If nothing else, I can claim to have been the last President to receive that particular perk under that heading. I remember using the cash (£20, I think it was) to buy a Bulgarian suit in Next's discount store.

A more pressing concern was the problem of the Union's bottom line. By the early 1980s, the 'new' building ('Legoland' some called it due to its external appearance) was a building under stress. Designed a decade before for around two thousand female students, not all of whom were expected to be in the building at any one time, by the time I was elected it now appeared to be attempting to cope with at least twice that number of female and male students every day. So the lunchtime queues got longer, as did the ones at the bar; the latter were, in many ways, more important; we lost money on catering, but made it on alcohol sales.

The bar was always a focal point of concern, and one where we needed to maximise income. I tried retiring the two elderly doorkeepers who were supposed to ensure that, in line with local licensing requirements, no one under eighteen years old entered the bar. It wasn't a particularly efficient system and it seemed to make more sense to have members of the bar staff do the checks, since after a short while they would know who was old enough and who not. But more radical members of the Board of Management decided I was condemning them to pension penury and the doorkeepers were reprieved.

Any Union President will recognise the kinds of requests, demands and complaints coming in each week: colder beer, more stock and cheaper prices; in our case, these were legitimate concerns. In the first place, Queen Margaret Union hadn't actually been designed with a bar: lady students weren't supposed to drink alcohol, they were supposed to have their hair done. So the first floor bar was originally a hairdressing salon and its conversion into a bar hadn't allowed for a separate cold room, meaning kegs of lager and beer were kept at a higher than optimal temperature. Of course, advised our suppliers, we could always knock through to the basement and set up a cold store there.

Yes: we could have done a lot of things, but money was always the problem. In essence, Queen Margaret Union had been using present income to pay past debts for several years; a quick check of the books suggested the deficit was around forty thousand pounds.

Increasing income became a priority; the bar needed redecorating, but we couldn't afford to have it completely rebuilt, so volunteer painters, cheap re-upholstery and re-carpeting would have to suffice (but then Board members complained that by not using professional decorators we were doing them out of a job). Constructing a separate bar in the white elephant that was the main hall would help; a brewer's loan did that. Thinking of all those future high-earners, the high-street banks wanted a higher profile and were willing to pay for the privilege, so ATMs appeared in the front hall.

Could we make better use of the space available inside the building? Two under-used dormitories were converted into much-needed study rooms, and the non-earning library was converted into a Games Room. In the latter case, Margaret Thatcher might have praised the intention, but probably not the deed.

Did we actually need Union diaries (used as proof of membership)? Couldn't we replace them with a photo ID card? There wasn't much debate about the decision; the (mild) screams only came once Freshers' Week was over and returning members had been deprived of something to write phone numbers in. I think the diaries came back the following year.

A potential money-earner was Entertainments; a Convener who knows his or her stuff can generate lots of publicity and much income by booking acts who are just about to become big, or who are already big but still affordable. And wth a licensed capacity of one thousand two hundred, we had a lot of space to fill. The higher the booking fee, the higher the ticket price; the higher the ticket price, (usually) the lower the turn-out, so the more drink students needed to consume for us to break even. One answer was tempering the cost with drinks promotions from companies under the impression that once you'd spent an evening drinking their product, you'd stick with it. How foolish can these people be? The most visually spectacular promotion during my year was with Pernod; it went down so fast the supplier had to raid local pubs asking for more; it came up so fast we had Technicolour toilets for the entire weekend.

Hiring a band is not just a question of the booking fee. There's a PhD awaiting someone who analyses the history of music contract 'riders' – the clauses dropped into a contract to specify what 'extras' a band needs in order to do what you've just paid for. One band's contract – and this was for four or five players performing for ninety minutes or so – specified the necessity for a green room equipped with four cases of lager, two cases of Coke, two bottles each of whisky, vodka and rum, and enough food to host a small convention. I seem to recall striking out almost everything, to the horror of my Ents Convener, convinced that his already advertised band would cancel if there weren't enough crisps on the table. I think they still turned up.

If this sounds like I spent much of my year acting as an accountant, it's true: the Honorary Treasurer resigned shortly after I came into office (nothing to do with me) and I spent much of the year leaning on the Student Representative Council's Permanent Secretary for advice.

A President should also be able to rely for advice on his or her General Manager, and a near-retirement one at Queen Margaret Union (inherited from Glasgow University Union) posed a challenge. A good General Manager can be worth his or her weight in gold, especially in terms of knowing what needs doing and how to do it; which University personnel need keeping on side; and what the boundaries of action are (especially when it comes to students taking decisions affecting permanent staff). A new Board of Management every year, each with its own agenda and wanting to make a difference, takes its toll, and few union managers last more than five years: intolerance (sometimes, downright rudeness) from students at the pace of change or the inability to achieve change at all, compounded by regular financial crises, causes too many sleepless nights. Early retirement enabled 'my' General Manager to leave with dignity, but it remains a largely thankless job and only for the thick-skinned.

And then we burned the place down. That is, someone dropped an insufficiently extinguished cigarette into a pile of rubbish inadvertently placed directly below a service duct inconveniently running all the way up the building. Cue one fire, the complete destruction of the building's core, and a two thirty am wake-up call. That this should happen just before our busiest and most lucrative period of the year, the end of the Easter term, made it worse. Add insurance cover that hadn't kept pace with inflation and you've got a financial hole that becomes almost impossible to fill as the bills roll in to a building that's closed for repairs.

So the tenure of the first male President – immediately followed by the second male President (my Honorary Secretary) – ended in smoke-tainted semi-darkness, with rebuilding work that ended just in time for the new academic session. But if the immediate feeling was downbeat, the overall experience of being President was a huge personal learning curve, and one that has stood me in good stead professionally and personally in the (gosh) decades since.

Selection of pictures from bands that played Queen Margaret Union

Queen Margaret Union LIVE!

Mark Graham
President 1983-1984

Anyone experiencing the nerve-tingling atmosphere of a sold-out gig at Queen Margaret Union could be forgiven for thinking that they were simply enjoying the same experience as thousands of other music fans in the (almost) forty years since the new building opened. While they would be mostly right, this wasn't always the case and anyone with an interest in music who was around Glasgow in the mid eighties would have recognised that 1983 to 1986 was the period in which Queen Maragret Union finally became established as one of the premier live music venues, not only in Glasgow, but in Scotland as a whole. I was fortunate enough to have been President during part of this period and while I'd like to believe I had something to do with it, as with all of the successes we have had, it owed a bit to circumstance and a lot to the hard work of all of the people on the Board of Management and supporting committees who made it happen.

In common with many student unions, Queen Margaret Union had hosted many top bands throughout the 1970s. This was partly because it had a captive audience but also because the Glasgow licensing authorities refused to allow licensed premises to charge audiences to watch live music within the venue, unless it was a club. When this law was changed at the beginning of the 1980s it had a dramatic effect on Queen Margaret Union and many other student unions as new live music venues like Tiffany's and the Mayfair in Sauchiehall Street sprang up almost overnight. The problem was compounded for student unions as these new venues had an 'open' drinks licence and could admit anyone over eighteen while student unions had club licences and could only legally admit members and their guests. This issue famously came to a head when Joe Strummer of The Clash met some fans outside Strathclyde University Students' Union where the band were due to play and was told that they couldn't buy tickets as they weren't students. When Strummer himself was knocked back when he tried to buy tickets for himself (obviously the ticket-seller had no idea who he was!), the concert was immediately cancelled and live music in student unions in Glasgow suffered another blow.

By the mid-1980s, the only real gigs Queen Margaret Union could possibly host were focused during 'Week Nothing', 'Daft(er) Friday' and the 'Mad March Ball' where guaranteed sell-outs allowed us to spend a bit of money to bring in bands who ordinarily wouldn't play there. We were also in dire financial straits (some things never change) due to a fire in March 1982 which led to massive losses so, absolutely no money could be spent on anything (including band fees) unless there could be a good return on the investment.

Another fire, this time at Tiffany's in early 1983, provided an opening for Queen Margaret Union to venture back into live music. Guessing that Tiffany's promoters would have a whole roster of acts with no venue to play in, Mark Mackie, our Entertainments Convenor, arranged a meeting with them to discuss the possibility of relocating the various gigs to Queen Margaret Union. While it became apparent early on that this wouldn't happen, for various reasons, we got enough encouragement to put together plans to re-launch ourselves as a premier live music venue in Glasgow.

Working with the promoters we'd met previously, and others, Mark identified a number of bands who were touring who he felt we could put on and make a profit from. Mark went on to become a successful promoter in the music business and actually ran Regular Music, Scotland's premier music promoter. His contribution was crucial to the development of Queen Margaret Union as a live venue. Like all good music promoters he has the knack of spotting the right band for the right venue at the right time and it was very much our good fortune that he first displayed this talent in his time there as Entertainments Convenor.

It was clear that the existing stage at about a foot high was far too small so a much larger one was built. The financial strategy

Selection of pictures from bands that played Queen Margaret Union

QMU

13TH OCTOBER 1982

THE HIGHEST EVER!

PRESIDENT AT CASINO! BOARD SPOTTED AT AYR RACES! well perhaps not but here LYNN JARVIE tells the true story of the QM's finances .....

BROADSHEET

The Union's deficit is at present £32,000, a great reduction from that of £93,000 which we had over the summer. This may seem an exceptionally high sum, however we are still expecting to receive £16,000 in insurance, £5,000 as a grant from Scottish & Newcastle Breweries and £1,500 from the caterers ARA Services, for stock purchased from us when they took over QM catering.

Asked how the Union had got into such financial difficulties in the first place, President Abdul Ibrahem explained that the debts had occured for two main reasons.
(1) The building was underinsured. Our insurance policy had not been upgraded since 1975/6, when the cover for QM was £78,000. It should have been insured for £180,000.

This was due to an oversight both on the part of QM and on the part of the insurance companies, and meant that we did not receive as much money from our insurance as we had expected.

(2) Last year's President, Dominic D'Angelo, had given assurances after reading the policy that the Union was covered for staff wages, but it was later discovered that it was not, and QM had no way of recovering the money paid out to staff.

Other factors: Catering made a deficit but this has now been taken over by ARA Services, so this loss will not recur.

So you see, folks, there is light at the end of the tunnel. Our bank are quite happy with the present situation, and we hope to be back in credit in 2 years' time. So when we pass the hat round please give generously.

QMU Broadsheet, October 1982

210

was pretty basic; identify the number of tickets required to break even, undertake an aggressive marketing campaign to sell them and make money on bar sales on the night. Colourful 'dayglo' posters advertising gigs soon became a permanent fixture in the west end of the city and the Publicity Convenor became one of the most important members of the Board of Management as we relied on his team to get the message out. If we were concerned that a band might not do enough on their own to shift the required tickets, we leaned heavily on suppliers to give us large discounts so that we could run a drinks promotion in tandem. New and unknown brands like Furstenburg Bier and Finlandia Vodka made their debuts at rock-bottom prices to make sure we could coax people out to gigs they might otherwise not have attended. This wasn't always a success as we found out when we attempted to promote another Furstenburg type bier – Hagerlocher - on the same night that The Lords of the New Church (a punk super group comprising members of The Damned, Sham 69 and fronted by New Yorker, Stiv Bators of the Dead Boys) came to town. Stiv Bators decided to welcome the audience by asking; 'Any Catholics out there tonight? Any Protestants out there tonight? You're all a shower of f****** wankers!' Given that the Old Firm had played earlier that day, it was almost endearing to see the way in which the audience, as one, decided to respond with their very own 'Bottle of the Bands'!

On the issue of alcohol in general, we were obviously worried about having a 'club' licence and concerned that this restriction might impact on the number of people we could legitimately allow to enter the building but we got round this by scrapping the old elitist rules around reciprocity and recognising students from any and every organisation which could conceivably be described as a further education establishment. We weren't too religious either about limiting the number of guests members could sign in or indeed the requirement to actually know them. As it turned out, the majority of people attracted to this 'new' music venue were students from the University of Glasgow itself.

Our strategy was successful almost overnight. From having very few gigs in a full academic year we started hosting them at least every second weekend during first term which culminated in our biggest success to date. For Daft(er) Friday, we booked Slade who hadn't had a hit for a while but who we knew would sell-out easily. Little did we know that by the time of the gig, they'd be at numbers 1 and 3 in the singles charts and we could have sold the tickets three times over. The gig itself almost didn't happen as some of the limitations of the old Queen Margaret Union venue almost scuppered it. Although we had put in a new stage we were still relying on the old power supply and while the existing supply wasn't quite a couple of three pin sockets, it wasn't much better. We were told that unless we could install a state of the art power supply the gig wouldn't go ahead. This was six weeks before the gig and normally it would take three months to install the new one but as ever we found a way round all of the obstacles. Normally I go blank at technical details but I still remember that we installed a 'three phase sixty' supply because it's all I thought about for six weeks.

Armed with our new power supply we moved onto even bigger and more frequent gigs in the second term. In one fifteen day period in March we put on five gigs including the first ever to be held on a Sunday and a Wednesday night. During this spell we had acts as diverse as The Smiths, Ian Dury, John Peel and Runrig. Another first was when we held a gig outside of term time and re-opened the building during the Easter holidays to allow Jamaican Reggae star, Yellowman to put on a show. Third term continued in the same vein with my own particular highlights being The Psychedelic Furs and Glasgow's own Lloyd Cole and the Commotions.

In the following years this success was built on. The Saturday before Christmas 1985, the Pogues, who were at the height of their success, played at the newly-opened Barrowland which had replaced Tiffany's but just to show that Queen Margaret Union was now a fixture, they also played to a sell-out audience there on the Friday night before it. At the Mad March Ball of 1985, a pretty unique event took place as for one night only, Queen Margaret Union became two major live venues. The massively-hyped punk and new romantic super group, Sigue Sigue Sputnik, with a number one single under their belt, were booked to headline. Also booked was Robert

NOT THE GUARDIAN

Anyone reading the article on the Queen Margaret Union's finances in today's Guardian might think that we would be just as well to lock the front door of the building and throw away the key. (The original Guardian article suggested that this was the case but the threat of legal action led to a withdrawel.) In fact nothing could be further from the truth. In October 1982 the Q.M.U. reopened following a 6 month enforced closure due to fire damage with a £100 000 defecit due to a lack of insurance cover. It was hoped at the time that the debt could be substantially reduced within two to three years. However, essential redevelopment has resulted in this not happening. For example, major necessary changes have taken place in the bar and the common room. In the summer of 1983 almost £40 000 was spent in the common room, transforming it from a lookalike to the Stevenson Building's Badminton Court to a top Entertainment venue which has hosted some of the best concerts in Glasgow over the past two years. Over the past two years an additional £25 000 has been spent on improvements to the first floor bar.

The benefits resulting from these changes are becoming evident now. Whereas in the past takings from second term onwards have been reletavely low, this year the discos are attracting crowds of 500 plus at the weekends. Bar takings are also much higher than in the past as the new bar proves its popularity with the students.

The Guardian stated that on last year's figures a debt of £20 000 is expected by June. This figure is less than half that of previous years, and with takings on the increase it may be even less than that. The Q.M.U. has set up a finance committee (not an emergency one) to review the debt and to consider areas where further investment within the building may be made. In response to this a scurrilous Guardian journalist, with one eye on the 'Glasgow Herald Student Journalist of the Year Award', has come up with a story based on an out of date minute provided by a source who was not present at the Board Meeting when finance was discussed.

The Q.M.U. Board of Management feel that it is unfortunate that the need for this statement has arisen, and blame it on the, at best, unwillingness of the Guardian to allow the Q.M.U. to state its position within the article, and, at worst, its totally misleading and inaccurate version of a statement made by Jill Simmons, President. For example Jill's explanation that the debt is due to a fire for which the building was inadequately insured by a board over three years ago is changed to : 'debts are the result of the inefficiency of past board members', giving the impression that the Board of Managements since October 1982 are to blame which is decidedly not the case.

Finally, while Guardian staff are congratulating themselves on fabricating a front page story based on an out of date minute, perhaps they should ask themselves how the Q.M.U. was able to obtain a copy of the story before it had even gone to the printers. We would put it down to another case of typical Q.M.U. efficiency.

Article stapled to the cover of Glasgow University Guardian following publication of an article about Queen Margaret Union.

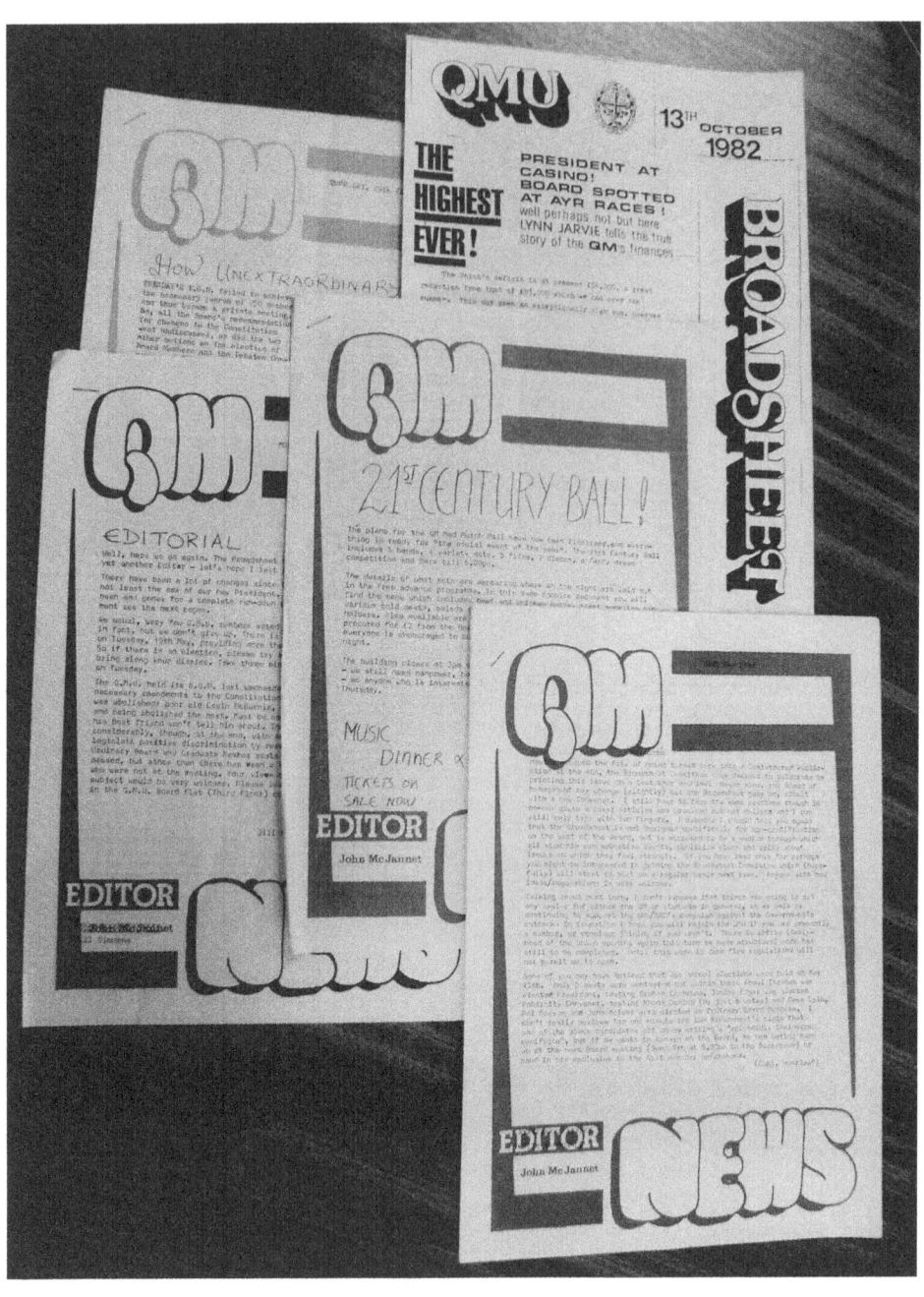

Selection of Queen Margaret Union broadsheet magazines

Cray who was not only one of the top Blues singers in the world but also one of the top Blues guitarists too. Realising that they would be blown off stage, Sputnik utilised some of the small print in their contract which stipulated they could veto the support act and duly informed us they wouldn't be appearing on the same stage as Mr. Cray. Having contracted to pay both acts the money; a separate PA and lights rigging was hired, and a small temporary stage built at the bottom end of the second floor dining room. To this day, Robert Cray in the Dining Room is still one of my top ten gigs of all time while all I can remember about Sigue Sigue Sputnik is their hair and make-up.

Any Scottish band who were going places during this period played at the Union including The Bluebells, Love and Money, Wet Wet Wet and Hue and Cry. The Waterboys played while *The Whole of the Moon* was in the Top Ten. One of the biggest Scottish bands of this time was Hipsway who had a top five single – *The Honeythief* – and a top ten album. As they'd already signed for a tour they couldn't play our venue for contractual reasons so they simply changed their name to The Honeythieves for one night only and played anyway.

It wasn't just the best of UK talent who played in this period. German electronic fashionistas Propaganda showcased their new rhythm section comprising former members of Simple Minds while The Bangles from the United States ensured that the shoe-gazers who used to watch gigs from the darkest recess of the Common Room (as the main hall was quaintly named at the time) were all at the front of stage for one night only. Perhaps the weirdest rider came from American rockers, The Blue Oyster Cult. They arrived with four forty foot articulated lorries clearly believing they were on a stadium tour as their rider requested 'a twenty five foot fire breathing Godzilla and two Harley Davidson motorbikes' for their stage show. This was indeed our own Spinal Tap moment.

Twenty years on, Queen Margaret Union remains a major established music venue in Glasgow and probably the number one student venue in Scotland even though it faces even more competition than it did then. Like all former Presidents and Board members, I look back with very fond memories on my time there but without doubt my proudest memories are related to my involvement in helping to establish it as such.

Student leaders meet the Principal in the Quad

Charities Week

Richard Gass
President 1985-1986

At the start of the 1980s, back in the days of the student grant, it was accepted that going to University was more than just about gaining an academic qualification. I however took the pursuit of non-academic activities to the extreme, leaving little time for any academic study. As sabbatical President of Queen Margaret Union in 1985 I have an excuse for lack of academic progress for that year, but what of my earlier years? Prior to rising to the dizzy heights of the Executive Committee I was first elected as an Ordinary Board member in 1982. As part of my enthusiasm for student participation I volunteered to take the *ad hoc* position of Charities Convenor. This meant that I represented Queen Margaret Union on the Glasgow Student Charities Appeal (GSCA) Committee.

The purpose of the GSCA was to raise money for a variety of charities in the Glasgow area through a series of annual events culminating in Charities Day. The Charities appeal in Glasgow was just one of many such appeals across the student centres in the UK. In other areas the Charities Appeal may have been referred to as their student RAG, which was short for 'Raise and Give'. The structure of the Charities Appeal was in many ways similar to the structure of student unions in that there was a committee comprising of elected individuals with a dedicated few who devoted all their spare time and efforts in ensuring the success of the appeal. In the mid-1980s the main drive and enthusiasm for organising GSCA came from representatives of the smaller colleges in Glasgow with an obvious lack of input from the majority of universities. It goes without saying that there was a large social aspect to it all and having fun was central to many of the activities.

As with such organisations participation with any degree of enthusiasm ultimately leads to either seeking or being persuaded to take on more responsibility.

In 1983 I became Queen Margaret Union Publicity Convenor and thought it made sense to also take on the role of Publicity Distribution Convenor for GSCA. Not content with the demands of the two convenerships I allowed myself to be persuaded to be the 'Charities character' for that year. Every year a character would be created for publicity purposes and their name was always a play on fund raising words. My predecessor was called 'B Jenny Russ' but I had been given the far grander name of 'Ceasyer Cash'.

The publicity distribution part was easy enough. This involved little more than arranging for promotional materials to be given to the different representatives from the colleges and taking the Charities van out on evening fly posting runs under the cover of darkness to publicise different events. The fact that the Police Benevolent Fund was on the list of charities was our get out of jail free card on the occasions that we were pulled up by the police.

With the Charities character however, I didn't really appreciate quite what I was letting myself in for. Firstly, I had to look the part and this involved a trip across the road from the GSCA offices in Buchanan Street to the Royal Scottish Academy of Music and Drama (also at that time in Buchannan Street). Here I was kitted out with all the clobber for a Roman centurion, an outfit that I was to wear several times before Charities Day. I cannot recall all occasions but there are a couple of occasions that are clearly printed in my mind.

In the run up to Valentine's Day there was a phone call to the GSCA office; it was the BBC looking for details of any stunts that we were intending for February 14th. It was commonplace for Charities Appeals to pull stunts through the year to gain publicity for fund raising events and ultimately for Charities Day itself. Although there was nothing in particular planned for Valentine's Day we could not let the obvious chance for publicity pass. The person from the BBC was advised that we had arranged a romantic 'Flan your Lover on Valentine's Day'. They liked the sound of it so invited themselves along to televise one such incident.

Welcome to the Q.M.U. Entertainments

ENTERTAINMENTS CONVENER

The following pages are a summary of last years entertainments at the QM.

Both the photographs and the rundown of last years bands show the high quality of entertainment here at the QM, and prove that the QM is easily the best student venue in Scotland.

We have our disco and band nights on Fridays and Saturdays from 8.00 p.m. until 1.00 a.m. (the latest licence on campus!). To try to compensate for the meagre grants dished out by the government, the QM always guarantees cheap ticket prices, as well as cheap drinks promotions every 2-3 weeks.

Also starting this year we will be having disco and band theme nights on several Thursdays, featuring alternative, rock and 60's nights.

For any of you who are interested in entertainments there is an entertainments committee who do all the work on band nights and even get paid for their troubles. So if you are interested please contact me by asking for me at the porters box.

If by any chance you are in an up-and-coming band yourself don't hesitate in giving me your demo tape or asking advice on anything about the music industry.

Last of all I'd like to wish every newcomer to Glasgow University all the best in the years to come.

Graham Paling,
Entertainments Convener.

From a 1980s QM Handbook

The scene for the 'flanning' was St Aloysius' school in Garnethill. In my full Roman outfit including sword and laurel wreath I hid behind a van and waited for the victim, a student teacher. I can't remember now how I was able to identify her and there was the possibility that I got the wrong person. What I do recall is darting out from behind the van and across the playground attracting the attention of lots of school kids. Well, it's not every day you see some Roman geezer chasing across the school playground hotly pursued by a television camera and reporter. As I stood in front of the teacher and she walked towards me I held out a single red rose in my left hand; behind my back on a paper plate there was half a can of shaving foam. As she saw my smiling face I greeted her with the words "Happy Valentine's Day" and gave a gesture for her to take her rose. As she took the rose she was whacked in the face with her real Valentine's present, the romantic flan in the face for one. A simple 'thank you' would have sufficed but either it was the surprise of being attacked in front of her school or she was playing for the camera when she uttered the words "Help! I can't breathe": words that I would remember uttering myself on a Charities Day another year.

That night the edited clip was broadcast as the lighthearted closing news item on the six pm Scottish news. As I write this I am a bit concerned that this could this be an early version of happy slapping.

A few days earlier there had been another opportunity to wear my Roman outfit in public, and I must point out it was not at all comfortable, didn't keep you warm, and was not particularly flattering. On this occasion it was for a photo opportunity in *The Scotsman*: to publicise the start of the 1984 Charities fortnight, the Lord Provost, Michael Kelly (who would later that year be elected Rector of Glasgow University) had agreed to hand over the city to Ceasyer Cash for the duration of the Charities fortnight.

The end of the Charities fortnight culminated in the highlight that was Charities Day. On this day Glasgow students from across all the colleges and universities would dress up in fancy dress and take out collecting cans. The buses and underground allowed free travel for students with collecting cans and the public at large knew to expect that they would be harangued on several occasions to put some money into a can. A full collecting can would entitle the student to a free pass to the Charities Ball held that evening. As part of the Charities Day programme there was the procession of floats from all the different colleges. Local businesses would donate the use of a lorry and driver and each college would design a float of some description. The floats would assemble on Kelvin Way and then head off towards George Square. This particular year some bright spark had arranged for the donkey from Possil farm to lead the procession and sitting pride of place on this donkey was to be none other than Ceasyer Cash. Fortunately, this was the last time I had to humiliate myself and I am relieved to hear that there are no surviving photographs of the occasion.

A major fund raising part of the Charities Appeal was the annual production and sale of *Ygorra*, the GSCA Rag Mag. In essence it was a collection of jokes, and humorous cartoons interspersed with adverts. I seem to recall that on at least one occasion the Magazine was banned from being sold in Queen Margaret Union due to it containing jokes of a sexist nature.

There was of course the conventional activities such as the annual sponsored walk from Drymen to Glasgow, something I must admit to having never attempted. And every year GSCA would buy a van as an essential tool to organising much of the appeals work, which at the end of the year would be donated to one of the charities.

The fun part for me however was the less conventional events and stunts. I can recall an intended pre-Christmas busking competition descending into an impromptu punk rock Carol Concert complete with alternative lyrics. The whole idea of pulling a stunt and getting away with it because it is for charity has always had a childish appeal for me.

As I understand it, the whole Charities fortnight including GSCA has faded over the years and is now a distant memory. Perhaps this excuse for collective high jinks should be restored if not at a Glasgow wide level at least at a local student union level.

However, when Guardian remarks about the QM's account-

GRAHAM WINS AT QM

MARK GRAHAM, a third year Arts student, has been elected President of the Queen Margaret Union for the session 1983-84. Mr. Graham received 224 of the 391 votes cast.

Jill Simmons was elected unopposed as Honorary Secretary and Rhona Dunlop defeated Paul Coyne by 67 votes to become Assistant Honorary Secretary.

The President-Elect, has been a QM Board member for the past two years. He told Guardian that this experience was a major factor in his being elected.

Mr. Graham believes the QM's major financial difficulties have been overcome. He hopes that the £100,000 deficit accumulated from the 1981-82 session would be reduced to £15,000 by September 1983.

"We would wish to renegotiate the ARA catering contract to give the QM a bigger say in catering and thereby exempting the ARA from charging the 15% VAT. This money could be pumped back into catering to improve prices and food quality."

The QM receives 5% of all gross takings, minus VAT, made by ARA. This is based on the agreement made in October 1982 with ARA following a £35,000 loss made in the previous session.

Plans were also proposed for the improvement of the disco equipment and facilities, including extending the bar. Work on this is to commence during the summer.

The candidates for the convener positions Broadsheet, Entertainments, Social and Publicity were all elected unopposed. They are filled by Lynn Jarvie, Mark Mackie, Keith MacDonald and Richard Gass respectively.

Elected to the six ordinary positions were Jean MacFarlane, Laura Peaston, Grace Lindores, Cliff Smith, Ronald Woodger and John Wilson.

David Lyle, Paul Coyne, Alison Connachan and Alan Greer were also elected unopposed to the Board.

Paul Gallagher

Glasgow University Guardian article showing Graham winning seat of President at Queen Margaret Union

Main Venue of Queen Margaret Union

Queen Margaret Union

1982 BY—ELECTION

CONSTITUENCY 'E'

NOV '82 — NOV. '83

4 VACANCIES

(MARK 1,2,3, etc against candidates of your choice)

RICHARD GASS	
CHAS. RODGER	
SCOTT KERR	
MICHAEL DYER	
JOHN McGOWAN	
ALEX. FERRIE	
CLIFF SMITH	
RICHARD TAYLOR	

NOVEMBER ELECTION   **TUESDAY 16th NOVEMBER**

Ballot paper, November 1982

Inspiration, Innovation

Marion Neill
President 1986-1987

It was a bright sunny morning when I found myself for the first time at the bottom of the Queen Margaret Union's steps. A 1970s vision of concrete and glass, it is not a building that will be remembered for its grandeur or style. For the five years of my university career it was to become my second home. The memories of that time would leave a lasting impression, having an impact on me for years to come.

Like the majority of Freshers, I didn't quite grasp the differences between the unions. I wanted to join the 'real' union, the 'Glasgow University one' at the bottom of Gilmorehill. Soon I was avoiding that long walk to the bottom of the hill after lectures at the Adam Smith building. As the autumn wind blew leaves down University Avenue, it was the vibrant Queen Margaret Union that beckoned to me, an altogether warmer option in more ways than one. In my first year, that black Glasgow University Union diary became less and less something to be proud of and more like something of an apology as I had to show it going into Queen Margaret Union events, gigs and discos.

My first impression of Queen Margaret Union was 'what a racket'. Just getting in the front doors involved running a gauntlet of students shouting slogans of the day, hawking newspapers, shaking money buckets for political funds, charities and causes.

Climbing up the steps I was showered by the confetti of a hundred different leaflets; join this; come to that; vote for the other. Anti-Apartheid, Friends of Nicaragua, CND,

Glasgow Womens' Group, they were all there. As a newcomer from Dumbarton Academy it was overwhelming, but it had a vibrancy about it. I felt like a student should. Laden with twenty sheets of A5 propaganda, I made my way to the canteen on the third floor. I wonder in these days of green politics, what do students use for leaflets?

Right from the first time I entered, Queen Margaret Union always had an 'open' feel about it. The bar's big u-shaped seating areas encouraged sitting with, and meeting, other people. The canteen was bright, light and open and I would quickly scan the sea of faces, more than a little desperate to pick out a familiar face from my old school.

That would change so quickly for all of us. I was to meet so many people over the next few years because of the place. It drew like-minded people together. It certainly had its characters. It didn't take long before you started to recognise the President, Abdul Ibrahim, and the Board of Management regulars. I looked up to them tremendously. They just seemed to belong, to rule the roost - and if any of them said hello to you, well, you were really chuffed. Little did I know that I was later to work my way up those ranks. By my second year (and now a fully fledged member), I knew with certainty that I wanted to become involved somehow in the running of the Union.

In the 1980s, Queen Margaret Union was right at the heart of 'the hot bed of political activism'. For those on the humanitarian and left wing of student politics, it was where all the best meetings were held. More often than not, it was sitting in the bar that things were really discussed, not in the Students Representative Council across the road. Views and opinions filled the air - direct actions were hatched. Thatcher had been in power since 1979 - it already seemed like an eternity for many in Scotland and for those of us in higher education, her policies began biting.

It was a place to really learn, to be politicised. In many ways, I think the fact that the Glasgow University Union existed, made Queen Margaret Union what it was. It pulled together all ends of the left and alternative thinking and was a bastion against apathy and old fashioned thinking. On women's rights, gay and lesbian politics, the two Unions were polls apart.

As a politics student, my lectures provided learning - but Queen Margaret Union's continuous roll call of meetings, debates, and film shows gave awareness. Importantly, it was awareness across a whole range of issues, not just education, not just Scotland. There was a world of politics going on.

The student of the eighties had a lot to be concerned about and we cared about what was happening in our community. The University of Glasgow had a high percentage of home students and I never felt any alienation from the greater community in Glasgow.

In 1985, Queen Margaret Union buzzed thanks to the miner's strike; meetings, rallies, fund raising. It became a focus for the frustration of years of Thatcherism. Students joined in marches to Glasgow Green and collected money in Argyll Street on Saturday afternoons. When Ayrshire miners came to speak at the debates, they got a rapturous reception from the Queen Margaret Union membership.

Things came to a head when the Glasgow University Union held a debate where Michael Heseltine (Thatcher's cabinet 'troubleshooter') came to speak against the strike. Led by Queen Margaret Union members protesting at his presence, the police became heavy handed, pushing and shoving protesters into metal barriers. Ringleaders were picked off and arrested. It was a violent and unsettling time, not just for the University but for the whole country.

Billy Bragg was going to play during 1984. He had become a minor celebrity in Britain, as he appeared at leftist political rallies, strikes, and benefits across the country; he also helped form the Red Wedge, a socialist musicians collective featuring the likes of Paul Weller. Billy was the real darling of the left and Queen Margaret Union student body loved him. He was going to be playing a fund raising gig at our Union for the Miners' strike fund. We were all in great spirits for the show.

I was the Assistant Honorary Secretary at the time and was on duty, busy getting things ready. The building was starting to fill up with students wanting to pay for tickets and eager to get to the bar before the queues got too long, or their feet got too cold – it was bitterly cold outside.

Richard Gass (the President at the time), called all the Duty Board members and security together. He told us that the police had called. There had been a bomb threat. A coded message had been received and we'd have to evacuate the building immediately. Thankfully, it was still quite early in the night, people hadn't had much to drink and left right away. Those walking towards Queen Margaret Union came across police cordons and were sent to the end of University Avenue to wait at a safe distance.

The police arrived and started to search the building. Most people waited at the end of the Avenue for more news. I remember feelings of real anger. We would have to cancel the show. Although in my heart of hearts, I thought it was probably a hoax, designed to ruin the gig and claim a small victory for those who opposed us, I was still worried. A very brave Richard Gass was leading police around the building in the search. Just days before, a small bomb had exploded in a locker at a major train station, the action claimed by right wing extremists.

As the painstaking search of the building went on, it wasn't long before people started to disperse from the freezing conditions outside. Then he did it; Billy Bragg saved the day. He appeared out of nowhere with his guitar case in hand and mounted the steps of one of the faculty buildings. Leading with, "We're not going to let these ******** beat us!", he launched into the anthemic 'New England', at the top of his voice. Everyone joined in immediately and rallied around the bottom of the stairs to hear him, matching his every word. It was turning into a street party. He stayed there entertaining us until the police gave the all-clear to return. More than a little late, the gig went ahead and the coins rattled in the collection buckets.

I'll never forget how I felt that night. It was more than just guitar music in the cold night air. It felt like we were all together for one cause, that we were standing up against Thatcher and the bullyboys that would silence us. In reality it wouldn't affect anything, but it felt like a victory. It was such a special time. I remember it with real affection. It was a time when everything was black and white, right and wrong and we were young with so much work to do. I truly believed that we could make a difference, no matter how small.

The miners' strike lasted a full year before the leadership conceded without a deal. The defeat of the miners' strike led

Queen Margaret Union Board of Management 1986-1987

Glasgow's Lord Provost, Dr Michael Kelly, was threatened with being thrown to a lioness when the Romans took to the streets yesterday. Dr Kelly had to appeal to 'Ceasyer' before being saved from a fate worse than seeing Meadowbank beat Celtic . . . It was all part of the Glasgow Student Charities Appeal campaign with Richard Gass (right) as 'Ceasyer Cash.'

Later the Lord Provost turned down an invitation to stand for the Lord Rectorship of the university. He had been approached by some Labour students who preferred his nomination to that of Yasser Arafat, official choice of the Labour Club. He had first consulted Labour party members in Glasgow who took the view that his standing against Arafat would be seen as a breaking of Labour's ranks. The group who approached the Lord Provost, wanted a working rector whose ties would be strong with the academic world and the City of Glasgow. The Liberal choice is Mr Menzies Campbell, the advocate and former Olympic sprinter who was president of the Liberal Club in the early 1960s.

Ceasyer Cash and Michael Kelly

230

to a long period of demoralization in the whole of the trade union movement. I remember the day it ended, with disbelief and disappointment.

The result of years of Thatcher's rule really made itself felt. The University grants paid to fund the Union were going to be cut. Students' unions were attracting the attention of certain Conservative MPs looking to end state funding, and in return silence the voices of dissent. When I was President, I remember only too well the meeting with University Council members where we were told, in no uncertain terms, that in years to come "self-sufficiency was going to be the future". We had to start running Queen Margaret Union more like a moneymaking business. Bearing in mind our customers were poor students with ever dwindling grants, this was going to be difficult. And, although in 1986 students had defeated proposals for the introduction of loans - helped by a massive campaign countrywide by the National Union of Students (NUS) - it was clear that the student loan was looming.

Like many student unions, we made more money from our bars than anything else. We were the second biggest customer of Scottish and Newcastle Breweries in the country. Queen Margaret Union was a member of Northern Services at the time, a Scottish universities purchasing consortium, put together to improve buying power from major suppliers. Not having the muscle of the NUS behind us, it seemed like a good move for Queen Margaret Union. The NUS referendum had taken place in 1985 and the students of the University of Glasgow had voted 'No' to joining. This was a huge disappointment to our Students Representative Council and the Board of Management who had fully supported the campaign to join. But, we were able to join together with other unaffiliated Scottish Universities and together we got good deals from our bar and student shop suppliers, which we could then in turn pass on to our members.

As President, I approached the brand manager for McEwans Lager. With some basic designs and a proposal. I got on the train to Edinburgh with Alex MacDonald, the editor of Queen Margaret Union Broadsheet. We persuaded Scottish and Newcastle that we were not only a great existing customer, but that we gave them direct access to a future market. We tied in their recent music-led ad campaigns with Queen Margaret Union's leading role as a groundbreaking live music venue. In return for on-ticket advertising we received funding for concerts and a facelift for our main Union bar. Student Unions could work hand in hand with business.

However, it also seemed that while we involved ourselves in the practicalities of keeping the Union functioning and afloat, perhaps we would lose some of the time and energy to organise and politicise our members.

A few years later, students were leaving further education with massive debts to repay; a shift had taken place. There were changes, which made it harder for political groups and other student minorities to organise on campus. Was the government being challenged on their education policies? I feared for the future of Queen Margaret Union. We would have to depend on those who came after us to define the Union's purpose in the next decade.

We already had a tradition of being a good music venue. Our downstairs common room saw many famous faces play over the years. During the 1980s our links with Regular Music saw us become a great venue - one of the best in Glasgow. Mark Mackie and his successor, Scott Fyfe, were our entertainment conveners. With Mark and Scott working hand in hand with Regular we became part of the UK touring circuit for many artists and the standard of the acts improved immensely. Students came from far and wide to see the likes of Motorhead, Erasure, The Waterboys, The Mission, The Smiths, Nirvana and The Bangles. This brought lucrative business to Queen Margaret Union, introducing us to new customers, who returned again and again. Our reputation was forged as an exciting concert venue.

It was at that time the Scottish music scene exploded into the mainstream. Nearly all of the bands that were having chart success had started their careers playing there - and many were to return. Hue and Cry, Lloyd Cole and the Commotions, Wet Wet Wet, Goodbye Mr MacKenzie, Hipsway, Texas and Love and Money. The list went on and on. It was probably the most influential time for Scottish bands in memory, and Queen Margaret Union made the most of it.

This introduction to the music industry made a big impression on me - I have been working in the live music industry since. As a production assistant, I still bump into members of the old stage crew, many of whom also followed careers in music. It's hard not to get nostalgic, and harp back to the good old days.

I can trace all that back to Queen Margaret Union. The place certainly made an impact on my life, as I'm sure it has on others. It was my social life, it was where I sought advice, where I studied, where I didn't study, where I fell in and out of love, where I made friends that have lasted my whole life; it was the heart of my time at university.

I think a part of me still misses it. I wish I could stand at the bottom of those stairs and listen to Billy Bragg playing his guitar again, and feel what I felt. It was a special time and a special place, and I know it will remain so.

Major posts contested in QMU elections

By JOHN PENDERS

QUEEN Margaret Union today holds its annual Board of Management elections.

People entering the Union will be showered with leaflets and emblazoned with stickers in an attempt to woo them to this or that candidate.

Competition for the various seats has been disappointing with no one being opposed in any of the ordinary constituencies.

Most of the executive positions however are being contested although only that for the important sabbatical position of President has more than two candidates.

Of these, two are serious contenders, the others, 'joke' candidates. Richard Gass is considered favourite but faces stiff competition from David Hutcheon.

Mr Gass, a fourth year science student, has been on the board since 1982. During this time he has held positions as Publicity Convenor, and his present post, Assistant Honorary Secretary. He has also been involved in various campaigns

Richard Gass

against what he calls "this vicious Tory Government."

He claims that the post of President is not a political one but does require political awareness.

"If I am elected, I would not like to see the QM ignore the injustices of the outside world but to continue with its present progressive policies on such issues as racism and sexism."

He is also keen to see the foyer shop back under QM control.

David Hutcheon, a third year social science student is best

David Hutcheon

known for his humorous 'What's On' spot in *Guardian*.

However he stresses that his candidature is in no way light-hearted.

"I am the only serious challenger to Mr Gass and I believe that the ordinary members want and need their own President and not someone to whom the board has given the nod."

Less serious are the manifestos of the other three Presidential candidates Tony McElvie, Hugh Bradley and Satnum Singh.

Last year Hugh Bradley claimed to know "24 things, seven concepts and four ambiguities." This year his platform is a vote for Bradley is a vote for a fish." While Mr Singh advocates amongst other things renaming the Union 'Glasgow University Union Annexe' and awarding Margaret Thatcher an honorary Degree!

Of the other executive positions, that of Assistant Honorary Secretary will be filled by Marion Neill who is presently an Ordinary Board Member. Miss Neill, a 3rd year politics student was elected unopposed.

The competition for the position of Honorary Secretary should be keen; both candidates are popular in the Union. John McGowan, whose less cerebral antics gained him notoriety in 'Watchtower' is nevertheless a strong contender. He has been active in almost every aspect of Union Management in his two years on the board and is the current Publicity Convenor.

His rival is Lois Calder, a

(Continued on Page 3)

Glasgow University Guardian article covering the Queen Margaret Union elections

A Change in the Air

Grahame Riddell
President 1987-1988

The year was 1987 and the week I got elected as President, 'Nothing's Gonna stop us now' by Starship was number one; 'Cheers' starring Ted Danson was one of the top television Shows; 'Lethal Weapon' was on at the cinema; construction began on the Channel Tunnel; and Rangers had sewn up the football league. In politics the anti-apartheid movement was at its peak; Margaret Thatcher was just about to be re-elected for a third term; and future Prime Minister, a youngish Gordon Brown addressed students in the committee rooms of Queen Margaret Union.

I'm sure that I wouldn't be far wrong in saying that students were much more politically active back then than they are now. By being 'active' I do not mean that students nowadays don't care about politics, it's just that during the eighties the University of Glasgow was a very political place and there was always an Extraordinary General Meeting on some topic or another. Chairing these meetings was never my favourite pastime as no matter what you did you always upset someone. The Students Representative Council (SRC) was always arranging a demo and marches to George Square; up to two thousand students would take to the streets on a regular basis with the main focus being the Tory Government's education policy, Campaign for Nuclear Disarmament (CND) or Anti-Apartheid. These marches quite often involved a few arrests. One of my most memorable times was picketing the Glasgow University Union when Tory ministers spoke. There was always a run for eggs in the Gibson Street grocers as students stocked up for the picket. The Glasgow University Union walls always got a good splattering of eggs; the stains usually there for some time after.

When I first got involved with Queen Margaret Union as an ordinary member getting the balance right between politics and running the Union was not always easy. Talking about making money and improving services was often followed by cries of 'capitalist' – usually from the Socialist Workers. I seemed to offend these same people even more by trying to secure a clear path for students who were often intimidated on the Union steps day after day. Although we had the SRC, which, with the unique set up at the University of Glasgow, was supposed to represent students and make policy on behalf of the students, it seemed that there were a number of groups who wanted us to take this role on as well. I'm not saying Queen Margaret Union should not have taken a stance on a number of important issues but you could argue that this affected the overall focus on delivering good services for its members.

Around the mid-eighties the government had been making noises about student unions having to become self funded by the end of the decade. It was therefore clear that we had to implement some major changes if the Union was to survive and be in a position to provide an improved level of service and facilities to our members. The fire in 1982 had really set us back financially and we were essentially broke. We had little money to invest in refurbishment and quite simply we had to start thinking about how to make money in order to survive. As Honorary Secretary, alongside President Marion Neill, I went to the University to seek their help and advice on how we could improve our position. The outcome was to appoint Coopers & Lybrand Management Consultants to review our working practices and come up with a plan of action primarily focused on the implementation of more stringent financial controls, up-to-date working practices and a short-term refurbishment plan.

The blueprint galvanised the Board of Management and we came up with the slogan 'The Union that is fighting back'. We wanted to be the biggest and best union on campus and we took the fight for members during 'Week Zero' right to

QUEEN MARGARET UNION
ANNUAL ELECTIONS 1985
POST OF PRESIDENT

Candidate	1st Count	2nd Count	3rd Count	4th Count
HUGH BRADLEY	101			
RICHARD GASS	312			
DAVID HUTCHEON	90			
TONY McKELVIE	28			
SATNUM SINGH	18			
N/T	/			
TOTAL	549			
QUOTA	276			
SPOILT	9			

RETURNING OFFICER _____   DATE 16/3/85

Tally sheet of results for recent President election in 1980s

Office Bearers

the doors of the Glasgow University Union. We focused a lot on the heritage of Queen Margaret Union as the best student entertainment venue in Scotland and the 'cool' Union as opposed to the stuffy 'Beer Bar' image of our counterparts. This proved incredibly successful as we increased the membership, continuing the trend from previous years.

We undertook a period of refurbishment including building new offices to ensure that the Executive and Office staff worked as a team in an environment that created a more professional approach to how we ran the Union. The Disco was improved and the Bar got a minor facelift (much to the disapproval of 'Wasters' corner' a group of well known students and ex-students who seemed to spend all day in the bar for a period of around five years). The entertainments side did very well with great bands such as The Christians, Motorhead and The Alarm. The discos were always well attended and the bar takings improved.

In my year as president I also raised sponsorship from our key suppliers to attend a 'World Student Union' conference in New Orleans where we visited a lot of unions in the United States and saw how they did things over there. The trip made me even more determined that we should have the best services on campus with a focus on service, quality and value. Plans were drawn up to revamp the catering areas and bring in new operators. I believe the name 'The Food Factory' still exists today.

As with all presidencies there were challenging times and in a time of change it made the job even harder. The natural human inclination to fight change resulted in some resistance to the things we did, which were in our opinion, for the good of Queen Margaret Union. There is no doubt that this period was a difficult one for the Union but as each year passed things did improve. These changes were our legacy; the building blocks that we put in place during the late 1980s enabled the Union to flourish and finally overtake the Glasgow University Union in terms of membership.

I was proud to be part of what we achieved at this time, despite the challenges of having little money and convincing people we were doing the right thing. Overall, it was a great experience and there was a dedicated group of people who made things happen and moved Queen Margaret Union forward I even married one of them. We learned a lot that I'm sure has stood us all in good stead for later life – and we managed to have great fun along the way as well.

Memories of a Staff Member

Michael McGovern
Reception Staff,
Past-Honorary Vice President,
Honorary Life Member
and Resident

I started working at Queen Margaret Union in February 1984 as the doorman at the first floor bar, which was then known simply as the 'QM Bar'. It was soon after was re-named the 'Biko Bar' in honour of Steve Biko who was killed in South Africa for opposing Apartheid.

I remember that Queen Margaret Union, at that time, through the activities of its members, was heavily involved in numerous campaigns against injustices at local, national and international levels, particularly concerning Palestine and South Africa.

Almost every day at that time some activist or other would be trying to slap a sticker for their particular cause on me. I always had to remove it as the staff were, and are, discouraged from openly endorsing a particular cause and from becoming involved in the student politics (I never fell out with anyone by practising this policy).

One of the first things, which I enjoyed were the great bands that played. This was in the days when Morrissey was being 'this charming man' and Lloyd Cole was spending a 'lost weekend in a hotel in Amsterdam'. There were no mobile phones to speak of and the word laptop still had to enter the Oxford Dictionary. In the eighties I can remember constantly putting calls out on the tannoy for someone or other to come to the Porter's Box to take a phone call. This went on all day as the mobile phone was still to become the everyday icon that it is now. That is perhaps one of the differences in doing my job nowadays; all of the calls I answer are mainly business related now.

In 1986 on St. Paddy's Day, 'God' played Queen Margaret Union with his band, 'The Boomtown Rats'. Yes, Bob Geldof played the 'John McLean Common Room' (now Qudos) and of course, sold out in between the first Band Aid record and the first Band Aid concert at Wembley Stadium.

One of the features in the mid-eighties was the infamous, 'Wasters' Corner', which was situated in the far right hand side of the then Biko Bar. This was a real mixture of characters who can only be described as full-time boozers and part-time students, which of course was supposed to be the other way around. There was always a mess at these tables; glasses, full ashtrays and footmarks; and spilled beer (but not too much; after all these guys were professionals). Woe betide any unsuspecting genuine student who wandered into this mayhem. They didn't stay long and if they did it was usually forever having been converted to the wasters' philosophy, which was all about 'not giving a stuff' about lectures and other such distractions, devising ways of getting more booze with very little means and getting pissed at any time of the day. The ironic thing about the regulars at 'Wasters' Corner' was that they were all highly intelligent and skilled individuals who basically couldn't be bothered. Most survived but one or two fell by the wayside.

The late eighties at Queen Margaret Union saw some big changes. A new General Manager was brought in and one of the first tasks was to arrange a 'Centenary Fashion Show'. He needed thirty girls to fashion clothes from the past one hundred years and handed me the task of finding them among the members and staff. A couple of days later we had the models we needed, as well as about half a dozen males. The show took place at the Kelvingrove Art Gallery and Museum and was a great success, which everyone enjoyed greatly. The clothes were borrowed; mostly from the People's Palace and the students and staff models had a great time wearing them. There was loads of champagne and much congratulation afterwards. I even wore a bow tie for the occasion.

One of the strongest activist groups of the eighties on campus was the Glasgow University Women's Group. They concentrated mostly on feminist issues, but would sometimes lend a hand to others if it served their interest as well. They had one great success on campus, which involved a group of people at the Glasgow University Union. Every Thursday at noon a group calling themselves 'the Freds' would meet at the Glasgow University Union and show a 'Tom and Jerry' cartoon (this is where the group got their name from as the creator of 'Tom and Jerry' was Fred Quimby; thus 'the Freds'). Unfortunately, the cartoon was really a front for the real reason for the meetings, as every cartoon was apparently followed by a porn movie. This of course outraged the Women's Group as well as many others. So every Thursday at noon a group of women would march from Queen Margaret Union down University Avenue to the Glasgow University Union and protest at the showing of these movies, only to be greeted outside with shouts of derision, buckets of water and bags of flour. Every Thursday around one pm they would come back either soaked or covered in flour, but always still angry and determined to keep the protests going. The story somehow found its way into the pages of the 'Evening Times', which of course alerted the University authorities of the seriousness of the situation and almost immediately, 'the Freds' disappeared into history.

Many political characters have passed through the doors of Queen Margaret Union in my time here. I remember in particular sitting at the door of the bar when David Steele, the then Liberal Party leader, appeared in front of me - he had actually signed into the bar only to use the men's room. George Galloway was a regular speaker at the club meetings on the third floor on a Saturday morning. I remember one time he was protesting about something or other and had himself tied to the bottom of the banister on the front stairs - I had to untie him in time for him to get a flight down to London. I also remember Paddy Ashdown, the then Social and Liberal Democrats leader giving a talk at the Union. He was provided with a microphone, which he didn't use as his voice carried a long way without it. The guys at the Porters' Box got a very nice, personally signed letter from him a few days later thanking us, and the rest of the staff, for our help and hospitality. I can't remember what became of that letter. I also met Jack McConnell who came here before he was First Minister. I found him very quiet spoken at the time.

Band nights at the Union were always interesting. A group called Sique Sique Sputnik played and their tour manager was being a bit naughty after punching a member of the audience. He then did the same thing to a female and was duly arrested by the Glasgow police. Another time a band called Bad Manners were playing and someone kept jumping up on the stage and chanting into front man Buster Bloodvessel's microphone, "You fat b*****d", and then stage diving into the front row of the audience. After doing this about five times, the audience were getting fed up and when he attempted to stage dive once more, they parted and he flew face first into the disco floor. As one, the audience began chanting, "You stupid b*****d".

That's why I love working at Queen Margaret Union; something different is always happening. I'm sure it will always be like that. I could go into more detail about the many and varied activities and misdemeanours of the Board of Management over the years but all that shall remain private to protect the guilty.

1990

The 1980s were the darkest period so far but Queen Margaret Union wasn't out of the woods yet. Although 1990 was the centenary year, the celebrations were held at the risk of financial meltdown. Thanks to the installation of a new financial management committee, prudent running of the Union by the Executive Committee and the quick thinking of the new General Manager, Anthony McConachie, the events went ahead as planned.

The highlight of the celebrations was a fashion show at Kelvingrove Museum where many students could showcase the fashion of 'Q-Emmas' throughout the decades.

By 1993 the Union's finances were back on track and refurbishments and investments meant that Queen Margaret Union was starting to look much more modern. Membership soared and began to really challenge Glasgow University Union in terms of student numbers.

'Cheesy Pop' was created as the definitive student night and is still running to this day, every week without fail. The pub quiz became a regular feature in the weekly social line-up and more and more live acts graced the Union's stage. Legend has it that Nirvana's lead singer, Kurt Cobain left his footprint on a set-list, which remains safely locked away in the Executive Office.

Queen Margaret Union was proving once again that despite the worst possible odds, it could pull through and become something bigger than it was before.

Dafter Friday Poster, 1989

Queen Margaret Union foyer from 1980s

Bring on the Nineties

Stuart Buchanan
President 1990-1991

In July 1990, Queen Margaret Union was tentatively taking a few baby-steps towards a dim, vague light at the end of a long tunnel. This in itself was wholly remarkable, particularly given the fact that only twelve months earlier, the idea of closing the doors permanently was a stark possibility.

In October 1989, the Glasgow University Guardian newspaper reported that we had accrued debts of over one hundred thousand pounds, and President Dianne Wallace admitted that "the place was in a financial mess" and that it was "trading almost illegally". Dianne had inherited the Union in that precise condition and her tenure as President was almost entirely devoted to ensuring that the lights remained in the 'on' position.

As a relative newcomer, I wasn't fully aware of the precise course that had driven Queen Margaret Union so far into the red. It was obvious to all that there had been some major operational upgrades in the late eighties, including a total re-development of the Second Floor catering area, and there had also been some tragic losses in the Entertainments division (a disastrous turnout for 'The Men They Couldn't Hang' saw them affectionately dubbed as 'The Men They Couldn't Sell'). The extent, to which they were the root cause, or merely the icing on a much bigger cake, was not immediately clear at the time.

Following the departure of both the incumbent General Manager and the then President, Jennifer Roe, it fell to Dianne to a plot a course through the mounting losses and develop a solution that would keep the pints flowing in the Biko Bar. Part of that strategy saw Tony McConachie appointed as General

Manager. Both arrived in a bleak climate and were forced into a brutal cost-cutting exercise - the policy revisions they took to the Board of Management at the time were never going to be popular, but they were absolutely essential.

One such revision was so vital that it demanded a constitutional amendment, something that could only be approved at an Extraordinary General Meeting (EGM). The October 1989 EGM saw the introduction of the Financial Management Committee, with powers to control capital expenditure, approve contracts and generally interrogate the veracity of the Union's spread of fiscal arrangements. Although members feared a lack of student control over Queen Margaret Union's affairs, the formation of the committee was in fact the start of the Union's rehabilitation. Most importantly, it gave the University itself the required confidence to believe that we could sort out our own affairs. They had previously declared that there would be no new money injected into the Union to fix the debt, hence Dianne's call that "they could close the doors tomorrow".

The following six months saw Queen Margaret Union quietly pull itself together again, steadily navigating its way through the centenary year in an attempt to regain its dignity and pride. At the end of her sabbatical, Dianne handed the steering wheel over to me, and the full truth of the origins of financial mess were made perfectly apparent. It only made me respect Dianne and Tony even more, as I understood the scale of the difficulties they faced, and I absolutely believe that without them, Queen Margaret Union wouldn't be the Union it is today, if indeed it was still there at all.

Thankfully, our General Manager remained throughout 1990 and 1991 (and for a long time thereafter) and I gave him as much space as I could to continue his repair job. Whilst he continued his work on the engine overhaul, myself and the rest of the Board of Management got on with repairing the damaged reputation. Throughout the 1980s, Queen Margaret Union was one of Glasgow's premier live gig destinations, and, given the financial constraints that had been employed, taking risks on big-name bands was no longer an option. 'The Pixies', 'Red Hot Chili Peppers', 'The Smiths', 'Happy

letters

QM Deny Week "O" Profits

Dear Editors

The Queen Margaret Union Board of Management would like to clarify certain points made in the Week '0' edition of Guardian regarding the financing of Week '0'.

Although all four student bodies did agree that the cost of Week '0' should be greatly reduced, it was also noted that it was too late into the organisation for this to be carried out.

The board take great offence to the comment that "the SRC is deprived of considerable income.... because the Q.M. and G.U.U. keep the profit from beer sales."

The Queen Margaret Union has no income from the admission costs of Week '0', indeed our only income is from Bar Sales and the "predetermined lump sum" from the SRC which goes towards the costs of our two palais nights - Runrig and Transvision Vamp.

It must be remembered that although other Student Councils may receive a share of Union Beer sales, Glasgow University is not a Students' Association and consists of autonomous student bodies.

The small profit made in the bar goes towards paying for various Q.M. events such as the Bouncy Disco and the many promotions held throughout the week. This leaves only the sum from the SRC, who expected the same level of high entertainment in previous years for less than half the financial contribution.

Contrary to SRC claims, the Q.M. does not bill for use of committee rooms, or the hire of the Common Room on Band nights. Indeed the Q.M.U. has never sought to make a profit from Week'0'. We would, however, prefer that we do not make losses that reach four figures.

To the Board, it is rather ironic that the SRC Vice-President stated that the SRC "do not wish to impose any financial hardship on your Union."

Yours sincerely

Jennifer Roe, President
Matric. No 855190

Katy Love, Honorary Secretary
Matric. No 864136

Dianne Wallace
Assist. Honorary Secretary
Matric. No 870255

From *Glasgow University Guardian* 1988/1989

UNIVERSITY GUARDIAN

SCOTLAND'S BEST STUDENT NEWSPAPER

19th May, 1983 — FREE

QM FURY OVER MISSING CASH

A cash deficiency, believed to amount to £4,784, has been uncovered in the Queen Margaret Union's accounts for 1981-2, by auditors examining this year's figures. A discrepancy was noticed in the accounts for the latter part of 1982, but further scrutiny revealed that the cash deficiency had actually arisen in the *first six months* of last year. As a result of this, the figures for July-December 1982, which should have been presented at the QM's AGM last Friday, were not available for presentation.

It is understood that a loss of £2,850 cannot be accounted for in the figures for the first half of 1982, but further controversy has arisen over the revelation that the accounts for the latter part of 1981 also show an unexplained loss of £1,934. Mr. Abdul Ibrahem, QM President, claimed that the auditors' report, which details flaws in the QM's financial statement for the six months to December 1981, was never presented to the Board with the rest of the accounts.

The report of the auditors, Alexander Sloan and Co., was sent to the then president of the QMU, Mr. Dominic d'Angelo, on 10th June 1982, and listed three major flaws in the accounts. The report states that:—

"1) A major part of the Union's income comprises cash income over which there was no system of control upon which we could rely. Accordingly, this cash income is not capable of audit verification.

2) The books of account have not been properly kept for the six months to 31st December 1981.

3) There was an unexplained cash deficiency of £1,934 for the six months to 31st December 1981."

Mr. Ian Mowat, of Alexander Sloan and Co., told Guardian, "The cash deficiency was pointed out to Mr. d'Angelo but he could find no satisfactory explanation for it."

However, when Guardian spoke to Mr. d'Angelo he insisted that a variety of problems within the QM during that period had led to the breakdown of the accounting system. In particular, the absence of a treasurer for the latter part of 1981 and early 1982 had, he felt, been the main reason for this.

"The problem of the accounts was symptomatic of the Union at that time. The treasurer left in mid-1981 and there was no integrated system of accounting until Mr. Armour, the current treasurer, took over in mid-1982. The Board was dictating financial policy and students were handling the accounts when a professional should have been in charge.

"Attempts were made to find a treasurer but no one suitable could be found. During this period I had to do the job myself."

Mr. D'Angelo was emphatic that the auditors' report outlining the cash deficiency must have been presented to the Board with the rest of the accounts at a meeting on 14th June 1982, but he could not recall much of what was discussed because, he claims, the minutes of the meeting were not sent to him.

However, Mr. Ibrahem told Guardian that the auditors' report of 10th June 1982 was first seen by him when Mr. Mowat and he were going over the 1982 accounts last week. "Mr. Mowat's file contained a one-page reference to the cash deficiency of £1,934 and remarks about the QM's accounting procedures. That paper was not included in the papers given to me when I took office," he said.

Mr. Ibrahem's claim seems to be borne out by the minutes regarding the Confidential Business of 14th June 1982. Item one simply states: "Mr. Armour presented the accounts to the Board. The accounts are fairly self-explanatory." No further discussion on the accounts is minuted, which would be highly unusual if an unexplained deficit of £1,934 had been brought to the attention of the Board."

Mr. Armour cannot recall the occasion but believes that a cash deficiency does not really exist. "It's more a case of bad bookkeeping at a time when there was no treasurer," he said.

The QM's accounts should be ready within a fortnight and Mr. Ibrahem hopes to call an EGM to discuss the figures whenever this is possible.

Angus Macdonald

MEDICS

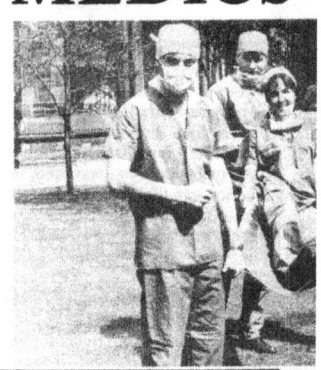

From *Glasgow University Guardian*, 19th May, 1983

Mondays', 'Motorhead' and 'The Fall' had all played over the previous few years, but, without the carrot of a guaranteed sell-out, Entertainments Convener Tim Laver had his work cut out for him. As flatmate and band mate, Tim and I were as thick as thieves, and our plan for rehabilitation partially focussed on the wider cultural changes that were happening outside the Unions doors.

The second 'Summer Of Love' (as it was lovingly known) was taking place over the country; the twin pillars of indie and rock 'n' roll were being demolished by dance and electronic music. Queen Margaret Union's competition was not so much the Barrowlands or other local venues; competition was happening in the middle of fields in the Scottish countryside as impromptu raves and sound systems (and the accompanying love of strange chemicals) drove students far away from the Union's doors. Early attempts to bring rave culture into Queen Margaret Union floundered, as the Friday disco gave way to dance parties, only a scant few were interested. By the time we hit December, things were starting to change, when Dafter Friday presented 'The Shamen' (possibly the country's best known dance act); we sold the place out; and it was comforting for us all to finally see that acid house had taken hold on the Ground Floor. The introduction of a new sound system the following January, and an accompanying free launch party, further saw the Union redevelop its identity as the local party-starter.

Of course, 1990 was the centenary year, and, despite the belt-tightening, we couldn't let it pass without some form of celebration. We corralled many past presidents into the Bute Hall for a centenary dinner, several of whom were not entirely pleased to see a male President at the top table, and, as the most recent female officer, I wisely passed speech duties onto Dianne. There was an equally awkward event at the Kelvingrove Museum, a Centenary Fashion Show, wherein various Board members took on catwalk duties to parade in front of an assembled crowd of friends and family as no one else would buy a ticket for such a thing. I do recall wearing both a 1930s tennis outfit and donning a Kaftan, whilst waving a bunch of fake flowers, which, given that I had newly shaved my head for charity, positioned me as some form of astral-projecting, transcendental nutcase.

There are of course many other tales to tell; the fall and rise and fall of the Labour Club on the Board of Management, the hopeless hilarity that always ensued whenever Social Convener Gordon Happer was present, Stephen Barret and Jake Scott's fight to get a disabled ramp constructed, the first time (and possibly last) Queen Margaret Union and Glasgow University Union made a joint speech on the first day of Freshers Week, the long-winded games of 'Alien War' that took place overnight throughout the building (much to the alarm of Mike and Allan, the Porters) and of course the year long fun with my much-loved fellow executive committee members Alison Rae and Kirsty Crawford (our hilarious 007-esque Executive photo still makes me chuckle).

It's always best to leave a place in a better condition than you found it, and by the time Jake Scott was ready to don the blue garb of office the following year, I felt that the Board of Management and staff could collectively claim exactly that. We were still going, and we had started to kick again as a venue and a Union to be reckoned with. If the current state of the Union is anything to go by, it is still doing exactly that.

(Above and overleaf)
The Centenary Celebration Fashion Show at Kelvingrove Museum

256

The Times They Are A-Changing

*Jake Scott
President 1991-1992*

Recalling time spent at Queen Margaret Union is actually an incredibly difficult thing to do. This is partly because much of it may have been hazed by alcohol, fazed by time and dazed by the sheer enjoyment of it all. There are simply too many happy memories to be able to tell them all. I loved the place. I was there for the Centenary Celebration, a fashion show held at the Kelvingrove Art Gallery with models selected from current members and a plethora of 'old' women, in the main, invited probably because they had not yet shuffled off this mortal coil. It was obviously a great reunion for many that attended but for the members at the time it grated with what we were allegedly about, the here and now, the future, a kind of deep need to be at the cutting edge of music trends with many competing to be the first to introduce friends to the next big thing and dropping them like a brick at the first sign of commercial success. Acknowledging Queen Margaret Union, the hub of all things new and trend setting, but also realising it was one hundred years old left some uneasy that there had been so many others before them. Although, some solace was found in a number of 'firsts' for which we had been recognised.

My earliest memory was climbing in through the third floor window to 'Dafter Friday' to avoid paying the five-pound admission charge in about 1985. An old school friend was at the University of Glasgow and had managed to secure the tenancy on one of the flats upon the roof, he had a number of 'contacts' which allowed him into the event to scale the stairs inside the building to the third floor and unlatch the window for a number of us to climb in. Roddy did eventually serve as a Board Member but for many years was only as a 'hack', I feel I should not give his full name for fear of incriminating him.

At the time Queen Margaret Union had an amazing reputation for live music and the long list of artists scheduled to appear or listed as having played in the past always struck me as akin to the list of bands appearing at the next Glastonbury Festival. It was quite clever marketing, as you wanted to go there to see one band with the romantic notion that it somehow connected you to all of them. Like Glastonbury, the list was more impressive each year. After a few trips to my friends flat on the roof, I found out that most of the concerts were run by students; booked, promoted, advertised, crewed and event managed by them. I had promoted a couple of small-scale events in my local village pub and hall and this knowledge inspired me to go to University, specifically the University of Glasgow.

As soon as I got to Glasgow I wanted to get involved with the running of Queen Margaret Union. It took me a couple of months from starting in October 1988 to first get involved with the Social Committee, which involved sitting on the door every Thursday night ensuring people signed in as guests properly and not as 'Batman' or any other such hilarious alias. After a couple of months I wanted more. I was told this had been necessary, as to be elected to the board required some sort of profile amongst the membership and proof of commitment by some sacrifice of oneself for the greater good of the Union. I was duly elected in March 1989 as an Ordinary Board Member. I went on to be a Campaigns Convener, Freshers' Week Convener and eventually President in 1991.

I was covering for the Entertainments Convener who was away for the summer when the Union secured 'Nirvana' and 'Extreme', both sell-outs, within a week of each other. I actually handed my phone 'hand set' to Souxie Sioux when she played with 'The Creatures' as well as showing numerous bands up to the dressing rooms upon their arrival. I had arrived, but suddenly it all stopped. Queen Margaret Union was under threat of closure and we had to comply with certain conditions for it to be allowed to continue to operate.

It was highly frustrating in some ways as just as soon as I became involved, revelations exposed a massive deficit in

1990 Queen Margaret Union Handbook Cover

Quodos at Cheesy Pop

the accounts. Members of staff left under a cloud and a new General Manager started to sort the mess out. The original plans for the Centenary were scaled down and for the next few years a variety of financial skeletons would fall out of closets or perhaps more accurately larders. Recent refurbishment of catering areas allegedly included strange deals where things such as the electrical wiring were 'leased' to us over an indefinite period of time.

In hindsight, it brought about a new era of co-operation and understanding between Queen Margaret Union and the 'powers that be' within the University of Glasgow, as well as with the other student bodies such as the Glasgow University Union, Students Representative Council and Glasgow University Athletics Club. We even set up a Freshers' Week Committee with equal say and funding for all the student bodies. During my first few years of involvement there was a culture of belligerence and rebellion, like an angst ridden rebellious teenager that huffed and puffed and argued about everything just for the sake of it. Now we had to negotiate with tact, had to work the system to get where we wanted. Instead of stamping our feet and being ignored, Queen Margaret Union began to seduce and be noticed.

I distinctly remember almost over night the Board of Management rising to the challenge of bringing well presented, researched and reasoned proposals to the Financial Management Committee and Board Meetings, with an excellent General Manager, Tony McConachie at the helm. The early nineties saw a surge in membership year after year due to a fantastically co-ordinated approach from all those involved in welcoming the new students and a realisation that catching them in the first year probably meant a loyal customer for four years. This was achieved by creative thinking rather than throwing money at problems. It is true that adversity is the mother of invention. In particular, I recall the centenary year Freshers' registration being scheduled in The Gilmore Hall right opposite the Glasgow University Union, so naturally their Board of Management assumed all the new students would simply cross the road for breakfast and duly sign on the dotted line as a member. However, whilst they were still tucked up in bed as the first new arrivals began trotting in we had forty Freshers' Helpers donning bright branded T-shirts extending a warm welcome and helping with bags all the way up University Avenue. At Queen Margaret Union they received a free cup of tea or coffee and were introduced to other new arrivals. By the time the Glasgow University Union had woken up and 'smelled the coffee' registration had closed up and Queen Margaret Union was full of new students.

The following year as President I managed to negotiate a donation of one thousand pints of beer from our Foster's rep the week before Freshers' Week and, as a complete surprise to the Glasgow University Union, announced this gift at the Principal's and President's Welcome speech in the Bute Hall, inviting all present back to the bar for a pint each. This again resulted in more feet heading up University Avenue rather than down it. On the one hand we became more proactive and creative in attracting membership and custom whilst on the other we had to become more efficient with expenses. I, with a couple of Board Members, actively pursued closing down 'known scams' such as the climbing through windows mentioned earlier, others included tightening ticket security to prevent forgeries, touting and reselling. This we did with dramatic effect by forging a current ticket in the Union on the day of a Board Meeting as proof of how easy it was to produce counterfeits along with a proposal to go to a more secure ticket printing company. The entertainments convener at the time was not best pleased owing to the financial implications for their budget.

A final memory that the financial management committee brings to mind was that I remember wanting to update the venue effect lighting as it had not been refurbished in about twenty years and consisted of about one thousand pin spots. I had seen these new 'state of the art' 'roboscans', a light with moving mirrors and four different 'gobos'. For that time they were quite stunning and were the very first 'intelligent' lights. At a cost of about two thousand pounds each I took a proposal to the committee to buy four which including fitting was about ten thousand pounds. After much deliberation they eventually allowed me the budget to buy one. I was devastated as they really are only effective in at least pairs and a lone scanning light would just look ridiculous. I decided to go ahead and get just the one. I was convinced they would see the error of their ways and allow me to add more on after it was installed. They did, but only in the next financial year. I had to suffer an entire year with a humiliating single scanner. It did have an effect though, some ten years later as a Venue Manager in England I attended a National Union of Students (NUS) entertainments convention and met a rather drunken entertainments manager who thanked me for buying that single light. He claimed he had been an entertainments officer at another union in Scotland in the early nineties. He had brought his entire union committee to see the light as the 'First Intelligent Light in Scotland' and it had persuaded them to allow him to buy a full set of four for his venue. So yet another first for Queen Margaret Union, and he even bought me a drink. Now if it is true I think that was worth a Centenary Celebration itself.

Logo for the 1990 Queen Margaret Union Handbook

Queen Margaret Union Board of Management 1990-1991

QMU "no confidence" vote crushed

REPORT: KIRSTY McCORMACK

The AGM of the Queen Margaret's Union on Friday 10th resulted in a clash with the QM board and Labour Club. After passing the minutes of last year's meeting, Simon MacFarlane put forward a motion to suspend standing orders with the intention of proposing a motion of no confidence in the Board of Management. There was a direct negative from the chair, Stuart Gosland, which was passed by the meeting. The AGM proceeded with reports from the President, convenors and auditors. The Honorary Treasurer's report was encouraging when it showed that the QM's debt has been reduced over the past year from £93,000 to £52,000.

The next point of contention occurred when Jake Scott, having taken over the chair, announced the election of the new ordinary board members. Simon MacFarlane complained that this was undemocratic and that it perpetuated "the board clique" as the availability of the posts was not properly advertised. The Labour Club then put forward two candidates and a vote took place. The three original candidates Raymond Donohue, Gerard Sennan and Peter Shea were re-elected.

The post of Honorary President went to Ronnie McDonald who is involved in the oil workers trade union. The two Honorary Vice-Presidential seats were taken by Iris Johnstone and Maria Fyfe, MP.

Under AOCB Ian McIntyre put forward a motion of no confidence in the board, on behalf of the Labour Club. A direct negative followed from Tim Laver. A open period ensued with empassioned speeches. When the motion was put to a vote it was overturned 56 to 12.

From *Glasgow University Guardian* 1991

265

QM EVACUATED DURING CONCERT

'That Petral Emotion' were rudely interrupted at their gig in the QM Union on Saturday 6th October by a suspected gas leak discovered on the first floor by a member of staff. QM President Stuart Gosland personally took a look, or rather a smell before the decision was taken to phone the fire-brigade and evacuate the building. Gosland commented, 'Everyone co-operated fully'. Apparently cleaning fluid had become overheated in its position under some machinery and had given off the odious, but harmless, smell. Within half an hour, the doors were back open and the band came on and finished their set.

From *Glasgow University Guardian* 1990-1991

Goodbye Mr MacKenzie, Hello Mr McConachie

Tim Laver
Entertainments Convenor
1990-1991

As a young fresher escaping from rural life to the big city, two gigs in my first term at the University of Glasgow shaped the rest of my life. The first was Transvision Vamp. As Wendy James shook her peroxide hair to yet another rendition of 'I Want Your Love' a Glasgow University Union helper came up to me on the balcony. "You know what, you should join the GU and play rugby, you don't want to join the QM," he slurred, "It's full of poofs, women and freaks with long hair that listen to odd music". It was the best bit of advice I ever ignored and I joined Queen Margaret Union the very next day. The second gig was part of that year's Christmas all night club, Dafter Friday. I stood expectantly at the front of the stage for headliners Pop Will Eat Itself to appear. "Where's the drum kit?" I asked the girl next to me. "Just watch" she replied. Suddenly a cut up of movie themes, sirens and sampled dialogue broke out of the PA and the band themselves bounded on stage. It was a revelation; you could have a laugh as a band. It was possible to take the Osmonds, the Twilight Zone, and Mel and Kim and bung it all into a mix, jump around half rapping over backing tracks, forget about conventional line ups and it could still be fabulous. My wonder was caught for eternity during a split second of the band's 'Can U Dig It' video that featured crowd shots from Queen Margaret Union. That holiday I blew my housing benefit cheque, bought a four track, plugged in my Casio SK1 keyboard and formed my first band.

At the tail end of the eighties Queen Margaret Union was in a rough and ready state, the Biko Bar was decked in comfy red seats that spilled stuffing at every seam. The décor matched the drink of choice, Snake Bite and Blackcurrant; and the 'cat weasel' king of the bar Graham Bell held court in 'Wasters' Corner' as the 'Defender' games machine chirped in the other. Most importantly Jim (who lends his name to the bar) was very much alive and pouring pints along with the rest of the Scott clan; Pat, Jessie, Catherine and Bryan. You could always tell when their caustic wit had annoyed one of the regulars as the B-side to Renegade Soundwaves' 'Kray Twins would come on the juke box and cries of "That's dain' ma heid in" would come from the staff.

It seemed at the time that 'Goodbye Mr MacKenzie' played every other month and that almost everyone had blagged at least one of their T-shirts for free. Queen Margaret Union became my home away from home. Michael the porter soon knew us all by name and Alan 'the master' Campbell, his cohabitant in the box would amaze us with his quiz knowledge and ability to cut anyone down to size with his quips. One of Alan's finest moments was a thirty-minute tirade against the television host of Scottish Television's pub quiz, who had cheated his team out of a place in the final. The porters truly were the heart of the Union and passed down legends and tales from generation to generation. Such as the riot during the Sigue Sigue Sputnik gig that had more glass thrown, and more policemen called, on each telling.

By the summer I became involved in the back stage entertainments crew and later got elected onto the Board. Band after band came to play and with many quality support acts too. The Happy Mondays played one of their first Glasgow gigs supporting James and at the end of their set everyone met up with people watching at the other end of the stage to ask if that bloke with the maracas actually did anything. The Pixies were the biggest gig of that time and the venue was bursting at the seams. Though less witnessed, possibly the most memorable set of the year was by a group from Belgium called Front 242. They turned the stage into a cage of lights and drum pads and bounded around in night vision goggles and head mounted laser lights. It was a Thursday night, half empty, but was the most exciting set I have ever seen and the band's only Scottish date. They looked like lost cyclists as they crossed the foyer,

Who is the Daftest of them all?

Craig Reece looks at end of term union entertainment

ITS nearly time for exams so that means it's time to decide how to party away the end of term. The choice, of course, is yours but here's the facts so far on (possibly) the craziest night of the year.

Daft Friday at the GUU, the traditional favourite, is selling fast, with a few tickets still left. They cost £40 for a double ticket from the GUU itself, but you'll have to hurry. There have been few details yet of the night's events, with the surprise theme being revealed on the night.

There's a twelve hour-long party kicking off at 8pm and rounding off early on Saturday morning with a Champagne Breakfast (for those still alive). So if you've not got a ticket you'll have to either start running down University Avenue, or find a lovely (preferably) lad or lass seeking a partner. Good luck either way!

The QM's Dafter Friday meanwhile, is a little clearer in its intentions for the evening, if not quite so popular so far. Tickets this year are priced at £12 (£3 less than last year). Sales so far have been low but President Sandy Cormie puts that down to students waiting to see the line-up of bands for the event before putting their hands in their pockets. The line-up is as yet undecided, but an announcement will be made later this week.

What can we expect to see down at the QM this year then? There will be a cabaret at the beginning of the evening with between two and three slots including "The Man" persuasionist with an entirely new show. This will go on until around midnight when the bands will play, followed into the small hours and beyond by various DJs.

The Food Factory, Jim's Bar and the Games Room all open throughout the night with special events throughout including Karaoke in Jim's and a disco on the second floor.

Tickets are on sale now from the Porter's Box. The date of both Daft and Dafter Friday is the 17th of December.

Alternatives for the evening include being sad and spending the time in Curler's, going out on the pull to the Volcano or getting a carry-out and watching "The Word". Pretty bleak eh? Don't you suppose you should have a night out at the Union then? Go on, show us how Daft you really can be!

From *Glasgow University Guardian* in early 1990s

Queen Margaret Union Board of Management 1989-1990

Queen Margaret Union Board of Management 1993-1994

but on stage they were like the cast of Alien coming out of the mist. When the peroxide quartet Birdland came to play, the entertainments crew were given the responsibility of handing out an exclusive vinyl record to every member of the audience. Rather bored we decided to start signing a few and made out to folk that they were so lucky to get one of the special, exclusive signed ones. The names got more ridiculous as the night went on. Since then there have been several occasions at parties when the story has been recounted and someone's face falls, especially the collector who had bought one at premium price at a Glasgow record fair.

Behind the scenes Queen Margaret Union was in crisis with spiralling debts. Without a radical shake up and support from the University of Glasgow it was going to close. It needed a President who was single minded, confident and 'bolshie' enough and in Dianne 'Danny' Wallace it got one. Over that summer a series of meetings guaranteed the continued existence of Queen Margaret Union. The University put in place strict financial controls upon the union in exchange for underwriting the debt. A new General Manager was needed and Danny and company decided to appoint out with the usual breed of student union manager choosing instead a candidate with experience in the hospitality industry. The choice would secure and shape our future. In Tony McConachie, or 'Mr. Mac', the Union found a dedicated, ambitious and commercially aware pair of hands. Changes came thick and fast, Queen Margaret Union regained control of the catering facilities and the games room, that had been leased out to external companies for a fraction of the income they could generate, and 'wee Michelle' got a variety of new lines into the shop. Most importantly the Food Factory got a pizza oven and Rab's legendary pizzas were born. With qualities unlike any other pizza tried before or since, they became a profitable hit and an institution.

Despite a ridiculously long commute Mr. Mac was always in early and away late getting a feel for all the aspects of the Union. Ever patient with the students and explaining honestly and clearly to the Board of Management what needed to be done and the choices that needed to be made. Some of the choices weren't easy and obviously times were uncertain for the staff but new relationships were built and terms and conditions agreed. Mr. Mac did once confess that if he'd know the state Queen Margaret Union was in before he was appointed and the battles that needed to be fought he might have passed on the offer.

After the year of crisis we again struck lucky with the choice of next President, Stuart Buchanan (although he will always be Gonzo to those who were there before the surname change). Queen Margaret Union needed to update its image and with an almost unhealthy obsession with 'Mute' and 'Factory' records, Stuart spearheaded the rebranding. The launch began in Fresher's Week with a very 1990's colour scheme of 'Day Glo' orange on black. Radiation symbols emblazoned with the new Queen Margaret Union logo appeared on giant posters, flyers, handbooks and all other publicity and publications. The Fresher's Helpers' T-shirts surprisingly became a much sought after fashion item. It worked, the membership numbers increased dramatically and the bar and Food Factory were rammed. In trying to recount the details of the re-branding for this article, everyone I asked had fond memories of the associated slogan as a truly clever play on words. No one could quite remember what it was. Publicity Convenor Fiona Pollard was the one with a preserved copy of the handbook and 'highly active' was the answer, to which we all commented disappointedly "Oh I thought it was better than that". Simpler times the early 1990's it seems. The Freshers' Week branding task was to fall to me the following year and moving the concept on, the logo became the heart of an atomic star with the tongue in cheek slogan 'Get a Life', widely used as an insult at the time.

Having been Publicity Convener from 1989-1990 I must admit a warm affection for the two letters 'Q' and 'M' written in a chalky scratchy font. The job of union publicity was far more a labour of love than it is now, as this was still a pre-desk top publishing era. Posters were a combination of cut out photocopies, magazines and pencil rubbed lettraset. You had to cope with the feeling of frustration when you realised you didn't have another 'S' in white lettraset in the required size and had to possess a steady hand to construct a new one out

Cover of 1992 Queen Margaret Union Handbook

Bomb scare at QMU

Lara Sanchez

QUEEN MARGARET Union was evacuated during its peak business time last Wednesday after an anonymous phone call at 1pm suggested the existence of a bomb in the building to Union staff.

Lizzy Toon, QMU President, informed the police of the scare only minutes after receiving the call. Police then advised Ms Toon to evacuate the premises immediately.

Students and staff were warned by the union's alarm and a tannoy announcement to leave the building. Despite most of the occupants being concentrated in the Food Factory and Jim's Bar areas, the evacuation took place in a swift but relaxed manner.

Once gathered outside, Ms Toon and the Union's General Manager informed students and staff that access to the building would remain evacuated for half an hour.

There is no firm evidence as to the identity of the caller. A QMU Board source has suggested to *Guardian* that the call may have been linked to events which occured at a Sepultura concert on Sunday November 29th. Many believe that troubles over the sale of unauthorised paraphernalia for the band at the concert may be one of the reasons for the scare. Other sources within the Union believed the call to be simple 'crank call'.

Two police officers arrived within minutes of the announcement and checked the security of the building. Meanwhile, some of the students outside waited patiently as they had to go back into the building for their food, although others decided to take their lunches outside.

The general manager informed that refunds on the food would not be available as it was impossible for the staff to determine how many people had lost their food. Access to the building was finally allowed in less than an hour.

Ms Toon expressed concern over the incident as, being lunch time, it represented a significant disruption and loss of money for the Union.

From *Glasgow University Guardian*.

RENEGADE COMMUNICATIONS
presents

NIRVANA

plus support

**LIVE AT QUEEN MARGARET UNION
GLASGOW UNIVERSITY**
on SATURDAY, 30th NOVEMBER, 1991
Doors open at 8.00 p.m.

Ticket £6.00
in advance   N°   486
(Subject to booking fee)

Management reserves the right to refuse admission
Over 18's   Entry according to reciprocity

The infamous ticket from the Nirvana gig

of other letter parts. You had to be inventive, have plenty of pritstick and be able to blag several photocopy cards off Enid in the office. One of the jobs that took the most planning was blowing up a giant poster of 'Mark E. Smith' from a single A5 sheet to multiple stitched together pages of A3, that filled the front common room windows to announce the headliners of that year's Dafter Friday. People actually excitedly stopped and pointed, as back in 1990 The Fall were riding the crest of their popularity. The poster that I remember most fondly was that for the Red Hot Chili Peppers. It featured a background created by dragging a sheet of lettraset across a photocopier as it scanned. Printed, of course, on to day-glo paper it just summed up their frantic energy and I was chuffed when the copy in the dressing room was carefully taken down, rolled up and pocketed by the band.

From being a member of back stage crew and publicity convenor I graduated to Entertainments Convenor in the year 1990–1991. As it turned out I became the last Convenor to bag a free 'Goodbye Mr McKenzie' T-Shirt and the first not to book them (I sometimes wonder if this may have had a butterfly effect on Shirley Manson moving on to form Garbage and Big John to play with Nirvana). Entertainments at Queen Margaret Union had a great reputation built upon the varied line up of bands that played each term, although for a number of years it was having to be subsidised by the bar profits. The thrice-weekly discos were under performing and a shake up was needed including the moving on of the wistful indie DJ Precious (who unless he was a doppelganger later found more success as the leader of Belle & Sebastian). Still very much alternative, but less obscure playlists built up the numbers so that the weekend truly began on Thursday. DJ's Stu, Gav and Goofy kept the goths two stepping, the ska kids skipping, the grebos frugging, the Belgium new beat fans punching, the indie kids swaying and the ravers building boxes of varying sizes. There were definite 'QM anthems' and you could always guarantee Debaser by the Pixies, Welcome to Paradise by Front 242, Def Con 1 by the Poppies, Personal Jesus by Depeche Mode and Primal Scream's Loaded at some point in the evening. With busier discos came the opportunity to take chances on bigger bands and probably my biggest coup was getting The Shamen in to not only headline Dafter Friday, but bring in their whole Pro-Gen experience with DJs, lightshows and projections. This didn't make me especially popular with other Scottish promoters who had been hoping to get them signed up for the Barrowlands. As my aim wasn't a job in the music industry, I wasn't worried about my popularity with other promoters and wasn't prepared to tie the Union to just one promotions company.

That year we also ended exclusivity and offered the use of the venue as a hired hall - we would staff it, sell tickets and help promote gigs for a guaranteed fixed fee. This paved the way for the hiring of Queen Margaret Union the year after my term of office by those promoting a little band called Nirvana. Although no longer Entertainments Convenor at the time, people are always impressed when I say I got to meet Kurt Cobain, however that credibility somewhat fades when it is revealed that he simply complemented the "fine array of snacks" I delivered on a tray into the dressing room.

My worst day as convenor came when ex-President Danny got married to John who was the head of our stage crew, though not because it broke many a heart. The wedding fell on the same day as Queen Margaret Union was hosting a sold out gig by Jesus Jones and so we had to hire in a crew from Glasgow's premiere live music venue. As they were erecting the safety barriers I pointed out to them that this was not the way they should be set up but was shouted down and told not to question the world famous crew of the 'premier music venue of Glasgow'. It was a battle I should have fought harder as the barrier gave way mid set and the crew, bouncers and Board Members had to jump in to hold it up so the show could continue.

When we put on That Petrol Emotion, I had to make my own 'big decision' and evacuate the entire building mid set as an odour of gas worked its way down from the upper floors. Front man Steve Mack did the announcement and mingled with the good-natured crowd outside. Trying to find the source of the leak the two on-duty Board Members had a heart-stopping moment when on entering the Food Factory the pilot light of the oven was spotted and they tanked it down to the foyer only to find out that the source turned out to be a detergent bottle left on top of the bar's automatic glass washer.

Another intense night was when my predecessor Ronan booked the legendary reggae and thrash metal group Bad Brains. The gig itself went off spectacularly well. However a sizeable crowd of 'crusties' besieged Queen Margaret Union demanding to get in. Looking like the cast of Doomsday the crowd started testing all the fire exits and the resolve of our bouncers. Any fears of a post apocalyptic style stand off ended when in frustration one of them decided to 'pelt' the bouncers by taking off and throwing his wellies. Big Yanis deftly caught them and locked the offending footwear inside.

The biggest diva we had come play was Siouxie Sioux when she visited with The Creatures. She insisted that the entire foyer be cleared not only of punters but of all staff who had to wait on the turn in the stairs so she could not be viewed walking to the stage. Her companion's electronic drums almost take the prize for most penetrating bass. This record was held by the industrial band Nitzer Ebb, who managed to cause all the bottles and glasses on the back wall of the downstairs bar to fly off the shelves; even the stoical bar hand Catherine had to cower for safety. Conversely, the nicest people to ever come play were Alien Sex Fiend, who ensured everyone on the crew got freebies and spent an hour painstakingly illustrating the visitor's book with intricate drawings of skeletons and gravestones containing all their signatures. The singer, Nick Fiend, was the sweetest of guys. So it was a revelation to see him as a man possessed on stage. At the end of the set he was led off by a mock psychiatric nurse to shuffle across the foyer in a zombie like trance. Waiting for the lift he turned his head tipped me a wink and quietly said "I'm buggered if I came all the way up the M6 just for an hour", dropped his head, shuffled back across the foyer and got the band to play another hour-long set. "He's totally out of it, man!", one excited Goth exclaimed to me as the band went back on.

My favourite page of the guest book, which I kept for my year, was not Mr. Fiend's, nor Paul Weller's, the Shamen's, Jesus Jones', Pop Will Eat Itself's or any of the other bands that played during the year. It is the one from Edwyn Collins because as a home coming gig his family came to see him play. So he also got his mum to sign it too; "All the best, Mrs Collins".

After my stint as Entertainments Convenor and Stuart's stint as President came to an end, we both served as Graduate Board Members. The Board of Management at the time wanted to take on the clubs in town at their own game. They wanted pure techno nights with named DJs and decided this would make the students come flocking. Us two "old hacks" looked at each other and said, "If you want to get students into the discos, what you really need to do is to throw credibility aside and go for the ultimate cheese". Our suggestions were met with a less than warm reception and the discos went totally techno. A year and a bit later, I met one of the same Board Members, who enthused that they had come up with this brand new concept that had totally revitalised the discos and got folk flooding back in. I enquired what it was. "Cheesy Pop!" came the reply.

The 'QM' stage holds fond memories for me for two other important reasons. Most importantly it was where, sixteen years ago to the month of writing, I shared my first kiss with my wife and soul mate Mairi. Secondly, it was the location of my first ever gig. Both of these events have shaped my life right up to this day and both almost never happened. The kiss was due to an overdue video needing to go back to Blockbusters and the gig due to a bloke called Mark Chapman. Fortunately, he was less dramatic than his namesake, (despite the way he twirled his zippo lighter). He stole our backing tape of samples and beats, but was caught just in time - scissors in hand. Megaphone in one hand, toy electronic drumsticks in the other and for some reason climbing on a step ladder, I (as Tim-Boy-L) joined DJ-SG and Rod Prinz D on stage. At first dumbfounding and then entertaining the assembled crowd, we hit bits of metal, crooned, rapped and somehow obtained a good review in the University newspaper and were invited onto Glasgow University Student Television. KEN (named after Craig from Bros) became a bit of a cult hit and with MC DAWG joining on bass and the dancing SKW security guards Russ and Gav, we went on to lead the West End answer to

Madchester with a sold out event at Queen Margaret Union called 'Hillhead Rave Off'.

To help bolster the line up of an end of spring term band fest, I along with other assorted members of the Entertainments crew, the President and regulars of the Biko bar decided to form an eight hour band. The appropriately called MESS formed, rehearsed four tracks and played the gig with a cast of thousands hitting percussion, dancing to the backing beats, and yeehawing. I'll never forget the guy from the next band who came up excitedly, asking how long we'd been going as it was "the most amazing and psychedelic set he'd ever seen". When I told him, he said, rather angrily, "No...really. I might as well just give up".

A few years later a chance conversation with the then Freshers' Week Convenor revealed they were short of a support for Pop Will Eat Itself, so I went away put together some tunes on the four track (including a Grange Hill sampling rant against censorship that compared PE teacher Bullet Baxter to Jesus, which in the early 1990s made perfect sense) and brought the tape up to the Convenors Office. Then, in one of my wisest moves, I made my excuses and left, coming back later to find it playing on the stereo and the band booked. Despite almost failing to breathe during the first track due to an allergy to smoke fluid, the set went down incredibly well and Clint Mansell of Pop Will Eat Itself watched us from the balcony before telling us later backstage that we were "bloody good". Sometime after, I was accosted by a girl on the dance floor at Mish Mash who said, "I know you. You played my Fresher's Week. It was great, that's why I joined the QM". As Mr Miyagi probably never said, "Things always come full circle".

BEAT THE CLOCK

QMU OFF-SALES.
OPEN AFTER ALL THE OFFIES
HAVE SHUT

From the QMU Handbook in the 1990s

Heart of the Nineties

Jennifer Paterson
President 1994-1995

In September 1991 I was bombarded with information during Freshers' Week about the University of Glasgow, the city, clubs, societies, where to go, what to do, but there was only one big decision to make and it concerned the student unions. The choice was between the beautiful old building at the foot of the hill or the 1960s concrete monstrosity, which was full of dyed hair, stripy tights and lots of music. The concrete won.

It wasn't thanks to the talk by both Presidents at the Freshers' Address, the aesthetics or even the rumours that rippled through the new fresh faced recruits about the popular Glasgow University Union or the smaller Queen Margaret Union. There was a gritty excitement about that modernist building at the top of the hill. Queen Margaret Union - different and alternative to where you had just come from, a bit of street cred, heightened by the first year hysteria and the fact that you were new ensured that you found friends wanting to hang out there too.

Even though I didn't quite feel alternative enough to be a Queen Margaret Union type, that's where I landed in 1991. One year on I was a fully-fledged Board Member and Freshers Week Helper, two years after that I was President. It became the love of my life for a few years, in what many people term the best days of your life.

The awe of walking in and the sights, sounds and smells of alternative students - goths, indie kids, crusties, freshers, older students all present as Freshers' Week Helpers, and numerous others that were part of the woodwork. The Wonderstuff, Rage Against The Machine, The Smiths, pints of beer and cider and black, the dings, dongs and bleeps permeating from the Games Room and a bar and disco that smelled of years of stale booze, not to mention the haze of cigarette smoke spilling down the stairs from the Biko Bar. All of this with the intermittent interruption of the tannoy announcing that there was a phone call for Mr McConachie or the Executive Committee, or that someone was wanted down by the Porter's Box.

The initial excitement of what your newfound social playground could offer was intense. Whether spending a day sitting in the Food Factory, despite the bright pink paintwork, with its salad bar and pizza oven and cappuccino machine that never worked, or a pint in the Biko Bar, where you might be entertained by a local band or a pop quiz or even get to play bingo on a weekday evening, there was always something going on. Of course there was the sense of wanting to be there all the time, which did affect many a student's (and especially Board Members) attendance at lectures.

Many people became involved in the running of the Union through various outlets, especially the Entertainments committee; helping with sign-ins on a club or band night, making sandwiches for the crew or buying the rider for a band upped the excitement stakes. Through the mid 1990s, bands like Spiritualised, Belly, Pop Will Eat Itself and Inspiral Carpets played at the Queen Margaret Union. Not as many as today (having full time entertainments staff allows for more frequent gigs), but we were one of the venues to play in Glasgow when a band was on the verge of breaking into the charts. One of the highlights of those early days was working on the Nirvana gig just when *Smells Like Teen Spirit* exploded onto the scene.

As the decade progressed so did the hold Queen Margaret Union had on my peers and I. Becoming a Board Member, spending more and more time within its walls (occasionally this even meant a night sleeping in the board flat), caring about what was happening and watching changes within the student population happen; it all became your reason for being there. The musical tastes of students shifting from Indie to Britpop and Clubbing Culture, and with it the shift

Display from the 1994 Bazaar celebrating 100 years since the first woman graduate

The 1994 Bazaar celebrating 100 years since the first woman graduate

union update
By Alistair McGhie

THERE'S SOME people on the grass. They think it's all over. It almost is. As the sun has appeared at last, the academic year is fading fast. The exams draw to a close, the summer plans come out of the wardrobe, and the Unions pick up the debris from the year past.
I.E. - Nothing is happening at the Unions. David McGhie, it. So did Sandy Cormie. This is reflected in the fact that the Basement Bar Season has come to a premature halt, and Marcella Detroit has pulled out of performing at the QM (50 tickets sold).
While the QM was pleased with the hypnotist and Bar Fly which drove people up the wall, the GUU has decided to sponsor a tree in Pollok Park. (Branching out, eh?) It's a gesture in the fight against the motorway which is splitting the southside.

The QM AGM (could almost be a techno band) saw Jim Wharvell chosen as the Honorary President, while Lady Fraser and Johnny Ball stay on as VP's. These honorary posts don't really mean much; they're just allowed to turn up to board meetings, if they want!?!
Solar is due on the 25th June, while the 75 pence a pint promotion is going down well!

The most dramatic happening at the Union has been the arrival of Planet 24 TV company which was looking for trainee producers for The Word and The Big Breakfast. The debates chamber saw the Huffty's and Terry's of the future sook for a job; but with 2 being chosen from 1000 around Britain, it will take a lot more than sooking to get the job. The in/out board has been a 'big hit', and Union publicity is due for overdrive with a new scanner.
You see? Nothing's happening.

The Unions have limited opening hours throughout the summer, but if you want to pop in, I'm sure they'd be glad to see you.
The waffle's dying out.

It really is all over.

From *Glasgow University Guardian* updating on the Unions

284

of what night was busy in the Union, most notably the death of alternative Saturdays to the rise of Thursday night, Cheesy Pop, and DJ Toast (who is still there now, and is a Glasgow institution).

Gradually as time went by, the Union became more financially stable and during Sandy Cormie's Presidency in 1993 we had our first year of being in the black. A chance to improve the Union surroundings and reinvest in what was becoming quite a run-down building meant new chairs and a lick of paint in what was now Jim's Bar (renamed from the Biko Bar after long-time bar staff member Jim sadly passed away). We refitted the shop, the Games Room and eventually the Common Room (now Qudos). Initial designs and interest from two different architect firms in 1995, allowed Stephen Rixon, President the following year, to secure a loan, realising the dream of finally being able to refurbish one of the most seminal stages and clubs in Glasgow.

Despite Queen Margaret Union being primarily a social Union, many political parties (those sitting more left of centre) used it as their meeting place. We even had our very own campaigns convener who focused on issues such as the supply of baby milk in the third world and the anti-Nestlé campaign, which saw the Queen Margaret Union boycotting all Nestlé products – a slightly trickier task than at first thought with the realisation of how many companies Nestlé actually ran.

It was also time to try and persuade students to campaign against student grant cuts and protest about the introduction of loans. Sadly many students no longer received a grant and apathy set in with regards to their passion about it, despite efforts by students such as Aamer Anwar (now a prominent anti-racism lawyer and campaigner), and Board Members such as Andrew White (now a Labour councillor). What attracted students attention more were campaigns for the Rector of the University of Glasgow, with the lure of celebrities such as Pat from Eastenders and Jonny Ball hanging out in the Food Factory.

It took becoming an Executive office bearer to realise the responsibility and what an organisation the Queen Margaret Union was. Not only were you a figurehead for students, you were running a business with nearly one hundred employees whilst staying true to your values, making the Queen Margaret Union the most welcoming and social place at the University and trying to achieve your election promises. The little things pale into insignificance when you're making decisions over beer suppliers, licenses and pay rises. A change of Executive, and its priorities, every year make it a fascinating yet sometimes frustrating place to work.

Although the Queen Margaret Union is often thought of as the concrete 1960s building, it is the people that have really made the Union, and its memories and stories, what it is now. That's why it is in such a unique position within the UK University setting, and perhaps why it still has a hold on you fifteen years on.

Space late cancellation prompts legal action

Paul O'Hare

The Queen Margaret Union has taken unprecedented legal action against Liverpool chart toppers Space following the band's withdrawal from the Big Kahuna, in breach of contract, one week before the show was due to go ahead in order to appear on Channel Four's TFI Friday.

The chain of events which led to much confusion among the Union's annual showpiece event, was unforseen when the band were contracted to headline the event in mid November. According to one of the evening's main organisers, Ben Martin, all the indications were that the band were 'completely up for the gig'. Problems began to surface on Friday 5th December when the band's agents indicated that they were unsure as to whether or not they could play, following receipt of an offer to appear on TFI Friday on the same evening.

Martin believes, however, that the band could easily have played both gigs given that TFI is recorded on the Friday afternoon leaving sufficient time to travel to Glasgow on the last shuttle from Heathrow and remains adamant that the QMU 'totally accommodated the band to meet their needs in light of the changed circumstances'. The revised plans included arrangements to transport Space's equipment to the QMU, clear Qudos for a soundcheck and finally for the band to be on stage around 11pm, which was later than originally arranged. Despite initial doubts, the band agreed to do both gigs and a potential crisis appeared to have been averted.

One week later and seven days before the event, on Friday 12th December, the Union received a fax from the band's management stating that they would be unable to play due to their appearance on TFI Friday promoting a forthcoming single.

The breach of contract that this decision signalled – alongside the insufficient time afforded to organisers to book a replacement – jeopardised the whole event, as despite the claims of the band's management in a recent edition of New Musical Express, that Space were 'only part of the attractions', it was stated in the contract that Space alone would headline the night and this was borne out in posters promoting the event which were dominated by the band's logo.

QMU President Sam Phillips, talking to Guardian, claimed: 'The Union has been left really sad at the inconsiderate manner in which the we have been treated by the band.' Phillips added that the QMU felt they were left with little choice other than to take legal action, whilst conceding that financial compensation will do little to correct the reality that the Space's withdrawal 'ruined our Christmas party'.

Fuelling the Union's despondency that the band could have managed both TFI and the Big Kahuna are strong rumours suggesting that the band stayed on after the programme to attend a party held by the show's host, Chris Evans. Although this rumour has been unconfirmed, the broadcaster and DJ is believed to have hosted a party to coincide with his takeover of Virgin Radio and the last of his weekly shows before Christmas and it is no secret that the Space have been friendly with Evans since he championed their debut hit single, Female of the Species, when it was released in May 1996.

A spokesman for Space told Guardian that the management were refusing to comment on any matters relating to the Big Kahuna and the impending legal action.

The extent of the Union's claim will become more apparent this Friday (23rd) when the Finance Committee will attempt to arrive at an estimate of how much the Union lost in ticket sales. Given that only a few hundred tickets had been sold prior to the event and that the vast majority are sold in the last week of term and on the day itself, Phillips believes that the Unions losses could be anything between £10,000 to £22,000, but concedes that 'the Union will never really know how many tickets would have been sold.

Indeed the decision to give the tickets away free could detrimentally effect any forthcoming litigation as it could be claimed that the QM failed to take sufficient steps to cut their losses by not charging any admission to the event which went ahead without Space on Friday 19th December. The picture will become clearer in the next few weeks. However, at present the Union continues to feel cheated at the group's actions, for as Ben Martin stressed: 'Most bands fell they can walk all over student unions. This is not the first time this has happened to the QMU or, I'm sure, a student union and I doubt it will be the last.'

SPACE JAM!

SPACE have announced details of their new album, 'Tin Planet', plus a UK tour starting this month. The album is released by ... st Records on March 9.

Space singer Tommy Scott said: "I feel a lot more at ease with this record than anything we've ever done before. It's still us, totally schizophrenic – one minute I'm Noel ... oward, next it's like '70s disco. And there's a song of Jamie's called 'Piggies' which sounds like being shot through a cannon, backwards!

He added: "There's stuff on 'Spiders' (their 1996 debut album) I can't even listen to now, but it was our first record and we're a better band now."

The tracklisting for 'Tin Planet', which includes current single 'Avenging Angels', is: 'Begin Again', 'Tom Jones', 'One O'Clock', 'Be There', 'The Man', 'Elvis', 'Unluckiest Man', 'Piggies', 'Bad Days', 'There's No You' and 'Disco Dolly'.

'Tom Jones', which is likely to be the next single, features a duet between Tommy Scott and Cerys Matthews from Catatonia.

Intriguingly, the tracks are numbered from one to 14, but with 13 missing.

A spokesman explained: "It's a track for luck. There's a track there, but it's a track of silence. Space are very superstitious, as Stevie Wonder would say."

Prior to the album release, the band play (including North Wales Conference Centre (26), Glasgow Barrowlands (30), Stoke Royal (31), Manchester Academy (February 2), Newport Centre (3), London Shepherd's Bush Empire (4) and Ipswich Corn Exchange (5). Support has yet to be announced.

Meanwhile, Space are facing legal action after pulling out of Glasgow University's Christmas Ball in order to appear on TFI Friday. The band had been booked by the Glasgow's Queen Margaret Student Union to headline the festive bash on December 19. They pulled the show on December 12. Organisers say that £20 tickets for the 1,500-capacity event had almost sold out. A student union spokesman told NME the band initially thought they could do both TFI and the ball on the same night, but that they changed their minds.

He said: "It is clearly a breach of contract and we will be taking them to court. They wrecked our one big night of the year. It's a rotten thing to do to us before Christmas."

However, a spokesman for Space's management told NME: "We're sad that we have had to cancel a gig, but it's a situation that couldn't be resolved. We tried a number of possible resolutions. But it was a university Christmas ball, not a Space show. The band were only part of the attractions. However, it's a disappointing situation and they're sorry for those affected."

● See Space feature, pages 24 & 25.

Local press coverage of UK group Space pulling out of a gig at QMU

Outside the old bar in Queen Margaret Union

Former President Craig Egdell on the top of the Union

Words of Wisdom

Stephen Rixon
President 1995-1996

As the nineties were in full swing and the Queen Margaret Union was financially better off, I found myself elected as President, having served for a full year as Honorary Secretary. This was achieved either because of the 'hard work' and countless hours I put in on the Executive Committee or possibly down to the fact I had secured a CD Jukebox when I was Games Convener.

On my election night, in the days before Glasgow's notoriously strict licensing laws came into force, I got so smashed on 'K' cider at only 50p a bottle that I fell asleep between the main entrance doors, thus providing members with the opportunity to give the President a swift kick on their way out – a worthwhile service that should be repeated annually.

As my tenure began I seemed to get through the long summer months unscathed despite reaching a level of frustration with the other student bodies on campus at the time that would be difficult to convey. Afterwards, I resolved to either befriend all of them or simply have them assassinated. Unfortunately, I had to settle for the former option.

For a number of years, the Queen Margaret Union had been a member of Northern Services, a buying consortium of various Student Unions from around Scotland. This allowed us to obtain better prices for our respective members. I managed to get myself elected as President of this organisation as well, much to the chagrin of our friends across in Edinburgh who, as it was one of the rare times that all the Glasgow student bodies voted the same way, were politically outmanoeuvred for the first time in a long while.

The first serious challenge in most Presidents' way is always Freshers' Week. I believe I managed to get through the period with only twelve hours sleep; not so good for an 'old man', as I was constantly reminded by my so-called peers. There were many more challenges along the way, especially during our Board Meetings. I think I must have set a record for the greatest number of 'challenges to the Chair', mostly from people who seemed to have a difficulty in accepting that I was usually always right. Others followed suit as it became a bit of a ritual (and often only for a laugh).

It was also during this time that we got a handle on the notion that the Queen Margaret Union was running really well financially. This presented a very different set of problems. With the General Manager's contract approaching its end, I managed to persuade the man who had helped keep our doors open, Anthony McConachie to agree to a lengthy contract, or perhaps he got me to agree to it, either way it was a good deal for the Queen Margaret Union.

The elections for University of Glasgow Rector stand out as well, as Ken McCallum, (a former Honorary Secretary) had managed to get Johnny Ball to stand for re-election to the coveted position. He was seen as a 'QM Candidate' and it was thought to be a good thing if he won again. Richard Wilson, however, won the hearts of the student body. I do remember however that Johnny Ball was in Jim's Bar toilets after the results were announced only to discover that the loo roll had run out. Let's just say he found a creative use for his flyers.

I remember getting so upset when the 'restructuring committee' (formed to sort out the Board of Management) managed to get the Board to ban me from attending that I actually made a future President burst into tears. I was right in what I said, but it was far from my proudest moment. The Committee was a complete waste of time and I struggle to remember any significant output from around seven months of closed meetings.

It was also this year that we got to change the Common Room. It was a Goth-haunted relic and badly needed to be updated. Unfortunately, as we discovered, it was not going to be cheap either. We got some people to have a look at it and were told we were going to need a quarter of a million pounds. I diligently set about composing a proposal to send off to the University of Glasgow Court. Our Honorary Treasurer, Terry Murphy, added the numbers and thankfully the University Court agreed to lend us the money, interest-free, over ten years. To this day it's still the best deal I've ever been a part of.

One moment of panic that stands out from those twelve months or so was when I got the news that our Honorary Secretary had not renewed our Thursday night late-licence. A potential disaster was thankfully averted by simply moving Cheesy Pop (our weekly club night that does exactly what it says on the tin) to a Friday evening instead. Unfortunately it all happened in the run up to the Annual General Election and the Honorary Secretary was one of the candidates and a good friend. With a bit of a heavy heart, I advised her to withdraw. She ultimately ran a very low-key campaign, which did her a dis-service and I believe led to Craig Egdell taking the top spot that year.

After my time at the top, I tried my hand as President of the Students' Representative Council, which was a whole lot less fun than the Queen Margaret Union in every way. However, I will always have my name on that Board in those shiny, gold letters to remind me of the good times.

Queen Margaret Union Executive 1996-1997

Toast to the Union

Sam Phillips
President 1997-1998

This speech was given by Sam Phillips in 2009 at the Annual President's Dinner. It is presented here in full.

To many people the Queen Margaret Union is a 1960s ugly concrete building. I first came here with mum. I was nine. My mum and her friends fought sexism from this building. This was a time when women weren't allowed in the pubs of Byres road and, of course, the Glasgow University Union. My Dad was on the Board too – we're the first father-son team – he fought racism and apartheid from this building. I marched with them to the BBC to protest against the National Front getting a Party Political Broadcast.

Our friend Dominic fought homophobia from this building. He went on to become the first male president. The Union was at the centre of political change in this city. Things we take for granted now. And I had fizzy pop and sausage and chips here.

But the QM isn't about politics and it also isn't about sausage and chips.

My first gigs were here in the QM. I saw countless forgotten bands here, most of them gothic, some were even good. And I saw Zigue Zigue Sputnik.

I learned to dance like Morrissey here. I had daffodils in my trousers and a shirt undone. I won a silly dance contest without realising I'd entered – and tickets to see Half Man Half biscuit. I have seen Billy Bragg perform on the front steps after a fire alarm; the Clash perform out front after Mick Jones left. I wish I saw Nirvana here.

The QM has been right at the centre of this city's music

scene. Countless musical careers have been launched from this building. And a good many have finished here too. But the QM isn't about music.

When I came to University I already had a young daughter. Me and her mother split up in our second year. I walked into the Board Flat and Stephen Rixon put his arms around me and a cigarette into my mouth and lit it. I didn't smoke at this point. From then on this building became a second home to me and a play-place to little Georgie. And the QM became a second family.

It was the QM that took me and Georgie in when we were heartbroken.

If it wasn't for the QM I would never have met Julie and Sandy and Jack and Rachel and Craig and Jacqui and Ken and Ben and Lizzy and Zoe and Parky Alison and Aleks and Corky and Austin and Francis and Jeremy and Steven and Rick and Steve and Paul and Alec and Shona and Fraser and John and Laura and Kat and Kirsty and Stuart and Tom (and these are just the ones on my Facebook page).

If it wasn't for the QM Rick would never have met Ruth; Shona wouldn't have met Fraser; Stacy wouldn't have met Tony; Paul wouldn't have met Louise; Steve wouldn't have met Kat and so Michelle wouldn't have met Steve (and again these are just the ones on my Facebook page).

If it wasn't for the QM; I would never have got a job at the BBC; I would never have met Katy and Katy would never have met Sandy; Sandy and Katy wouldn't have two little girls.

If it wasn't for the QM; I would never have met a young Campaigns Convenor called Chelle and we would never have had Noah and Alfie and Sauly.

Baby Noah lived for five months in Great Ormond Street Hospital. It was my family, my school friends and my QM friends who visited us when baby Noah died. It was my family, my school friends and my QM friends who came to the funeral.

When I have been ill it is my family, my school friends and my QM friends who have been there.

The QM isn't a building. The QM isn't a political movement or a shared musical taste. My QM friends are the people I see at weddings and at christenings. They came to my baby's funeral and I have been to their parent's funerals. And we will no doubt go to each other's funerals.

I am not sure I would have so many of these people if it weren't for the QM. So, I am truly grateful for the QM.

Ladies and Gentlemen. Stand up please. Look around this room. Look at these faces. If you are lucky you will know some of these people for the rest of your life. Ladies and Gentlemen. I give you Queen Margaret Union.

Queen Margaret Union Board of Management 1997-1998

Cover of 1997 Queen Margaret Union Handbook,

The Presidents' Dinner

Lizzy Toon
President 1998-1999

At the beginning of my time on the Queen Margaret Union Board of Management, everybody came from somewhere; Jim's Bar, the television room, the games room, the various committees or clubs and so forth. I came from the notoriously militant and left wing Labour club and stood in a third term by-election in my first year along with another member of the club, and fellow politics student, Dara O'Reilly. After a few months on the Board, it didn't really matter what your background was originally, you became first and foremost a 'QM hack'.

When I was first elected to the Ordinary Board in May 1995, Jenny Paterson was President. These were in the days when the Board Meetings regularly lasted more than three hours in a smoke-filled room, were highly politicised and acrimonious from start to finish. Despite all the animosity, the President's Dinner provided us with an opportunity to put all the politics and bitterness of the recent past behind us and celebrate the strengths of Queen Margaret Union and what we had in common, and besides, everyone loved Jenny. I have it on good authority from Stephen Rixon that this was the first Presidents' Dinner in a long line which has continued since. This annual event has become somewhat of an institution in the modern history of the union.

Queen Margaret Union was always very proud of its lack of formality, ceremony and conformity to the imposed institutions of five hundred years of University history. Perhaps this was because we hadn't existed for as long as the other institutions or maybe it's because our 1960s breezeblock home didn't look very traditional. In truth, our attitude was probably a combination of being a bit dismissive of tradition, individual, forward thinking, but also absolutely bloody-minded. 'We don't do all that stuff at the Queen Margaret Union' was the generally accepted attitude of the mid-nineties. As a result, despite the nominally formal structure to the dinner, it was quite a uniquely 'QM' experience which celebrated our successes, rewarded the hard work of those involved and allowed us all to dress up, drink loads of wine and heckle the evening's orators. The most loved heckle was always to interrupt the speech maker in full flow by demanding that he or she 'stood up' or 'sat down' according to their vertical status and sometimes despite it. For most of the Board of Management, this was the only event in the annual calendar when we had an opportunity to wear a dress or suit. In fact, I think this may have been the first formal occasion where I had had a chance like this. We were all pretty scruffy in those days and 'that look' was practically the uniform and certainly part of our character.

However, our attitude to tradition meant that we definitely also missed out. For many years we neglected to adequately celebrate or learn about our respected past with the people who had helped support, build, mould and nurture the institution of which we were so justly proud. Excepting a Board Handbook from the 1980s, and a few photographs, the mace and the chair in the Board Room, our history might as well have only gone as far as the 80's.

Of course, the dinners were fantastic fun. The food and service was always superb and much better than the oh-so-famous Bridie Dinner down the road at the Glasgow University Union. The company was excellent (especially if the Honorary Secretary got the seating plan right), the atmosphere was jovial and buzzing and when everyone was fed and well watered, the speeches would begin. The toast to Queen Margaret was always first and then the smokers would be allowed to smoke. I've been to ten Presidents' dinners and I think that the speech to our namesake is always quite a tricky one to make, but was also historically quite short, as by this time most people would

Queen Margaret Union Executive 1998-1999

Queen Margaret Union Board of Management 1998-1999

be desperate for a cigarette and the longevity of this speech was the only thing standing in the way of them 'sparking up'. Most people usually do a bit of research, find out about Queen Margaret, make some witty comparisons and then talk about how great we are - and there is nothing wrong with that. The speeches have always provided an opportunity to praise what we have achieved together; however links with the past were often disregarded in favour of self-congratulation or deprecation at the behest of our nearest and dearest Board Members, hacks, mates or recent Presidents. The only exception to that I can remember in my five years on the Board of Management was at my own dinner. By chance, a good friend of mine who worked for the Department for International Development in East Kilbride had noticed that one of her colleagues was called Dominic d'Angelo, and had assumed correctly that he must also have been the first male President of Queen Margaret Union. As a result of this coincidence Dominic came to the dinner and delivered an excellent and very enlightening speech, toasting the union.

The other main speeches at my own dinner in 1999 were both amusing and touching, made by my very close friend and ex-Board Member Stephen Burns and ex-President, close friend and campaign manager, Stephen Rixon. The whole experience of having a dinner held in your honour was amazing if a little overwhelming, but certainly an enduring memory of a wonderful time of my life. My family and friends were all there and when I made a slightly tearful, heartfelt and passionate 'reply' it was a culmination of twelve months of emotional energy, passion and sacrifice in addition to a fair few glasses of wine. It is a hard and lonely job to be President and all those who preceded and succeeded me know it. But it is more than a job; it was and is a great honour and a privilege.

Since my own dinner, I have been lucky enough to have been to five Presidents' Dinners for my successors and have felt very proud of what they have achieved, but also reassured that the best of our inimitable character and values live on and help shape the nature of the University experience for so many students today. It is a fantastic feeling knowing that people are still being looked after and enjoying a similar feeling of belonging, which was such an important part of my own time at the University of Glasgow. Of all of these, my most recent, in 2007 was by far the most memorable and interesting, bringing together so many Presidents from seven decades of our history. It was such an amazing achievement and invoked a whole new level of pride that finally we have reconnected with our past and better understood what has made Queen Margaret Union so special for all these years.

The President's Dinner represents continuity but also change, pride and passion, solidarity and comradeship, dedication and commitment, achievement and success, an overwhelming feeling of belonging in an atmosphere of tolerance and understanding and friendship. These sentiments also encapsulate much of the essence of Queen Margaret Union itself, which is why it has such a special place in the hearts and memories of those of us for whom it meant, and still does mean, so much.

We Belong

Omar Kooheji
Honorary President

What is it about Queen Margaret Union that makes so many people feel so attached to it? It's definitely not the building. It looks like someone tried to put up a multi storey car park in the middle of the university but changed their minds half way through. The cliché is that it's the people that make the Union special, which I guess is half right.

There is some magical property that Queen Margaret Union possesses, it seems to appeal to a certain type of person, and fill them with a sense of belonging. Not only do they belong to the Union but the Union belongs to them. I spent a long time hanging around the place over the course of the eight years I was at the University of Glasgow. And I've noticed a pattern; everyone I meet who is attached to Queen Margaret Union is under the impression that it is their union, I don't mean 'their' as in they are members of the union I mean that they have a perceived ownership of it. It belongs to them.

Here are some examples:

There was a group of smokers who used to hang about in the Food Factory, by the juke box (back when there was a juke box in the Food Factory and you could smoke there), they called it 'Cancer Corner'. Every day one of them would arrive at eight am so they could get their table, strategically placed by the juke box, this person would then reach behind and pummel the free credit button until it had about twenty songs on it and run to the other juke box which would have the free credit on it. They would then put on whatever music they wanted to listen to. If during the day a song came on that they didn't like they would cancel it. There was no malice in this act they just wouldn't have any Hanson played on 'their juke box', in 'their Food Factory'. Woe betide anyone who managed to get that coveted table, for it was theirs.

The TV Room "Crowd" was another such group who owned the Union, they even crowned two of their number King and Queen of the Union – a practice which seems to be quite common among the people who frequent the union. This group of about 30 or so people would seemingly drift in and out of the TV room over the course of any given day, peaking whenever Countdown or Neighbours was on. They would initially be extremely suspicious of anyone else who came into the TV room, for it was their domain, but given a little time they would accept almost any misfit into their ranks.

In Jim's Bar I recall there was a man who seemed to live on a diet of Guinness (and Guinness alone), he had his menagerie of merry followers who would come in and out of the pub between lectures, but he had decided that the pursuit of the perfect pint was much more important than an education. He'd be in the bar from opening to closing most days, and as far as any of his friends were concerned Jims was his realm.

When you walked into the games room for the first time it's hard not to notice the odd looks you get from some of the people, it's as if they are sizing you up. Do you belong here? Are you any good at pool? Or are you just here looking for somewhere quiet to get your lunch? Within a day or two of frequenting however you are inducted into its ranks and everyone is your friend. It's bizarre how quickly one goes from being an outsider to a member of the tribe.

There are so many more examples; Io (Science Fiction Society) and GUGS (Glasgow University Gaming Society) both think of the Food Factory as 'their haunt'. The people who frequent events like Unplugged, Revolution and Cheesy Pop seem to do so with an almost religious zeal. These events belong to them. In their eyes they are as much a part of the union as the union is a part of them.

I've spoken to several people who regaled me of Queen Margaret Union 'celebrities' whom I'd never heard of. They were apparently cornerstones of the union, and the place would not be Queen Margaret Union in their absence.

So the Union really is about the people, and somehow it magically imbues those people with a sense of ownership and belonging. Queen Margaret Union belongs to its members and they can feel that seeping through the crack infested crumbling walls, and though they may move on in four, five or even ten years time, a little part of it will always remain with them.

QMU to start record label

Promotional material for the QM's new album

News Team

The Queen Margaret Union has started its own record label over the summer. The Union has recorded an album, entitled *Penguins in the Sand*.

The venture follows on from the success of its 'Unplugged' nights, where people are invited to perform an acoustic set comprising original songs. The album was recorded and mixed in on campus, in the studios of Subcity Radio.

However, this caused a degree of controversy in the Students' Representative Council, as the Executive protested about the use of facilities belonging to the publications department for commercial purposes.

Sources within the QM and the SRC expressed concerns that the Executive members were 'kicking up a fuss about nothing', and pointed out that the album was good publicity for Glasgow University as a whole. However, the Executive still insisted on conducting a n investigation' into the alleged improper use of SRC equipment.

The QM has succeeded in securing a deal which will see the album being retailed on the high street. Virgin, HMV and the Fopp stores in both Glasgow and Edinburgh have all agreed to sell the album; and the QM have plans to release the album in conjunction with BBC Digital some time this month.

From *Glasgow University Guardian*

UNPLUGGED

**JIM'S BAR
SUNDAY EVENINGS**

Unplugged is the QM's very own open stage night. For those of you new to the concept of an open stage I shall explain... an open stage basically means you come down with your instrument, whatever it may be, digeridoo, bodhran, saxaphone, or just the guitar. If you don't play an instrument you could always treat us to a bit of acapella singing or maybe even some beatbox!

Over the four years of Unplugged's existence we have seen free-form jams, the occasional comedy double act, the odd star turn (Badly Drawn Boy) and heard lots of great music.

Unplugged wouldn't be anything without you guys, so come along, bring your instruments and let us hear your songs. Who knows, as well as a free pint you could end up on the next Unplugged album!

NORTH PARK COMMUNITY

North Park is the QM's record label. It was formed a couple of years back so the QM could release the first Unplugged album 'Penguins in the Sand'.

Now, however, plans are afoot to turn it into something bigger and better. So if you're in a band, drop a demo into reception and who knows what might happen...

From a 1990s QMU Handbook

Members of Student Theatre at Glasgow and Amnesty International

Inside the old Games Room at Queen Margaret Union

Andy's Year at the Top

Andy Whincup
President 1999-2000

During my time at University, the Queen Margaret Union had been somewhere I went for a cup of tea, a pint of Guinness, a game of pool or a spot of dancing. It was where I had always met friends, often ate pizza, occasionally been sick and frequently left at the wrong time of day or night. On one particular morning I was a little nervous, and I approached the doors with more than a little trepidation.

This morning, as of the point when I crossed the threshold, I was President of Queen Margaret Union. It was enough to scare anyone. It certainly scared me. They say that the 'other place' has all the tradition, they're wrong. I felt the weight of generations of my own family who had been there and the expectations of the current members bearing down on me. I looked up at the wooden plaque with the names written in gold and thought to myself "Oh God, I'm one of them."

Part of the reason I was worried was that I hadn't followed the typical Presidential career path. I hadn't done my time in the trenches of the Ordinary Board, I hadn't paid my dues as a Convener and I certainly hadn't had the responsibility of an Executive Board Member. I was the breath of fresh air, the new blood to take the Union in a new direction. I was known as 'Krusty' on account of the huge dreadlocks, a name that still haunts me all these years later. So not only did I have the weight of my own expectations but there was an entire Board of Management waiting to see what this complete stranger was going to be like.

I needn't have worried. It was a young Board and we bonded pretty quickly, especially those of us who were there over the summer. I quickly got my head around what was going on and got used to the fixtures of the building; the General Manager, the Porters, the cleaners (who really run the place). To the casual observer, all the big moments in our history were behind us when I took up the reigns: the emancipation of men, the building of the Union as a cultural force in the city, nearly going bankrupt and the mythical fact-finding expedition to the Caribbean. In some ways that was correct. My memories of the year are of small battles won and lost, of anecdotal moments and things going on behind the scenes that the ordinary member would not have noticed. That didn't make it any less of an exciting year for me.

It didn't take long for the roller coaster to pick up momentum until I was just going along for the ride. There was all the political jiggery-pokery involved in planning Freshers' Week and all the egos to be massaged between the Unions and the Students' Representative Council. I'm sure that every President says this, but Freshers' Week itself was a never-ending festival of madness. I can't remember everything that happened but I do recall being awoken from behind my desk by the cleaners one morning. Now that I come to think of it, the most exciting event of that week actually happened down the road at the other Union. Their annual 'Iron Stomach Competition' reached a head when the competitors were asked to drink a pint of water - the only difficulty was a live goldfish still swimming in it. Needless to say there was uproar, and that the Glasgow University Union couldn't see what all the fuss was about.

Not that it was an issue for long because their President had forgotten to do something important: matriculate. He was summarily sacked without ceremony, which left them, in October, looking for a new one. While I followed the election, I had no idea who most of the people involved were. Then one day the Glasgow University Sports Association representative on our Board came to see me looking a bit embarrassed. Apparently he wanted to resign. As excuses go, "I need to resign from the QM board because I've become GUU president," is a pretty good one. I have fond memories of our Friday afternoon tea meetings.

A forgotten and mysterious space – known as the Rat Hole – under
Queen Margaret Union used to store the many random things
created over the decades

President Andrew Whincup at his desk in the Executive Office

Having spent a paragraph laughing at the Glasgow University Union's woes, I suppose it's only fair to mention our biggest controversy of the year. Most Friday nights the Board Flat was packed with people. Often I knew who they were, but there were usually a few I didn't. The party in there seemed to go on until the next day and there were usually a few casualties lying about. To begin with it wasn't a problem: everyone was having a blast, myself included, and there didn't seem to be the usual in-fighting that can split the Ordinary Board. The only problem was that the waft from the partying began to percolate its way down the corridor. Even in the era before smoking bans the herbal tint to the aroma meant that you could tell exactly what was happening. By November it was getting difficult to ignore the excesses in the Board Flat and some of the tales were frightening. It was agreed at the next Board Meeting that we needed to behave ourselves or things might get unpleasant. So that was supposedly the end of it... only it wasn't. I don't want to rake over old coals but to cut a long story short, I found myself without an Honorary Secretary and Discos Convener in January after indiscretion made their posts untenable. In all honesty it was pretty heated for a few weeks as people from both the University and the real press poked round to find out what had happened. Then, once they discovered there was no juicy gossip to be had, they went off in search of other things.

More behind the scenes fun was to come though. Money, or lack thereof, has always been an issue at Queen Margaret Union and this year was no exception. One of the Union's most staunch supporters and unsung heroes is Terry Murphy, who headed our Finance Committee. Anyone who's met Terry will know that he gets a bee in his bonnet about injustices, and he has seen many of them perpetrated against us. I recall one particular university meeting where there had been discussions of 'temporarily' redistributing the block grant funding of the student bodies for some project. Terry fumed and got a bit irate so Dougald Mackie, the Clerk of Court, tried to get his own back by asking if we should maybe look at the way Queen Margaret Union spends its events money. I listened in horror as he told him to "come and have a go if you think you're hard enough". Never talked to me again. Never mentioned redistributing the block grant either.

Meanwhile, our Entertainments Manager was winding up some serious stuff. Over the years we had waxed and waned. There had been massive bands, some of the up and coming ones like Death in Vegas still wanted to play and Badly Drawn Boy blew up our telly, but we had never really broken into the dance market. With 'Bugged Out' that changed completely. It was marketed as a proper club night, with multiple rooms and dancing until three in the morning. The Lone Swordsmen played, Tom Middleton was there and others who I forget. It was brilliant and it was always packed. There were some licensing issues as I recall, but they were dealt with in usual fashion; "what can we get away with"? I think we ended up putting as much water out as possible when our license ran out at two am so people could carry on dancing for another hour as the license only applied to the sale of drinks. Paul Oakenfold even came for a night. There were other forays into the club scene such as 'Ouch!' It didn't do quite so well however, but the half dozen or so people who came seemed to have fun.

We had discos throughout most of the week in one form or another, whether it was bands or big dance nights. There was a night that was a bit different to the others and really showcases some of the things that make us special. I can claim no credit for it save being there and taking part, but every Sunday night Jim's bar was packed with about two hundred people. Unplugged was our open stage acoustic night hosted by the irreplaceable Kenny 'Fluppet' Thom. Every week, without fail, talented (and not so talented) musicians would get up on stage and perform for the princely sum of a pint of Carlsberg. Unlike so many events it really was down to the members and the people who were there. Without them it would have been pretty dull. By the time I left Unplugged's second album was recorded and awaiting production.

For all these trials, tribulations, fun and games, it's probably the little things that have left the lasting impression. All the people who, by doing what they did every day, made the place what it was. I remember the coterie of smokers who sat by the jukebox in the Food Factory and cancelled any tune they didn't like. It became known as 'cancer corner' and one of them went by the name of 'One Lung' because of the habit. I remember the massive clique of people who met in the television room every day without fail. I can recall being kidnapped and ransomed by the metal society. There was a game called 'punter fishing' that involved dangling things out of the committee room windows. There was a fellow at Cheesy Pop every Friday night who was the absolute spit of David Beckham - poor guy must have got really tired of people pointing it out. There were even the people who worked out you could save money at Cheesy Pop by buying vodka on its own and buying coke from the machine, saving them about ten pence a shot.

There are a lot of memories; some sad, many happy. It was a long year, but it was an exciting year for me. I've never yet regretted putting my name down for it, and certainly never doing it. In fact, I met someone a few weeks ago in the Midlands who recognised me because of it. It was brilliant. It's a magical place that has a special place in my heart and in my memories.

Queen Margaret Union Board of Management 1999-2000

Queen Margaret Union Board of Management 2000-2001

2000

Queen Margaret Union began the 'noughties' on a high. It was clear that the troubled times of the 1980s were gone and the successes of the 1990s meant that the Union was now one of the best in the country. By mid-decade Queen Margaret Union made another 'first' in University of Glasgow history when it finally overtook Glasgow University Union in membership numbers.

Social life on campus was now more important to most students than ever before. Queen Margaret Union developed its programme of events to include several weekly quizzes, a pool competition, interactive game shows, film evenings (Jurassic Park trilogy being an annual feature at one point), local band nights, an unplugged acoustic guitar evening and more live acts than ever before.

A fortnightly magazine, 'qmunicate' was created that eventually rivalled Glasgow University Magazine (GUM) and *Glasgow University Guardian* in terms of quality of storytelling and campus news.

Student elections were becoming more contested and the campaigns were starting to rival those of the United States Presidential Election candidates (albeit on much smaller scales).

The decade has yet to close and Queen Margaret Union is in perhaps its strongest position yet. No longer simply a place for people to meet, it now acts as the venue for enhancing the University experience. Friendships for life are made and networking that will stand you well in future career moves usually tends to begin in Jim's Bar.

It is clear that Queen Margaret Union is an essential part of life at the University of Glasgow and will continue to be for future generations of budding and enthusiastic Glasgow freshmen.

President Caroline Johnston outside Queen Margaret Union

Cheesy Pop

Laura Kane and Alec Nicolson
President 2004-2005
and Resident DJ Toast

The biggest student club night in Scotland. The longest running student club night in Scotland. The longest haired DJ in Scotland. The original and the best – Friday nights *are* Cheesy Pop.

Since its inception, Cheesy Pop has been a staple of nightlife for students at the University of Glasgow and the evening torch bearer for Queen Margaret Union's appreciation of diversity, openness and, most importantly, fun.

In 1993, responsibilities for the Unions night-time activities were divided between between the Social Committee, which organised things like quizzes in Jim's Bar and the 'smaller' club nights held on Thursdays, and the Entertainments Committee, which ran gigs and the popular weekend discos. Attendance at the Thursday club nights had lately been somewhat lackluster and so the Social Committee scratched its collective head to try to find something that could at once appeal to enough people to stand a chance of becoming popular, while also retaining something of Queen Margaret Union's slightly quirky nature. Many ideas were tossed about but the one that got the room buzzing came from a young man named Paul Crabb, who honed in on the idea of 'popular' — what if we played pop music? This was a much less obvious suggestion than it might now seem all these years later, given that the weekend nights (and the most popular jukebox selections upstairs) consisted mostly of various shades of punk, metal, goth and industrial music.

The idea for the new night was to throw out anything connected with *serious* clubbing and see how it could be as fun, silly, and almost musically irreverent as possible. There was a rich vein of suitable chart music at that time—Take That's *Relight My Fire* and Jazzy Jeff's *Boom! Shake the Room* are perhaps good examples—and the eighties were sufficiently recent to be readily plundered.

The first task was to find someone to man the decks, so the then Social Convenor, Debbie Halcrow, asked if anyone at the meeting knew of anyone suitable, and a young student going by the nickname 'Toast' was thrust forward by a friend. The reluctantly volunteered student was to be trialed for the next two Thursdays, so his parents were duly called and a parcel of seven-inch records was posted up from London where he had cut his cloth DJing at parties for school friends.

Thursday night arrived and at nine pm prompt, the doors opened under the night's original moniker of 'Snap, Crackle and Pop' and Toast and another Social Committee member, Ros, nervously started playing records. The Board of Management watched with interest and the punters were at first reticent to buy into the idea of dismissing credibility in favour of foolishness, but alcohol gradually worked its magic and the dancefloor got steadily busier. By the end of the night, more up-to-date records like *Boom Shak-a-Lak* had given way to *The Lion Sleeps Tonight*, *Wake Me Up Before You Go-Go*, *Nelly the Elephant* and such unashamed pop. People left elated and the night was an institution from that moment on: the Board of Management's decision was an easy one; the night should stay. Toast became 'DJ' Toast (a name familiar to any student who has since passed through the cloisters) and before long Snap, Crackle and Pop was renamed Cheesy Pop as it was thought more descriptive. It was also how many people referred to the night in any case.

Friday morning lectures became a bit of a struggle for many, not least for the DJ whose digs at the time were on nearby Kersland Street, meaning his head hit the pillow each week as merry students ambled along outside his window still singing the last song he had played.

A couple of years later, Queen Margaret Union found itself in a good financial position and the Board of Management decided to update the venue. The dark, dank common room was to be refurbished and transformed into a modern and

From a 1990s QMU Handbook

fridays are cheesy pop

with dj toast

scotland's biggest student night
now in its tenth year

stella £1 / bottle
vodka 60p a shot
all night every week

ps: we're here all through the holidays too!

flexible venue named – after tremendous debate – Qudos. Shedding its previous guise as a dark room where students got drunk and snogged each other, it became a 'proper' venue where students got drunk and snogged each other.

The refurb also signaled a change for Cheesy Pop – Thursdays became Fridays, to the relief of lecturers around campus. There was no longer that guilty feeling about going out the night before lectures and the students took to it with gusto. 'Friday nights *are* Cheesy Pop' wasn't a marketing effort by the Board of Management – it was a mantra invented by the students and subsequently adopted by Queen Margaret Union. The improved venue combined with a later licence saw numbers climb steadily and throughout first and second terms the Union was usually filled to capacity on Friday nights.

Its Friday night residency meant that it now occupied the annual space previously reserved by 'The Big Kahuna' – the end of Martinmas term party held by the Union. Twelve-hour Cheesy Pop had its first outing in 1998, and immediately became as much of a staple as its weekly equivalent. With Daft Friday at Glasgow University Union demanding formal dress and a formidable ticket price, Queen Margaret Union welcomed people who just wanted to let it all hang out on the last day of term – good tunes, wear what you like, and don't pay through the nose for a ticket.

Twelve Hour Cheesy Pop was a hit as soon as it started – our very own DJ Toast playing his mix of cheese, dance, rock and everything in between, as well as a special act that was traditionally never announced in advance – and sold out in advance every year. Over the years, there have been some great acts playing the event including Musical Youth, Urban Cookie Collective, N-Trance, The Foundations and B*witched.

The most special night of the year is, undoubtedly, the Friday night of Freshers' Week: the first Cheesy Pop for new students. The pinnacle of Freshers' Week, Cheesy Pop has always been *the* way to finish off a great week. From a president's point of view, standing on the balcony watching one thousand two hundred people have the best time of their lives so far, as they watched The Proclaimers sing *500 Miles* and knowing that I had a part in that, is a really special moment.

At the time of writing Cheesy Pop has been running for approaching sixteen years, which translates to about sixty thousand records played, something over five hundred thousand tickets sold (or to put it another way, not far off the population of Glasgow) and enough pints of Tennents sold that if they were stacked up they would reach beyond the earth's atmosphere! The night also spawned a spin-off for one year, dubbed 'Cheesy Pop Gold' and aimed at those people who enjoyed the retro component of the music the best. Held on Saturdays, it was a dazzling affair, with the whole of Qudos bedecked in golden foil.

There have been numerous notable moments over the years. The most poignant was the first Cheesy Pop after the death of Kurt Cobain, when in response to Toast playing the Nirvana song *Lithium*, all 500 people present ended up sitting on the dancefloor in tears. Not the usual aim of a frivolous club night but an extraordinary moment. At the other end of the scale was the prank played by the crew, where they set up the smoke machine *inside* the DJ booth with the aim of filling the booth with smoke. Unfortunately, since the machine was pointed at one of the decks, the burst of smoke emitted by the machine was powerful enough to blow the record right off the record player, and out the front of the booth onto the dancefloor, leaving the club in silence – an interruption which took some time to rectify, as what had occurred didn't become clear until the smoke had cleared! But the fun-loving nature of the average Cheesy Pop punter meant that the cheers were all the bigger when the music was eventually restored.

Cheesy Pop exemplifies what is great about Queen Margaret Union – completely unabashed, open to anything and definitely up for a good time.

Cover of Queen Margaret Union Diary, 2002-03

Cover of Queen Margaret Union Handbook, 2004-05

Clubs and Societies

Sarah-Louise MacAdie
Honorary Secretary 2007-2008

I was never really one for clubs before I came to the University of Glasgow. I was a Brownie when I was younger but I suspect that was mostly due to my mother wanting a break on Friday nights for a few hours. I was never in a band or a dance group, and I was definitely not into sports. However I became a club, committee and Board Member, and still had the time to make use of all the brilliant outlets the university had to offer before I faced the real world.

I discovered that clubs and societies could make or break your time as a student. They have the power to inspire, to challenge and to change the world. A society can be so much more than just a group of like-minded individuals: it's a place to hang out, something to do at the weekends and a ready-made group of friends always eager to find someone new with similar interests. All it takes is that first daunting step into a room of strangers and a little courage to find out what they are all about. Pretty soon you'll find you are moving your University course work around to try to fit in your club activities and trying to decide if you can still pass all your exams and write a dissertation whilst running for President of your favourite society. A former Board Member told me about the first time they got involved:

"In my first year at University I remember plucking up the courage to attend a meeting of People and Planet to voice my opinions of all things ethical. Imagine my shock to discover myself thrown into a meeting of the highly vocal Socialist Society with almost thirty opinionated and loud student activists between me and my only means of escape. I must admit though that although I stayed to the very end, I never did go back!"

The real power of clubs and societies on campus is revealed every year around about the time of Queen Margaret Union's annual election in March when the Presidential candidates attend meetings with as many of the major campus groups as possible in order to convince the student societies that they have their best interests at heart. Legend has it that one Queen Margaret Union President was elected with no former experience to the Board of Management thanks in main to a record turn out on election day from GUGS (Glasgow University Gaming Society).

Of course, political parties are well represented in Glasgow's makeup of clubs and societies just as they are in many of the other Universities up and down the country. It is seldom that political careers are ruined even before they have begun – however, I do recall that a front page story in one of the nationwide papers exploded the fancy-dress scandal of two students who perhaps made a questionable decision in their choice of costumes. Just as Prince Harry's Nazi ensemble sparked debate about the bad taste of his outfit, so did the students' 'master and slave' outfits leave their reputation in tatters. The paper had dug up the pictures from social networking site Facebook that just goes to show how, thanks to the internet, student politics can rock the world, although I'm sure it wasn't in the way those lads intended.

My personal favourite incident concerning a club happened just as I had been elected to the Board of Management of Queen Margaret Union. No less than twelve members of the theatre group STaG (Student Theatre at Glasgow) managed to squeeze into our tiny passenger lift and decided to "make it bounce", breaking the only disabled access available to the upper floors of the building. Needless to say a complete revision of Health and Safety Procedure was inspired by the incident. If the records of Incident Report Sheets are correct, I believe that our very own President of 2008-2009 Mr. Ally Hunter was one of the culprits who faced a petty fine and banishment from the building until the debt was paid.

I joined a club when I came to University and it helped get me get a job. This in itself is probably not unusual, particularly

Board Member Ruairidh Anderson voices his opinion on the University of Glasgow joining the National Union of Students

Stop the War Coalition society at a Queen Margaret Union event

Honorary Secretary Roslyn Scoular shows off the latest addition in the Games Room

Pause Gaming Society taking over the second floor of Queen Margaret Union

when you consider the wide range of clubs in existence at Glasgow. You may picture me working in a newsagents because of my affinity for comic books, or at my local church tearoom because I may be a member of the Christian Union; however my story is a little less logical. Upon going for an interview for a part-time job in a well known café chain, my future manager informed me that the reason I had gotten the interview was due to the information I had provided on my CV. Alas it was not my qualifications, but the part stating that I enjoyed knitting and that I attended a knitting circle at University called Glasgow University Stitch 'N' Bitch. She was ridiculously excited at the prospect and insisted on pawing at the scarf which I'd knitted. Needless to say I got the job, though I have never been sure if it was due to my fine personality or my new-found knitting skills.

My experiences with clubs over my time at Queen Margaret Union has been rewarding in many ways. I now know that a club can be friendly and frightening, disastrous and quirky, and that it works in my favour to be a little bit kitsch and be proud of it. Having worked with clubs professionally as Honorary Secretary I can safely say that they have been both the bane of my existence and some of the most fun and exciting people I have ever met. Club members are passionate, dedicated and friendly, and they are my kind of people.

The refurbished Games Room

President Laura Kane gazes out of the second floor window

The People Make The Union

Katie McDonald
President 2002-2003

I was shy at school and, like many people, never felt like I fitted in. The move to the University of Glasgow and the acceptance I found at Queen Margaret Union was amazing. I was not alone in feeling like I had found a home there; many students felt, and still do feel, the same.

The membership of Queen Margaret Union had changed dramatically in its one hundred and twelve years up until July 2002. It was originally created for the educated women of wealthy families who attended the College of the same name, firstly for women of all backgrounds, and then making way for students of both genders after the historic 1979 change to the constitution. The Union has had a long history of campaigning for the rights of different groups in society; the most vivid for me being the ban on all Nestlé products in the building due to unethical sales of baby milk to women in the third world who have no way of sterilizing equipment or bottles. This ban is still in force.

The membership of Queen Margaret Union post-1979 was considered 'different'. All groups outside the mainstream found acceptance here – gays, geeks, goths and just anyone looking beyond 'rugby-boy' drinking games for fun. Of the many groups, homosexuals were an early fixture in the Union as they left behind the macho drinking games of the Glasgow University Union (GUU) to come and sit with the girls. Queen Margaret Union still hosts Glasgow University Lesbian, Gay, Bisexual and Transgender (LGBT) meetings; giving advice and a voice to those in, and out, of the closet, or in the middle of a transition. The geeks came and formed groups of science fiction societies, so-called 'LAN parties' (where they colonise the Food Factory all night and play video games) and of course, the Glasgow University Gaming Society (GUGS), with a huge membership taking over half the Food Factory every week. The Goths have Bedlam (a club night that really does take seeing to believe) every once in a while, for which people would travel up to from as far away as London in years gone by. Revolution (a weekly Rock and Metal club night) on a Tuesday night also offered alternative music to the masses.

The most wonderful thing about Queen Margaret Union is that everyone celebrates these differences and it is not hard to find people from any of these groups (or other groups) sitting around together in the Food Factory, Jim's Bar, the Games Room, the Coffee Shop in the common aim of doing anything but go to lectures. I have known goths and hippies that sat together happily; gays and straights; Muslims and Jews; computer geeks and computer illiterates; metalheads and ravers. This list could easily be added to on a walk around the Union on a busy evening.

My love for Queen Margaret Union was formed during my own Freshers' Week, when I spent around half an hour in the Glasgow University Union and the rest of the time in the 'better Union'. I joined the Board of Management in my first year, solely due to a friend's persuasion. She had been elected after befriending some Fresher's Helpers and said, "Katie, join the Board – it's fun". I asked what 'the Board' was. The reply, "it's just really fun" closed the deal, and so I filled out a nomination form. I did not know what the Board of Management was or that there was a heckling meeting to get through. If she had told me about the heckling meeting, I don't think an eighteen-year-old me would have even considered applying. I made it through, luckily, and was elected to the Ordinary Board for a good while, then became Honorary Assistant Secretary. The decision to run for President only happened because others who were going to run dropped out, and the thought became 'someone has to do the job – why not me?'

The job is a strange one. Although considered a student by the University of Glasgow I was on sabbatical for a year and paid for the privilege. Suddenly the buck stopped at me. All complaints were directed at me. For someone who never had long term plans to run for President, the sudden election and start of the job were daunting.

We had a good summer. I had an excellent team of convenors, and Freshers' Week was organised brilliantly. The most frightening five minutes of my life were spent speaking to a packed Bute Hall as part of the Freshers' Welcome Address, however it went smoothly and the building was packed all week.

My year as President was the first time we were neck-and-neck with the Glasgow University Union in terms of current student members, and it was a source of great excitement comparing the updated membership figures each day. Since then Queen Margaret Union membership has been consistently higher than our companions down the hill, despite our much smaller building. In terms of developments, the addition of a coffee shop was the main project during my year, and it is now stocked with entirely fairly traded coffee in response to members' wishes.

The Board of Management is a brilliant platform, not only to lead but to learn. Few former Board Members would have difficulty writing a full page of transferable skills after six months in its voluntary employ. It was where we became the people we are today as well as the place where we perfected our social skills in Jim's Bar over the many years. A year as President is hard work, varied and, despite the fun, can be overwhelming at times. The position was the first full-time job for me, as it is for most who fill the role, and it certainly gave me insight that my future career would never be in management. I doubt I am alone in thinking I would do things differently if I had my time again. I am now a qualified doctor and will be far better at my job for the experiences I had in Queen Margaret Union, and the skills I learned there.

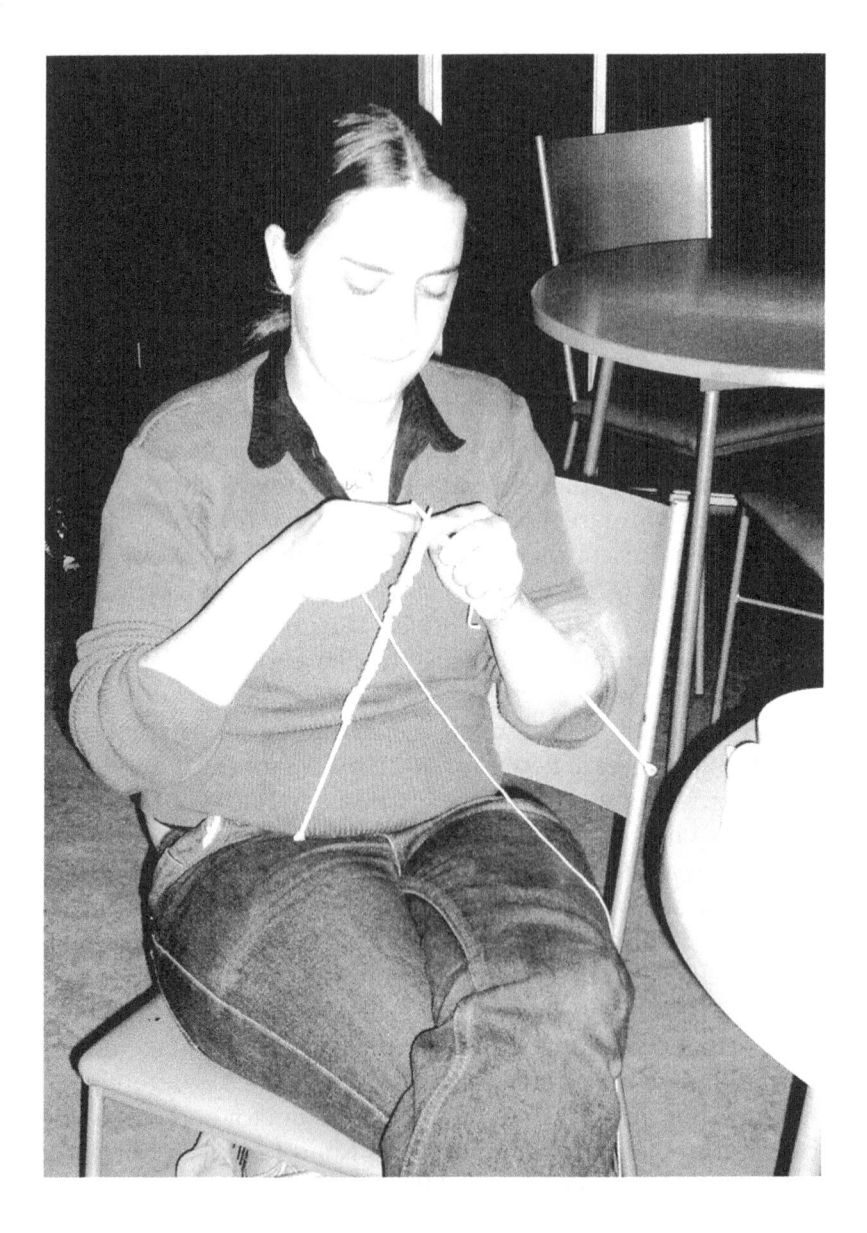

President Laura Kane gets stuck into a session with the Stitch N Bitch society

Queen Margaret Union Executive 2001-2002

Queen Margaret Union Executive 2002-2003

Queen Margaret Union Board of Management 2001-2002

Queen Margaret Union Board of Management 2003-2004

Freshers' Week

Jamie McHale
President 2005-2006

My first few days on University Campus I spent playing pool in the Glasgow University Union, drinking weak beer, and chatting to the people I befriended in the matriculation queue. Everyone was trying to act as relaxed as possible, chatting about student life, with the full experience of our five-minute stroll from Hunter Halls to the Beer Bar. I remember realising halfway through the day that I was dressed almost exactly the same as the guy I had been talking to for three hours. Obviously, we had both been packed off to University with a nice new Marks and Spencer jumper from our proud parents.

I moved into Maclay Hall at the top of Kelvingrove Park. It was the perfect distance and angle to the Glasgow University Union; in a straight line, down a steep hill. Most of my friends joined immediately, but I waited. Flicking through the incoherent babble in the Queen Margaret Union handbook. I felt a feeling of friendship. People often speak about being 'grabbed' by the Union during Freshers' Week, a hold that never loosens up. For me though, it took a few days to take a hold. I spent a little time in Queen Margaret Union with some new halls-buddies, enjoyed the music and the atmosphere, so I bucked the trend at halls and joined. I'd spent virtually no time in the Union during my own Freshers' Week, but I spent the next five years making up for that as much as I could.

My next experience of Freshers' Week was the following year as a freshers' helper. One of my friends suggested that I might like to get involved, as she had been in previous years. I went to the Union often enough, so I thought I should share my enthusiasm for the place. After a gruelling interview designed to make me feel as uncomfortable as possible - I was in. I willingly trouped in over the summer, sat in the Convenors Office with lots of people who were a lot cooler than I was. I stuffed hundreds of leaflets and diaries into wee plastic bags - an essential part of any pre-Freshers' Week summer for years to come.

Freshers' Week came, and I was higher than a kite. Up every morning as early as biology would allow, and to bed as late as the candle could burn. You couldn't hold me back and I was extolling the virtues of the Union to everyone and anyone that would listen, including my long-suffering helper friends. That freshers' week was really one of the best weeks I have ever had, meeting freshers and Helpers alike. Being part of the team, working hard, and partying even harder. It left the Helpers physically exhausted.

In order to meet Freshers our team set ourselves up as 'Matriculation Card Inspectors' outside the Bute Hall. One person would check the photos of the newly signed up students, whilst the others dealt them a hand of flyers and Union-related banter. It was about an hour before the University Staff realised and kicked us out.

Just before the end of the week, during the Friday Night Cheesy Pop finale, I was taken onto the balcony by the Freshers' Week convenor. It was around one am, when the crowd was at its largest and the music at its loudest. He chatted to me about how good the Union was, pointed down to the packed crowd and told me; "you could make that happen". I hadn't thought about working for the Union before, but my path was well and truly set. I spent the next two years of my life organising Freshers' Weeks. I'm pretty sure I wasn't the only one to have the 'balcony chat', but I made sure I gave it to a fair few people in the following years.

Freshers' Week 2004 was by far my favourite time in the Union. The Union had found itself without a Freshers' Week Convenor about two days before the Helpers were to be picked. I had organised the week the year before, so I knew the formula. The Honorary Secretary had previously worked as the Social Convenor. We volunteered to put the week together. This year it was a team effort. That's what makes a Freshers'

Cover to the 2005 Queen Margaret Union Handbook

A gathering of Freshers Helpers in 2006

Executive Committee members Gill Turnbull and Roslyn Scoular lead Freshers to Queen Margaret Union

Freshers Week edition of Queen Margaret Union Magazine
qmunicate

Rock band *The Automatic* during Freshers Week 2006

Week turn from a good experience to a great experience. Everyone played their part. Everyone was involved. Everyone had a stake in making sure it turned out all right.

Picking the Helpers was difficult. Neither the Honorary Secretary nor myself had been in the helper interviews, which take about three weeks at the best of times. We decided to try and compress the interviews into just a few days, inviting applicants out on the Friday night so we could try and meet them all. The Honorary Secretary undertook one memorable interview conducted during the night. The guy didn't know who I was, so when I asked him later how his interview went, he said "pretty good, but the amount of lies and rubbish you have to make up to get into these things..." It's safe to say he wasn't selected. The rest of the picks were potluck. The result was an eclectic mix of enthusiastic Helpers, who didn't really know each other. This gave the whole week a great energy. It was the Helpers that were making friends too, not just the Freshers.

Everyone had Freshers-flu by the first day. Lemsip consumption went through the roof. I carried sachets round in my back pocket. Helpers ate, slept, danced, drank and worked together. Of course, someone always ends up crying, and there is the helper couple who decide that after kissing on the first night that they are going to be sickeningly attached to each other for the rest of the week. Still, there isn't any other feeling like being part such of a great team.

It's being part of such a good group of people that makes many people decide to dedicate more time to the Union. The brilliant experience I had in 2004 convinced me to run for President, and I know that several other Helpers were also inspired to join the Board of Management.

One of the most nerve-wracking things you can do as President of Queen Margaret Union is the Freshers' Address. Standing in front of a packed Bute Hall and welcoming the freshers to University seems like a daunting task, especially as you have a lot of 'thinking-time' over the summer. It's the first impression many people will have of the Union, so you have to make it good. Having never spoken in public before, I was a little apprehensive. I was even more apprehensive as Richard Wilson was performing the Rector's welcome address. It was pointed out to me that my speech, "didn't bring the funny", but you try telling a decent joke when following a career comedian.

I expected to be jittery, I expected butterflies in my stomach, I expected to fall over and curl up into a ball sobbing. I didn't. Walking to the Bute Hall, with Helpers all around, some of my best friends at my side, the carnival atmosphere, and the sun shining I felt totally relaxed. I had realised the simple fact - I was there to speak about Queen Margaret Union and there was no one else better qualified than me to do so. I had the chance to speak to an audience of Freshers, to pass on the friendly welcome that I had felt from the Union. For those few minutes no one knew the subject better than I did, and no one cared about the Union as much as I did. It was as if I was speaking about my own family. I finished the speech on a high and I think, I hope, that some of the Freshers' felt a little more welcome than they would had I not been there. That's what mattered to me. I wanted them to realise how much I loved the place, and that they could love the place too.

It's easy when talking about Freshers' Weeks to compile lists of bands that have played, numbers of people through the doors, and the membership numbers for the week. Those kinds of lists don't do the Freshers' Week experience justice. You can't place a value on being part of a great team, the friendships that you make, and the energy you experience. It's all about the little stories, and memories. It's the feeling that you have passed on the enthusiasm for the Union to the next generation. That's what Freshers' Week at Queen Margaret Union is all about.

Photo of local band *The Dykeenies* at Queen Margaret Union

Queen Margaret Union Executive 2003-2004

Queen Margaret Union Executive 2004-2005

Save the Green Planet

Molly Illife
Campaigns Convenor
2005-2006

By the time I joined the Board of Management in 2002, no one really seemed to know what the Campaigns Committee was supposed to do. Its continued existence was arguably down to the positive PR it generated for the Union, allowing it to sneakily claim to the higher echelons of the University of Glasgow that we provided 'student welfare services'. From its heady beginnings as a hub of resistance to the introduction of tuition fees, the Campaigns Committee's remit had gradually matured into an all-encompassing mishmash of student welfare and charity fundraising. It suffered from a kind of committee snobbery, being seen merely as the easy option for Board Members to attend their compulsory one meeting a week - during my tenure as Campaigns Convenor I only received less than half of the budget I requested.

However, despite our minuscule budget and reputation as tree-hugging slackers, we were blessed with insanely enthusiastic members, and became infamous for organising events which were fabulously off-the-wall. There was, for example, the legendary 'hugathon' when enthusiastic committee members attempted to hug one thousand startled Union punters, and the teddy bear's picnic in the Food Factory to raise money for Children in Need. There was also the reggae night on Bob Marley's birthday to raise money for victims of the Boxing Day Tsunami, with the only hitch being that the DJ was too stoned to operate the decks. The Christmas Party for the children of students and staff sticks in my mind as another highlight. The committee members bounced about like mad on the bouncy castles in Qudos once all the kids had gone home, and sat on Jimmy the Porter's knee to receive Christmas presents of their very own. The highlight of the year had to be the incredibly random, 'Be Excellent To Each Other Week', which culminated in a 'Be Excellent To Each Other Tag' at Cheesy Pop where punters were encouraged to swap messages saying how great everyone was.

For a 'campaigns' committee though, campaigning often seemed a bit thin on the ground. My tenure as Convenor was marked by only one truly gritty campaign, and it was not against an apathetic government or an evil multinational corporation, it was against elements within our own University and even at Queen Margaret Union. It was the campaign to make the University of Glasgow into a Fair Trade organisation. Really, given Queen Margaret Union's record of ethical procurement, including a long standing ban on Nestle products, you would have expected us to be chomping at the bit when it came to Fair Trade. However we found opposition in surprising places and it took the best part of a year to convince the key decision makers that Fair Trade was not a fad, a con or a sure-fire route to bankruptcy. We deployed a range of tactics including surveying Union members, writing an extensive report for the Board of Management and organising a diverse array of awareness-raising events. After much political manoeuvring and dissemination of information and Fair Trade chocolate, the Board unanimously passed Fair Trade policy, enabling the University to successfully apply for Fair Trade status. We thus proved not only that a few committed people can change the status quo, but that avoiding University work and eating yummy chocolate can save the world.

The impact of the Campaigns Committee also extended beyond these sorts of grassroots student activism activities to more subtle influence. Throughout its life the committee acted as a bit of a bridge between the Board of Management and various 'do-gooder' societies in the Union, with enthusiastic members coming along from clubs like Amnesty International and People and Planet. If they went on to become Board Members, these usually left-leaning committee members, leant a balancing weight to the profit-centric mentality that,

Helpers relax after another successful Kids' Christmas Party

Board Member Nicola Clark surveying members

Milly the dinosaur on campus before her brutal slaughter at the hands of the University Executive

although essential to the successful running of the Union, would have made the place soulless had it been allowed to operate unchallenged.

More than one member of the committee has gone on to pursue voluntary or paid work for a charity, putting to good use the skills they had allegedly picked up amongst the haphazard madness of the our activities.

Alas, the Campaigns Committee is now no more, its anachronistic name being updated to more closely reflect its modern activities and purpose. However, even though the name of the committee has changed, Queen Margaret Union still retains its commitment to Fair Trade and to the student welfare and charity work that were previously the remit of the Committee. And along with the world saving, I imagine there is still a fair amount of procrastination and chocolate consumption as well.

President Laura Kane as Santa Claus

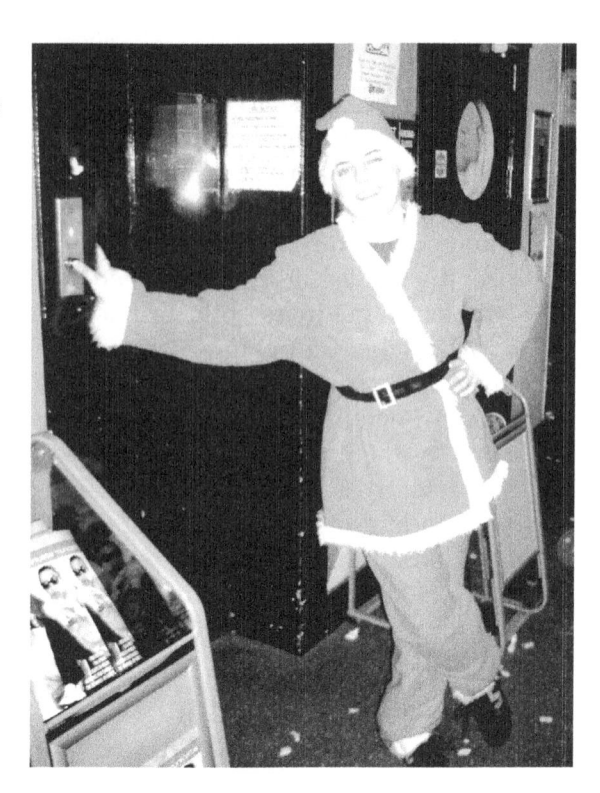

Honorary Assistant Secretary Gill Turnbull after a visit from Santa Claus

Roxanne

Erin Haig
Social Convenor 2005-2006

There were two names that were synonymous to the Social scene at the Queen Margaret Union; Mathew Davies and Richard Adams, the dynamic duo, who were known on campus as 'Spoonie' and 'Troutfish'. Spoonie was known for his extreme 'words of wisdom' while, Troutfish would spin beats that would allow his many fans to break into dance on stage. They would fill the lives of University of Glasgow students with themed quizzes including the memorable pirates and ninjas night. They were perhaps best known for their game featuring The Police track, *Roxanne*, where half of the bar had to stand up and sip a drink whenever the songs namesake was spoken and the other half followed suit after the words 'red light' were announced. Yes, these were brilliant ideas that would ignite the passion of the crowd, but they would also be the bane of my time as Social Convenor.

At the end of the University year in 2005, the legendary Spoonie and Troutfish were ending their quiz host reign, which meant that I had to find new hosts for the upcoming Fresher's Week. This would have been fine if we were the beginning of the year and not after all the students had fled from campus following their finals. On top of the timing, these two gentlemen had put their mark so deep into Glasgow, that to replace it would probably be to the ruin of the next convenors reputation. We decided that we had to change it drastically from what it was known for so that there could be no comparison between the two.

It was decided that the best course of action would be to put on a 'Quiz Idol'. I have always told everyone to own up to their mistakes and this one was definitely mine. Allowing people who have never hosted anything in their life to go on stage and try out being a host for the night was never going to be a good idea. The people who tried out were incredibly nice, but also extremely green. Needless to say, that one didn't work. The committee needed to go in a different direction, but with the end of term fast approaching and my plane ticket back to Canada booked, I had no idea what to do. Since term had ended and the committee was not meeting anymore, I had to take it upon myself to try and find people for the quiz.

Luckily for me, Spoonie was kind enough to point me in the right direction. His name was Ben and his partner in crime was Andy. To me, these guys were a breath of fresh air, they had great ideas and were full of life. After our initial meeting I knew that the year would turn out better that I originally thought. We now we had our two quiz hosts and all we needed was a DJ. Before the years of Gordon Brady as President of Queen Margaret Union, he did pose some interest in Entertainments. He had no DJ experience whatsoever, but he had the right attitude and mentor in DJ Troutfish. So with time and practice, Gordon Brady became DJ NuStart and the trio were branded as 'Ben and Andy's Excellent Pub quiz featuring DJ NuStart'. Mind you, there were moments where I thought I had made the wrong decision covering my eyes and ears with some of the risky, and risqué, things that were said, and performed, on stage.

At first people were very sceptical. I was not liked for my decisions; some people didn't even talk to me. What many people need to realize is that sometimes, you have to make decisions that people don't like, you are not a Board Member to make friends but to contribute to the success of Queen Margaret Union and at the end of the day they will respect you for sticking to your guns.

By the end of the year I knew that they were a success and I was proud. It was also my last year of University and just before I had to go back to Canada. Still strongly attached to what I had built, I frequently called to find out what was happening with the Social Committee and making sure the platform that I left behind would still be there. However, like all things they evolve and change shape with the influence of the new members of the Board.

Student participating in one of the many random games at the Union quiz

Two volunteers at the Union's quiz

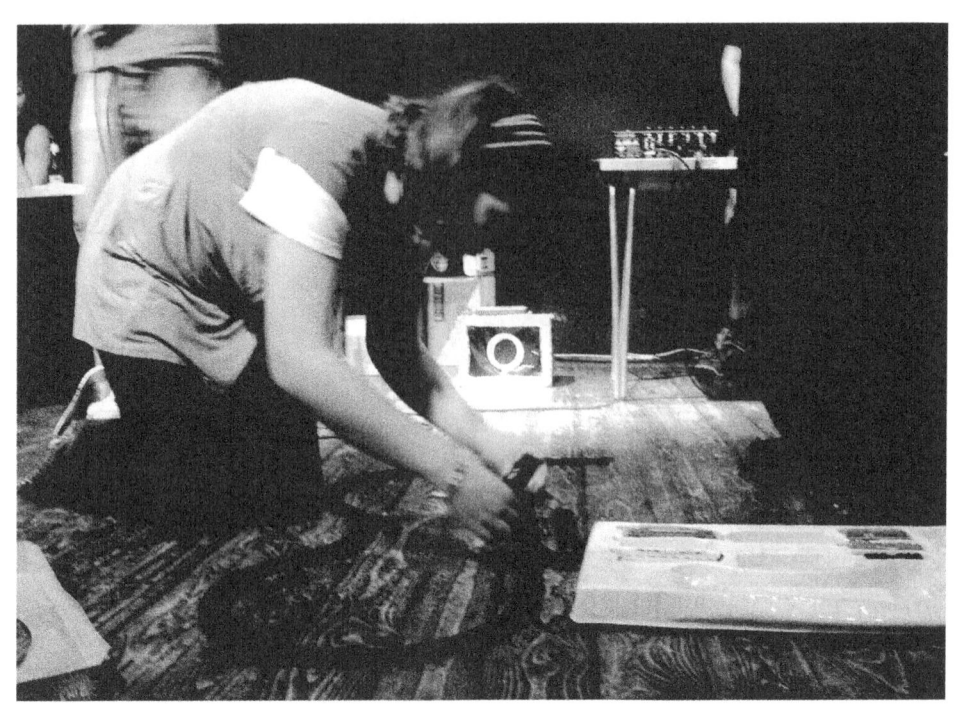

Former Board Member Beth Kahn tries to win prizes at the Quiz

Student participating in one of the many random games at the Union quiz

The Legend of Matron

Jimmy McLaughlin
Queen Margaret Union
Staff Member

It all began quietly and without ceremony on a bright and beautiful autumn morning. It was first term in the sanctuary that was the Games Room Bar. Drew was lying on one of the south facing recessed windowsills; he was well wrapped up, hooded and looking miserable. In addition to being used as extra seating space during the busier moments, the windowsills were a popular location with students who simply wanted to 'chill', reflect, ponder the wonders of creation or simply consider the pimple on their bottom. Making my way around the room collecting the empty glasses, I was made aware that Drew was having a bad time. All he really needed was a quiet day in the warmth and comfort of Queen Margaret Union. Arriving at his windowsill I found myself asking him if I should send for Matron. It was thumbs down. That was the moment from somewhere in the corridors and alcoves of my imagination that Matron came to life.

As the day progressed I checked on Drew, telling him that I had spoken with Matron. She had advised he stay in a warm and well-ventilated area and drink plenty of fluids. In the days that followed, Matron became my buzzword. I dropped the name into stories and conversations with students as they whiled away the hours on the pool tables. It became common knowledge that we had some sort of 'matron' living on the (imaginary) fifth floor of the Union. She was the sole reminder of times past. The old girl was now retired and was occasionally consulted by the Board of Management. As a close friend, I would accompany Matron to various functions and received messages and phone calls from her regularly.

Allegedly, in less formal moments, Matron could be spotted early in the morning, jogging around campus before arriving at the Food Factory for a 'Big Breakfast'. On Mondays, Matron was in the Laundry Room attending to her smalls, at Quiz Nights in Jim's Bar she enjoyed a glass of Guinness and a cigar with the hosts. Friday nights, pre-Cheesy Pop it was cocktails before stepping out for dinner. Never seen by anyone, Matron became a regular hot topic and part of student and Union life.

She seemed to capture the imagination and mood of that moment; 'Matron is living the student dream', 'For someone of that age, Matron is cool', 'Matron says you simply cannot have too many condoms during Freshers' Week', 'Matron is a legend'. One morning I was enjoying some pre-exam nervous chit-chat with a group of first years when they asked me if Matron had a name. None of them had ever heard her called anything else. I had never given thought to a name; they had taken me by surprise. Picking up on my hesitation they wondered if I was related to Matron or if I was trying to hide something. I confirmed I was not her relative and that I would ask her permission to reveal her name. If she agreed, I would tell them after their exam. When the group returned in the afternoon I was ready for them. I began with Matron's four names; her maiden and three married. Then I went on to tell how they were acquired.

Born at the end of the First World War into a wealthy Scottish medical family with numerous connections to the University of Glasgow she enjoyed a privileged but unspoiled upbringing in both the West End of Glasgow and the family ancestral country estate north of the city. She entered the nursing profession in 1936 before the outbreak of World War II. She joined the military nurse service and completed her training on the front line. Frequently mentioned in despatches she was an inspiration to many. It was at this time that she, Nurse Marion Glenclyde met her destiny; the dashing American military surgeon Colonel George Bacillus. The nursing brigade referred to him as Gorgeous George. It was love at first sight. They married in secret during a forty-eight hour leave. As the war neared its end, plans were made for civilian life. She would be giving up nursing to concentrate on marriage and motherhood, he had already accepted a post as head of surgery at a hospital in Boston. Before heading to America they would honeymoon in Scotland. Their great adventure was mapped out before them. Then, the unthinkable happened. On the last day of his military service Colonel George Bacillus was killed in a friendly fire incident. A devastated, shell-shocked young widow returned to Scotland, alone.

Marion decided to continue with nursing. She would use her maiden name once again as that would help to manage her grief. She accepted a sister's post at Glasgow Memorial Hospital in 1946 and became Matron in 1949. Having given thirty-two years service to nursing, she retired from the profession in the late 1960's and came to Queen Margaret Union as an assistant administrator. She remained in situ for the next fifteen years, retiring in the early 1980's. Matron carried a torch for her late husband and any relationships with me were purely platonic. This kept her life uncomplicated, the way she liked it.

However, shortly after taking up her post with Queen Margaret Union, Matron surprised and shocked her family and friends with her news. She would marry the following spring. The man was Captain Andrew Abernethy R.N. based with the Royal Navy training centre at Greenock. It was not a match made in heaven. Arriving home early one Friday hoping to surprise her husband, she found him in their bed with his former first lieutenant who had been best man at their wedding. Married for less than a year they divorced. Wounded, Matron was comforted by her nearest and dearest life-long friends, spinster Hilda McTavish and her brother Donald, known as Jock. The bold Jock fell into Matron's platonic category. All the more surprising then when she married Jock in 1971. This was a match made in heaven. Matron retired form Queen Margaet Union in the early 1980's and Jock, a retired policeman and security consultant, worked only when he wanted. This let the couple travel for several months each year.

All went well for some years until they arrived in Rome for a spring break. Waiting for them was an urgent message from Hilda. Matron called her friend and was bombarded with a hysterical rant. It was a bad line but the gist of it was, "Love… scandal…lies…sex…videotape…empty bank account…

A portrait of what members believe matron to look like as she is sighted around the Union

closing down...QM Union". Jock and Matron caught the first flight home. A calm Hilda picked them up at the airport and filled in the blanks. Now known in the press as 'The QM Two', the President and General Manager of Queen Margaret Union had emptied the Union bank account and eloped with the money. There was evidence to suggest that they had gone to a hot, sunny, South American country having no extradition treaty with the UK.

University of Glasgow authorities were sympathetic but unable to help. The situation at the Union was terminal and closure was inevitable. Matron refused to accept this however. She managed to secure substantial donations and Queen Margaret Union got back on its feet. Later, at an award ceremony, Hilda and Jock beamed with pride as Matron was made a Patron of the Union. After the formalities, Jock left Matron and Hilda to allow them to have cake and coffee with the old girls. He headed home to prepare a celebration lunch. Jock put champagne on ice and prepared melba toast for the caviar. Then he went to have forty winks on his favourite chair in the study. Later, Hilda heard the crash on the floor as the glass slipped from Matron's hand upon entering the study. Jock had died in his sleep. They had been married for seventeen years.

With Jock gone, Matron decided to downsize her home, moving into a flat on the fifth floor of Queen Margaret Union. She would be nearby if the Board of Management wanted to consult her and far enough away if not. At a time when most people her age were content in retirement, Matron wanted to work. Making use of her nursing and administration background she joined, part-time of course, the University of Glasgow Department for Holistic Hygiene and Human Welfare. Just as she had done after the war, Matron immersed herself in work.

That was enough for that day, it was now getting late and not a single glass had been washed in the Games Room. The group thanked me for the talk and they left to prepare for that evenings RAW, the local band night. It was the morning after the night before. Matron was about to gain some serious street cred across campus. The Games Room resembled the Green

Room at the Music Awards. Undergraduates at Glasgow hung around in their boy band guises, a world away from their various disciplines of study. We had the Kick, the Down and Outs, Serious Young Men, Grand Hotel and Corridor IV. The bands were talking about an old gig incident. A few fans had tried to get backstage but some 'old cow' accompanied by security had stopped them. Yes, apparently it was Matron. To this day there are still sightings of her both in Queen Margaret Union and around campus. Making my way through the bands and around the room collecting the glasses I noticed a sad and tearful Kristy lying on a south facing windowsill. I made my way over to have a word with her and had a strange sense of déjà vu.

Age of Innocence

Gary R. Brown
President 2006-2007

Hindsight is a wonderful thing. If I had known everything I did at the end of my term of office before I began as President of Queen Margaret Union then things would have turned out differently.

I can't remember the exact moment that I entered the Union for the very first time but I do remember being told in my final year of Cathkin High School that it was certainly the Union for me at the University of Glasgow.

When I think of Queen Margaret Union and what it meant to me in my early years at the University I don't recall anything terribly spectacular. I remember being able to leave my Psychology class at ten-fifty am, dashing towards Hillhead Underground Station, running down Buchanan Street to the comic book shop and still making it back in time to buy breakfast from the Food Factory before they stopped serving it at eleven-thirty am. Every day from eleven am until Philosophy lectures at noon was 'QM time'. My friends and I would buy our drinks from Qudos coffee bar, get our caramel shortcake from the shop and our slightly over-filled, bulging baguette from the Continental Café on the second floor before spending the hour debating the finer things in life including the existence of man and the inner workings of each others relationships, or lack thereof.

It didn't take long for the Queen Margaret Union bug to bite us all. One of our friends had been a Freshers' Helper in 2003 and one by one we were suckered into the fold. As I was about to embark upon my third year of single honours Psychology in 2004 I found myself donning a red Fresher Helper T-shirt and it was downhill from there. I spent the week oozing levels of enthusiasm that I thought to be previously impossible. Impressionable Freshers found my retro SEGA baseball cap and vast knowledge of the 1990's to be so incredible that I was given the moniker 'SEGA Gary', a name that is still attached to me post University.

They say that once Queen Margaret Union grabs a hold of you it is impossible to escape. I have no idea who 'they' are, but it seems to be true. From my humble beginnings as a Freshers' Week helper I found I suddenly cared about the place in a way I never had before. I quickly became involved with the fortnightly magazine qmunicate. Its quirky pages often featured campus scandal, film reviews and the strangest cartoons on the back pages. For years, 'the Adventures of Rob the Dog and Tony the Pony' kept readers amused as they procrastinated over lunch. The Campaigns Committee fast became my home from home as I suddenly had the chance to 'make a difference' in the lives of our members. One week we were promoting the Union's Fairtrade policies (and long-running Nestle product ban) and the next we were encouraging everyone to love one another hippy-style, holding a hug-a-thon in the foyer (I don't think we ever did reach our target of one thousand hugs but it was fun nonetheless).

As my final year of Psychology at University began I found the Union became my only escape from an otherwise exhausting period in my studies. SEGA Gary became the host of the successful Friday night 'Mousetrap', a quiz show, game show, freak show amalgamation of fun that preceded the long-running Cheesy Pop club night. I have no idea how I managed to get my upper second-class degree considering all the time the Social Committee and I spent drumming up ideas for the weekly interactive games that held the regular crowd at 'Mousetrap' in such awe week after week. Among the highlights were 'Escape from Jurassic Park' a game where a dinosaur attack could cost your team points, and 'Mariah Carey: Boob Job Fiasco Nightmare Game' where America's favourite diva had undergone one too many bouts of cosmetic surgery resulting in a mass of botched boob jobs (pink

Gary on election day with Board Member Louisette Baillie

Presidents Sandy Cormie (1993-1994), Jennifer Paterson (1994-1995),
Craig Egdell (1996-1997), Katie McDonald (2002-2003),
Laura Kane (2004-2005), Jamie McHale (2005-2006) and
Gary R. Brown (2006-2007) at a gathering in 2006

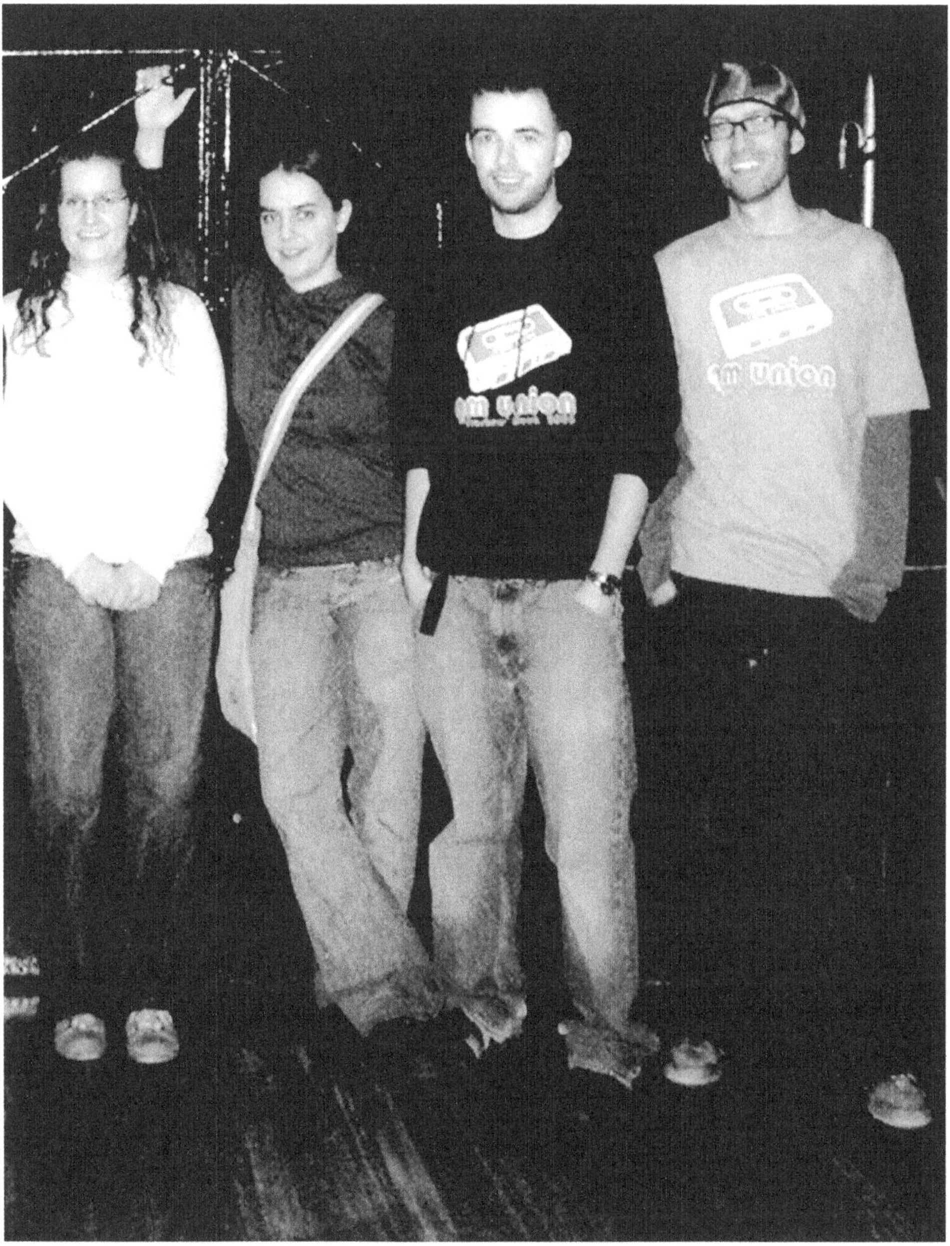

Presidents Jamie McHale (2005-2006), Laura Kane (2004-2005),
Margaret Fairlie (1966-1967) and Gary R. Brown (2006-2007)
during a visit in 2006

RED DWARF: THE MOVIE, FINALLY GETS UNDER WAY
FILM : PAGE ELEVEN

HOW I LOST MY VIRGINITY
THE BARLOW TALKS ABOUT HIS FIRST TIME IN HIS LAST COLUMN : PAGE 15

qmunicate

Wednesday 25th May 2005 Summer Special FREE

NEWS

GLASGOW UNI CUT JOBS
PAGE 2

REVIEW OF THE YEAR
PAGE 3

CHELSEA: LOVING IT
PAGE 4

TOP TEN SONGS TO STALK TO
PAGE 9

STAR WARS
PAGE 10

JURASSIC FARCE

DINO DESTRUCTION

- **DINOSAUR SLAUGHTERED AS STUDENTS SLEEP**
- **PROTESTS FALL ON DEAF EARS AT IVORY TOWER**

FESTIVALS FOR FREE
PAGE 12

MS. HONEYDEW'S MOTH/MAN PROBLEM CONTINUES
PAGE 13

LORNA LOVES VEGANS
PAGE 14

Mhairi Wilson

FOLLOWING a week of speculation, Millie the Dinosaur has been torn down from her home in the University grounds. The replica Tyrannosaurus Rex was secretly removed on Saturday 21st of May, despite the University Press Office denying there were any immediate plans for the dino to be demolished.

Students who supported the Save Millie campaign will be taken aback when they find an empty space outside the main building, as plans for the removal were not announced publicly. After repeated vandalism the model has endured, it was always clear that there were plans to get rid of Millie, but definite plans were never released. During the week, students past and present from the University of Glasgow, as well admirers from all over the world, pledged their support by signing an online petition (www.petitiononline.com/millie/petition.html) set up by an anonymous group of concerned students, after hearing a rumour that the University was planning to move Millie.

The University had previously commented on the proposed relocation. A spokesperson told The Evening Times, "(Millie) is very shabby – past her proper life-span – every time she is vandalised it costs approximately £2000 to repair her claws or tail – it's not acceptable for the University to use its very scarce resources on this. If any other organisation wishes to be represented by a dinosaur they are welcome to contact the University and offer Millie a retirement package."

Many will be disappointed the University has chosen to demolish rather than relocate the dino though. Employees from the Estates and Buildings service started to pull down the dinosaur at seven o'clock on Saturday morning, taking over an hour to completely destroy the model. Security were unappreciative when a News of the World photographer arrived on scene, asking him to move on, further displaying the desire to keep Millie's demise quiet.

CONTINUED ON PAGE 2

WHAT'S ON: PAGE 3   SPORT: PAGE 4   TOP 10: PAGE 9   ROB & TONY, CROSSWORD, I SAW YOU: BACK PAGE

Issue of *qmunicate* magazine featuring the destruction of the University of Glasgow's beloved dinosaur – Milly

371

Cover of Queen Margaret Union Handbook 2007

balloons with bits of paper inside them) all over her body with only her head, hands and feet recognisable. Contestants had to correctly answer a question about the singer (Wikipedia is such a wonderful tool) to be allowed to burst one of her balloon breasts to free the 'prize' inside.

In many ways it was quite literally madness from time to time at the Union, although I suppose University is like that. Only in Queen Margaret Union could you have had toilet graffiti that was added to each day by various students until the entire set of lyrics to David Bowie's track, 'Magic Dance' from the 1980's retro hit movie 'Labyrinth' emblazoned the walls.

My year as President, which I did post degree, was no different in tone to the rest of my time at Queen Margaret Union. Perhaps with the exception of driving one of my convenors insane, another fail to matriculate, a further get essentially fired by the Board of Management, another resign due to workload and bickering and a final one quit in protest, we had a fairly successful year. As a Union we played an essential part in keeping the National Union of Students (NUS) out of the University of Glasgow. We saw some incredible bands once again grace our stage (the Automatic, Dykeenies and Fratellis to name but a few), gained and lost an Electro night, tracked down most of our former Presidents, launched a late-night coffee service and saw a vicious attack on one of our mascots, Marty the Mouse. I never was the same after watching a random female Fresher rip his tail from his body at Cheesy Pop. He's been seen around since then but he doesn't seem himself anymore.

Life after University is weird, scary and also wonderful but that's what life is all about. If you've ever watched any American college drama in its final season you'll know what I mean. The people I've met, the things I've done, they all got me to where I am today and none of it would have been possible without that fateful day on 28 March 1890 when eighteen young women students were elected for the first time to create Queen Margaret Union.

Gathering of Presidents at the Dinner in 2006

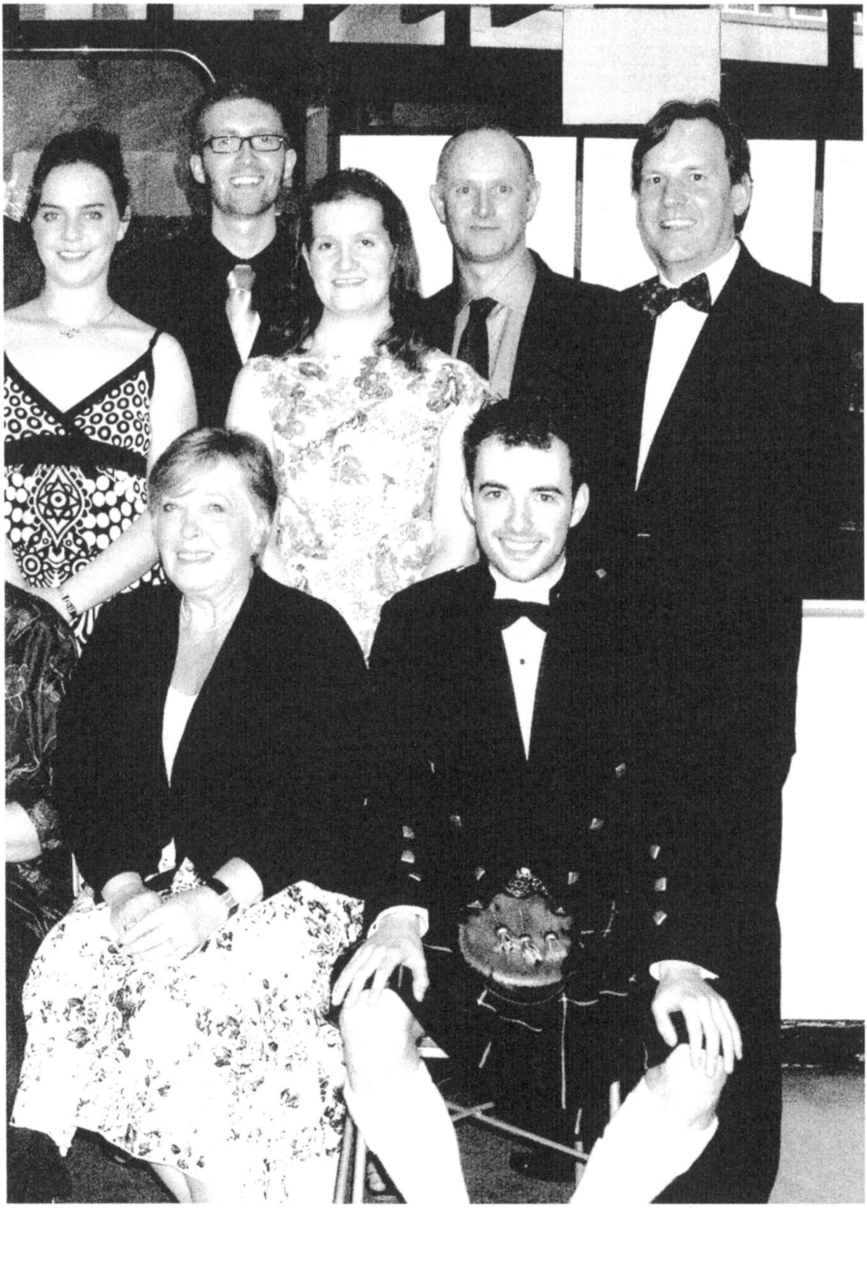

Queen Margaret Union Executive 2006-2007

The Space Between

Ally Hunter
President 2008-2009

While Queen Margaret Union is essentially nomadic in nature it has a couple of spaces, including the odd nook and cranny, and it would be silly not to mention them. The laundry room, for example, is so much more than simply somewhere to wash your clothes when your own washing machine breaks down. The industrial tumble dryers double as futuristic nesting pods for late night drunken challenges and photography. The room is also a well known sex spot of the Union, though everyone is aware that the stopping goods lift is a much safer bet.

The goods lift is not the only lift to have been known to stop between floors. An historic event took place in early 2006 when eleven members of StaG (Student Theatre at Glasgow), myself included, were late for an audition and decided the only thing to do would be to board the lift together. After a creaky start we realised that we were going a lot slower than normal. As it slowed to a stop between the second and third floor the panic began to set in That was my first encounter with Duty Board and my only, fairly traumatic, encounter with the Union disciplinary process on the receiving end.

Queen Margaret Union is full of secrets; not only in the rooms, but in the hidden spaces between the rooms. As well as much asbestos, the walls and the ceilings are home to hidden objects that include guitars, shoes, and more illicit materials. Shortly after I became President renovations were underway in what would become a new committee room. Found during the repairs to the roof was the Queen Margaret Union mace dated 1957 and lost sometime after. Who knows what secrets remain hidden in 22 University Gardens? Only time, and a little rummaging, will tell.

Glasgow University Union Executive 2007

The Love-Hate Relationship

David Tait
Honorary Secretary
Glasgow University Union
2006-2007

It has long been something of a surprise to me that one of the University's many anthropologists has not undertaken a serious investigation of the relations within and between the two Unions. Perhaps this has never occurred due of the scale of the task - in comparison the Augean Stables would be simplicity itself. Each of the Unions, with their (what can only be described as quasi-tribal) internal politics and mating displays that would make a peacock blush, are a complex mosaic of historical influences, cultural trends and modern practicalities.

However, to gain a deeper understanding of the relationship between Queen Margaret Union and Glasgow University Union it would perhaps be best to move to another academic discipline- that of psychology. Sibling rivalry is perhaps the best way to describe the fluctuating bond between the two buildings and their respective occupants. This is undoubtedly a 'love-hate; relationship.

Popular opinion (given only a slight prod by the occasional *Glasgow University Guardian* story) has it that Glasgow University Union's members are entirely woven from tweed. This being very much in fashion in the place since the Boer War- an event which many of the place's most venerable members claim to vividly recall and, in their more convivial moments, to have carried out some of that conflict's more distinguished actions. It is seen as a refuge for persons not entirely at home in this century (or perhaps even the last) and is how those less enamoured with Glasgow University Union portray it.

Board of Management meeting in 2008-2009

"i couldn't just sit in my room with a guitar and pen a little love song"
TOM VEK || PAGE 9

'You too could be a non-smoking health food eating stud'
LORNA MCKINNON || PAGE 14

qmunicate

Wednesday 13 April 2005 FREE

NEWS

SRC ELECTIONS NEXT WEEK
PAGE 3

GUST WINS NATIONAL STUDENT TV AWARDS
PAGE 3

MINORITY REPORT
PAGE 14

GLADIATORS, WHERE ARE THEY NOW?
PAGE 12

TROUTFISH'S FINAL COUNTDOWN
PAGE 9

QM PRESIDENT VOTE

- QM BY-ELECTION, 14TH APRIL

- VOTE FOR PRESIDENT AND TWO ORDINARY BOARD POSITIONS

On Thursday 14th April, the QM will hold a by-election for several positions on the Board of Management. The position of the President is open again after the vote at the General Election was declared void. Two of the original candidates, Molly Iliffe and Jamie McHale are standing, as well as two new candidates; Matthew Davies and John Stormonth-Darling. There are two positions available on the Ordinary Board, with six candidates standing, which could make for a competitive campaign.

Who will get the sword from the ballot box?   CONTINUED ON PAGE 2

TEN HOURS, EIGHT TURNTABLES, TWO DJS, ONE GREAT NIGHT

TEN HOUR CHEESY POP: SELLS OUT AGAIN

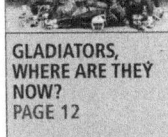

Euan Lindsay

The final Friday of term two saw 10 Hour Cheesy Pop devoid of any gimmicks; no fancy dress this time, just top class entertainment.

Early comers were treated to the ever improving Mousetrap in Jim's Bar giving anyone who had spent their student loans the chance to win some beer.

Starting the night in Qudos, Midas Touch were getting everyone into the groove with a collection of funk and disco songs played live to the obvious enjoyment of the revellers in Qudos. But in reality it was just a teaser for what was to come.

Rumours that Troutfish and Toast would hatch from gigantic polystyrene eggs during a smoke and laser show were proven false as Spoonie introduced the main attraction. Standing at opposite sides of Qudos stage the two DJs were prepared for an epic battle until 6 in the morning. Both Troutfish and Toast were in top form, playing Cheesy Pop classics and introducing a few new favourites.

Anyone who managed to tear themselves away from the battle in Qudos and stumbled into Jim's would have discovered Subcity DJs playing some great tunes, contrasting with what was happening downstairs. As the night went on the funk was replaced by some hip hop before Subcity's Cloudo was joined by DJ Mayhem to wreck havoc in Jim's with some Happy Hardcore.

Its sister Union in contrast is viewed by those of an extreme disposition as a youth club for a bunch of humourless, politically correct, 'giant-jenga-playing' Goths constantly looking to pass a motion banning something - anything! And it is a fact, oft repeated by Queen Margaret Union members, that the Executive Committee has a sheet of paper emblazoned with what is reputed to be Kurt Cobain's footprint. They even had it DNA tested to prove it.

Such mistrust and stereotypes have led to numerous outrages that are undocumented in any of the many history books on Level Eight of the University Library. One occurred as when a Glasgow University Union member, whose identity is obscured by the mists of history, once observed a large balloon anchored to the roof of the other Union for the purposes of the promotion of their Freshers' Week events. This 'gentleman' sallied forth suitably equipped with Land Rover, Wellington boots, tweeds (but of course) and (more alarmingly) shotgun to Queen Margaret Union where upon he shot a sizeable hole in the side of the balloon.

In retaliation Queen Margaret Union's membership released a number of, what can best be described as, unwelcome furry visitors into the dining area of Glasgow University Union.

Undoubtedly both of these stories sparkle with the sheen of ex-post facto embellishment. Regardless, the then-Secretary of Court decreed an embargo on such stunts at the end of the 1990s and relations have been far warmer between the two Unions ever since.

In the past five years the two Unions have joined together with the other student bodies to actively oppose membership of the National Union of Students and to ensure the election of Charles Kennedy as Rector of the University. The results of both of these speak to the virility and strength of both Unions at a time of unprecedented student apathy. For all the Unions are very different places – intentionally so – they are united by their members' earnest and pre-eminent concern with the welfare of their fellow members and their desire to preserve the communities they have gained so much from- the Unions themselves.

In the end then perhaps the discipline which illuminates best this volatile co-existence is the science of Biology. This is the archetypal symbiotic relationship – as both Unions work to shed the preconceptions which dog them and strive to welcome as many new members as possible they have come to recognise that the individual cultures they prize so highly can only be maintained by the growth and success of the other. One Union cannot exist without the other.

Executive 2008-2009

Board of Management 2008-2009

Thank You and Good Night

By Aaron Murray
President 2009-2010

And so we have reached the end, or is it merely the beginning of the next era of Queen Margaret Union? We have travelled a long road to get here and it has not always been easy. Our present mirrors a lot in our past, as we have a dedicated Board of Management, supported by an excellent staff. Similarly we have an enthusiastic, varied and ever changing membership.

As with all student unions in the country we face stiff competition and a student base with less money than ever before. Despite this, our union has never simply been a business; from listening to the tales of Michael the porter and talking to past-presidents it is apparent that, as a Union, we flourish when our backs are against the wall. Our 'them and us' attitude will always drive us to great achievements and to respond to our challenges with fresh ideas and determination.

As things change across campus in the coming years we must always remember that we have the most valuable asset that any organisation could possibly need – people committed to keeping the Queen Margaret Union at the high standard that we have always held dear. With their support, we can continue to overcome the various trials that will undoubtedly be thrown in our way.

Every year we are faced with a group of freshmen and women who know only our reputation as an outstanding student union. We are at an integral juncture in our history and we cannot let our predecessors, or our current members, down.

This book records but the first chapter of the history of Queen Margaret Union, its members and its characters. Long live our Union and all those who are lucky enough to have been a part of it.

Gathering of former Board Members and Presidents from the 1940s
with recent Presidents of the 2000s:
Back Row: Jamie McHale 2005-2006), Gary R. Brown (2006-2007),
Gordon Brady (2007-2008), Laura Kane (2005-2005).
Front row: Joy McCracken (Board Member 1940s), Nora Beveridge
(President 1940-1941), Margaret Sinclair (Board Member 1940s)

The Presidents

Marion Gilchrist

President 1894-1898

J R B Nelson

President 1905

Katherine C. Dewar

President 1910-1911

Jean B. Trench

President 1911-1912

E. R. Thomson

President 1912-1913

Elizabeth P. Cowie

President 1913-1914

Marion Watson

President 1914-1915

Jean St. C. Balls

President 1915-1916

Mabel Vaughn

President 1916-1917

Pearl S. Henderson

President 1917-1918

E. Y. Angus

President 1918-1919

M. L. Young

President 1919-1920

Margaret W. S. Glasgow

President 1920-1921

Nan D. Neilson

President 1921-1922

May D. Tennent

President 1922-1923

Ida Wylie

President 1923-1924

Violet M. Purves

President 1924-1925

Elizabeth M. Jack

President 1925-1926

Elizabeth B. Currie

President 1926-1927

Esther B. Hamilton

President 1927-1928

Mary V. MacGregor

President 1928-1929

Muriel O. Gibson

President 1929-1930

Marjorie E. Douglas

President 1930-1931

Hester Scobbie

President 1931-1932

B. Lesley McEwan

President 1932-1933

Irene F. Browning

President 1933-1934

Barbara L. Napier

President 1934-1935

M. Muriel Gibson

President 1935-1936

Lorna J. Tillotson

President 1936-1937

Carol M. Bennie

President 1937-1938

Landa M. Wingate

President 1938-1939

May C. Dryden

President 1939-1940

E. Nora Hamilton

President 1940-1941

Dorothy B. Raeburn

President 1940

Catherine P. Cathcart

President 1941-1942

Muriel B. Geddes

President 1942-1943

Anne L. Craig

President 1943-1944

Agnes A. M. White

President 1944-1945

Pamela A. Davies

President 1945-1946

Winifred A. Gibson

President 1946-1947

Mae Walker

President 1947-1948

Frances A. Melrose

President 1948-1949

Jean B. Geddes

President 1949-1950

Stroma M. Duncan

President 1950-1951

Elma Cant

President 1951-1952

Jean Reid

President 1952-1953

Marion A. Forbes

President 1953-1954

Jean Livingston

President 1954-1955

Mary Roger

President 1955-1956

Joanne McNiell

President 1956-1957

Margaret M. McNamara

President 1957-1958

Margo H. C. Budge

President 1958-1959

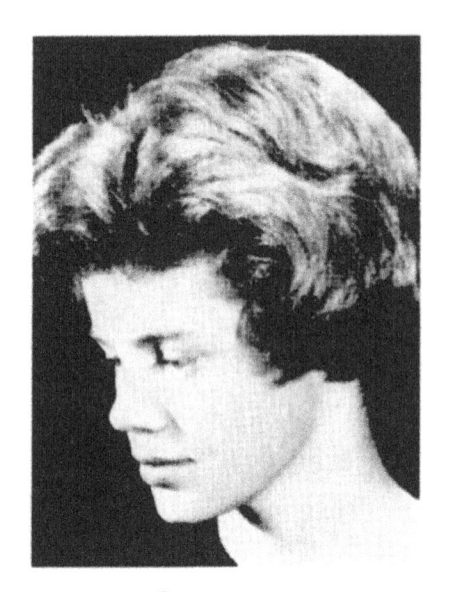

Deirdre V. Brown
President 1959-1960

Sheila Kidd
President 1960-1961

Elisabeth MacKinlay
President 1961-1962

Rona Davidson
President 1961

Marcia McKeand

President 1962-1963

Elizabeth Hamil

President 1963-1964

Maeve McDonald

President 1963

Christine Hurst

President 1964-1965

Sheila Crawford

President 1965-1966

Margaret Fairlie

President 1966-1967

Moira McBride

President 1967-1968

Maren Hunter

President 1968-1969

M. Jane Spence

President 1969-1970

Kathleen McDonald

President 1970-1971

Lesley Bell

President 1971-1972

Brenda Dowd

President 1972

Catherine Shearer

President 1972-1973

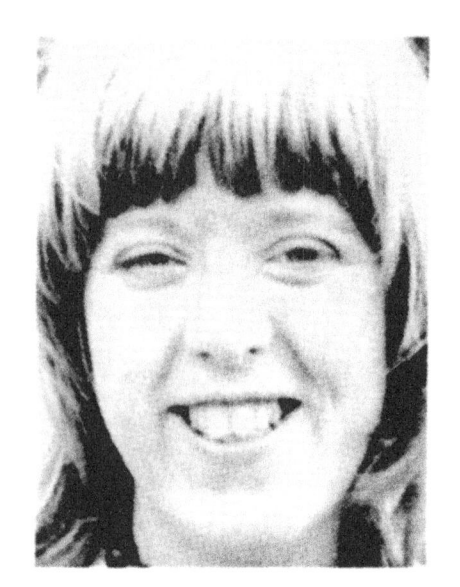

Dianne Savage

President 1973-1974

Christine Hamilton

President 1974

Ruth O'Beirne

President 1974-1975

Jane McMinn

President 1975-1976

Moira Corrigan

President 1976-1977

Catherine Savage

President 1977-1978

Rosemary Nugent

President 1978-1979

Gillian Govan

President 1979-1980

Mairi MacLeod

President 1980-1981

Dominic d'Angelo

President 1981-1982

Abdul Ibrahem

President 1982-1983

Mark Graham

President 1983-1984

Jill Simmons

President 1984-1985

Richard Gass

President 1985-1986

Marion Neill

President 1986-1987

Grahame Riddell

President 1987-1988

Jennifer Roe

President 1988-1989

Dianne Wallace

President 1989-1990

Stuart Gosland

President 1990-1991

Jake Scott

President 1991-1992

Emma Bamforth

President 1992-1993

Sandy Cormie

President 1993-1994

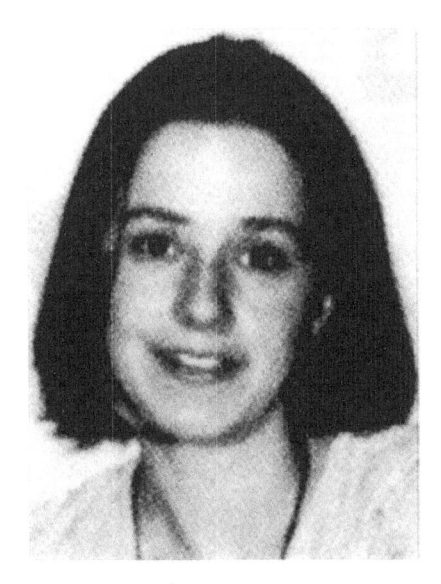

Jennifer Paterson

President 1994-1995

Stephen Rixon

President 1995-1996

Craig Egdell

President 1996-1997

Sam Phillips

President 1997-1998

Lizzy Toon

President 1998-1999

Andy Whincup

President 1999-2000

Caroline Johnston

President 2000-2001

Jamie Wakefield

President 2001-2002

Katie McDonald

President 2002-2003

Alastair Deutsch

President 2003-2004

Laura Kane

President 2004-2005

Jamie McHale

President 2005-2006

Gary R. Brown

President 2006-2007

Gordon Brady

President 2007-2008

Ally Hunter

President 2008-2009

Aaron Murray

President 2009-10

qmunicate

issue 62 • 1st december 2008 • free! • www.qmu.org.uk

RIP SATURDAY MORNING TV

Index

Photographs are not included in the Index

A

Aberdeen Students Representative Council 53
Adams, Richard 355
Amnesty International 308, 350
Ann Street 52, 63
Anwar, Aamer 285
Ashdown, Paddy 243
Association for the Higher Education of Women in Glasgow and the West of Scotland 7

B

Baird, Mae 85
Ball 82, 95, 96, 113, 128, 151, 186, 208, 212, 221, 285, 290
Barret, Stephen 254
Bazaar 15, 17, 18, 21, 63, 73
Bedrule 72, 97
Bell, Graham 268
Bell, John 177
Belle & Sebastian 275
Bennie, Carol 72
Beresford Hotel 97
Bernal, J.D. 92
Beveridge, Nora xv
Biko, Steve 241, 242, 249, 267, 279, 282, 285
Board Ball 96, 128
bomb threat 228
Boomtown Rats 242
Boyd Orr 85
Bragg, Billy 227, 228, 233, 293
Brichta, Irena 171
Bridie Dinner 298
Bridie, James 86

Brown, Deirdre 109, 110
Brown, Gary 17, 63, 77, 365
Brown, Gordon 223
Brown, Walter 23
Buchanan Street 218, 365
Buchanan, Stuart 249, 272
12 Buckingham Terrace 21, 63
Bugged Out 314
Burns, Robert 301
Butler, Rab 108, 117

C

Campaigns 258, 294, 349, 350, 353, 366
Campbell, Alan 268
Campbell, Menzies 109, 116, 129, 130, 159
Campbell of Tullichewan 7, 12
Camp Coffee 95
Ceasyer Cash 218, 220, 221
Charities Convenor 217
Cheesy Pop 245, 278, 285, 291, 304, 315, 319, 320, 323, 324, 340, 350, 360, 366, 373
Christmas Ball 128, 151
Coffee Shop 334
Cohn Bendit, Daniel 167
Coia, Paul 192
Cole, Lloyd 212, 232, 241
College Pudding 54
Collins, Edwyn 184, 277
Common Room 168, 192, 215, 242, 285, 290
Cormie, Sandy 285
Corrigan, Moira 175, 181
Crabb, Paul 319
Cray, Robert 215
Cuban Missile Crisis 130

D

Dafter Friday 208, 212, 253, 257, 267, 275, 276
Daft Friday 82, 113, 177, 186, 323
Daltry, Roger 157
d'Angelo, Dominic 197, 201, 301
Davidson, Rona 110

415

Davies, Matthew 355
Dawson, Miss 95, 102, 104
Debates 66, 85, 117, 119, 130, 131, 149, 150, 159, 160, 171-3, 181, 187, 201
de Valera 92
Dewar, Donald 109, 116, 129, 130, 139, 159
Dialectic Society 172
Distributists' Club 172
DJ Toast 285, 319, 320, 323, 324
Duncan, Stroma 96, 97

E

Edinburgh Ladies' Educational Association 7
Egdell, Craig 291
Elder, Mrs 8
Elliott, Sir Walter 92
Entertainments 116, 123, 127, 128, 144, 168, 184, 185, 190, 203, 208, 249, 253, 258, 267, 275, 276, 278, 279, 282, 314, 319, 356
Entertainments Committee 116, 123, 128, 319
Ewing, Winnie 117

F

Fairbairn, Nicholas 159
Fairlie, Margaret 139
Fair Trade 168, 350, 353
Fashion Show 242, 253
Food Factory 239, 271, 272, 276, 282, 285, 315, 334, 349, 360, 365
Forbes, Marion 109
Fork and Glass 102, 119, 151, 161
Frank, Hannah 45
Fraser 13, 25, 35, 57, 86, 109, 294
Fresher's camp 115
Freshers' Social Halloween Party 65
Freshers Week 177, 254, 281
Freshers' Week 3, 196, 203, 258, 261, 262, 272, 279, 281, 290, 310, 323, 334, 335, 339, 340, 346, 360, 366, 382
Fyfe, Scot 232

G

Gaelic 4
Galloway, Janet 11, 15, 18, 24-6, 57, 65, 67, 243
Games Room 192, 195, 203, 282, 285, 334, 359, 363
gas 86, 276
Gass, Richard 217, 227, 228
Geldof, Bob 242
General Adviser of Studies to Women Students 92, 101, 103
Gilbert Scott Building 65, 77
Gilchrist, Marion 9, 12, 13, 26
Gillanders, Farquhar 151
Glasgow Student Charities Appeal 217
Glasgow University Athletic Club 116
Glasgow University Gaming Society 304, 328, 334
Glasgow University Guardian 124, 189, 197, 249, 317, 379
Glasgow University Lesbian, Gay, Bisexual and Transgender Society 333
Glasgow University Magazine 33, 54, 78, 317
Glasgow University Sports Association 310
Glasgow University Student Handbook 78
Glasgow University Union xvii, 65, 81, 86, 161, 171-3, 177, 183, 185, 186, 187, 204, 225-7, 235, 236, 239, 243, 245, 254, 261, 262, 267, 281, 293, 298, 310, 313, 317, 323, 333-5, 339, 379, 382
Glasgow University Women's Group 242
Gordon, Jimmy (Lord Gordon of Strathblane) 109, 116
Govan, Gillian 187
Graham, Mark 207
Gray, Alasdair 97, 102, 113, 184
Greene, Elizabeth 135
Grierson, John 97

H

Haig, Erin 355
Hailsham, Douglas, Lord 117
Halcrow, Debbie 320
Hamilton, Christine 165, 171
Hanks, William P. 54
Happer, Gordon 254
Heals, Keppie Henderson & Glebe 97
Heath, Tim 190
Helpers 262, 272, 281, 334, 340, 345, 346
Heseltine, Michael 227
Hetherington, Lady 71
Hetherington, Sir Hector 61, 75, 78, 108, 131
Hook, Jane 157
hugathon 349
Hunt, Marsha 159
Hunter, Ally 328, 377
Hunter Hall 46, 33

I

Ibrahim, Abdul 196, 226
Illife, Molly 349
Independent Socialists 181
Ingleston, Ann 191
Io (Sci-Fi Society) 304

J

Jim's Bar 285, 290, 297, 304, 317, 319, 334, 335, 360

K

Kane, Laura 319
Kelly, Michael 220
Kelvin, Jean 67,
Kelvin Way, 72, 221
Kelvingrove Museum 245, 253
Kimmins, Marie 185
Kooheji, Omar 303

L

Laver, Tim 253, 267
Leslie, David 151
Lilybank House 57
Livingston, Jean 110
Louise, Duchess of Argyll 21
Lutuli, Albert 139

Mac

MacAdie, Sarah-Louise 327
MacAlister, Donald 39
MacBride, Brian 177
Mackie, Mark 208, 232
Mackie, Rona 115
Mackie, Dougald 313
McAllister, Lady 64
McCullum, Ken 290
McClusky, Rev. Fraser 86
McConachie, Anthony 245, 249, 261, 267, 271, 282, 290
McConnell, Jack 243
McCormack, John 97
McCormick family 109, 116
McDonald, Katie 333
McGovern, Michael 241
McHale, Jane 339
McIntosh, Miss 13
Mcintosh, Rev. Hamish 86
McLaughlin, Jimmy 359
McMinn, Jane 175
McNamara, Margaret 110
McNeill, Joanne 73, 109, 110
McQueen, Moira 149
McSkeane, Liz 181, 182

M

Maguire, Anne 159
Malone, Gerry 159
Margaret, Queen and Saint of Scotland 3
Matron 33, 359, 360, 361, 363, 364
Mavor, O. H. 54, 86
Melville 7, 56, 57, 58, 65, 192
Men's Union xvii, 43, 61, 65, 72, 86, 92, 96, 97, 109, 113, 116, 117, 127, 129, 131, 144, 157, 161, 171, 175, 177, 181, 183, 189, 190
Mercury, Freddy 168

Mixing Debate 161, 197
Murphy, Terry 291, 313

N

Napier, Barbara 103
National Union of Students 231, 263, 373, 382
Neil, Andrew 159
Neill, Marion 225, 236
Nelson, Janette R. B. 15, 17, 18
Nicolson, Alec 319
Nirvana 232, 245, 258, 275, 276, 282, 293, 324
Northern Services 231, 289
North Park House 8, 17, 25
Nugent, Rosemary 189

O

Oakley, C.A. 53
Observer Mace 109, 173
Observer National Debating Trophy 130
O'Reilly, Dora 297

P

Paterson, Jennifer 281, 297
Pattie, Jessie 51
Peel, John 212
Phillips, Ian 55
Phillips, Sam 293
Pearce Lodge 71
Pirie, Marie 123
Pitt, Margo 107
Pogues 212
Pollard, Fiona 272
President's Dinner 293, 297, 302
Princess Margaret 195

Q

Q-Emmas 18, 43, 53, 68, 73, 75, 89, 135, 136, 145, 245
Qudos 168, 192, 196, 242, 285, 323, 324, 350, 365
Queen Margaret College xvii, 1, 7, 8, 9, 11, 12, 15, 17, 18, 25, 26, 27, 35, 51, 53, 54, 57, 58, 61, 65, 67, 68, 192
Quiz Idol 355

R

Ramsey, Meta 110
Red Hot Chili Peppers 250, 275
Reid, Jean 103, 195
Reith, Lord 144
Riddell, Grahame 235
Rixon, Stephen 285, 289, 294, 297, 301
Rodgers, Mary 110
Roe, Jennifer 249
Royal Scottish Academy of Music and Drama 218

S

Savage, Catherine 183
Scott, Jake 254, 257
Shackleton, Ernest H. 21
Sinclair, Margaret 81
Siouxie Sioux 277
Slade 212
Smith, Adam 225
Smith, Dr Herbert 71,
Smith, John 109, 116, 130, 159
Smith, Mark E. 275
Snap, Crackle and Pop 320
Spoonie 355, 356
St. Andrews Halls 18
Steele, David 243
Stirling-Maxwell, lady 66
Stitch 'N' Bitch 331
Stray Pearls 21
Students Representative Council 53, 108, 116, 139, 177, 190, 226, 231, 235, 261, 310
Student Theatre at Glasgow 308, 328, 377

T

The Big Kahuna 323
Tillotson, Lorna 72
Toon, Lizzy 297
Transvision Vamp 267

Trinity College, Dublin 96
Troutfish, D J 355, 356
Turnbull, Gill 3
Tweedsmuir, Lady 92
Twelve Hour Cheesy Pop 323

U

1 University Gardens 64, 65, 72
2 University Gardens 65
22 University Gardens 21, 119, 377
Unplugged 304, 314

W

Wallace, Miss 68
Wallace, Vera 82
Wallace, Diana 249, 271
Whincup, Andy 309
White, Andrew 285
Whiting, Brian 115
Willocks, Edna 91, 104
Wingate, Landa 72
Women's Royal Naval Service 75
Woodburn, Winnie 117
Wyllie, ida 43, 64

Y

Ygorra 48, 79, 113, 221
You're Only Young Twice 89, 98

Lightning Source UK Ltd.
Milton Keynes UK
UKOW06f1834090615

253187UK00001B/2/P

9 781845 300616